Great Restaurant Innovators

GREAT RESTAURANT INNOVATORS

Profiles in Success

Charles Bernstein

Lebhar-Friedman Books
Chain Store Publishing Corp.
A Subsidiary of Lebhar-Friedman, Inc.
New York

Copyright© 1981, Chain Store Publishing Corp., 425 Park Avenue, New York, N.Y. 10022

Printed in the United States of America.

Design: db

Library of Congress Cataloging in Publication Data:
Bernstein, Charles, 1934-
   Great restaurant innovators.

   1. Restaurateurs—United States—Biography.
I. Title.
TX910.3.B47   647'.95'0922 [B]   81-18175
ISBN 0-86730-239-9

5 4 3 2 1

To my wife, Norma, and our children, Adam, Gregory, and Georgia.

And to all the great personalities who make the restaurant industry such a fascinating one.

Contents

Photo section appears at center of book

Acknowledgements

One day many months ago Bill Beard, a kind and thoughtful adviser, came to me with a brainstorm that "a book on leading restaurant personalities would be an excellent idea." Actually the idea had been germinating for some time, and this was exactly the spur I needed to put it into action. George Lang, a fascinating personality in his own right, was intrigued about the project's potential and offered particular encouragement.

I am grateful to the leaders of the Lebhar-Friedman book division, my publisher, for their devotion to quality. Barbara Miller, the division's chief editor, gave me steady encouragement to stay on the track even during the toughest periods. She was unstinting in support of my efforts. Thea Beckwith, who edited the book, showed tender care in preserving my style but molding it into a more cohesive format. Joe Morse was most helpful in devising ideas to promote the book.

Certainly the twelve diverse personalities who cooperated so much with my efforts on this book deserve thanks. I greatly appreciate their trust and hope it proves merited.

Unquestionably, there are many other individuals in the restaurant industry who would make interesting profiles both to the trade and the public. But a journalistic decision had to be made on a representative cross-section, and I am pleased with the results.

Most of all, I want to thank my wife, Norma, and our three children, Adam, Greg and Georgia, for their extreme patience and understanding during the many many hours of painstaking work necessary to finish the project. They gave me the inspiration to keep going. We all agreed it was worth the effort—after the book was completed.

—Charles Bernstein
Sept. 7, 1981

Preface

Charles Bernstein has combined his knowledge and understanding of the restaurant industry with his admiration for the qualities of character and personality of several men who have left their mark on the industry.

Obviously, he did not cover all the greats of the industry. Instead, he has selected as examples some individuals who perhaps are less well known to the general public, but whose ideas have had a marked effect on the development and trends of the restaurant industry.

The profiles of these individuals illustrate the qualities of character that make for success in the food service industry: courage, determination, innovation, confidence in one's ideas and, above all, an energetic pursuit of the objectives.

That these qualities appear in individuals of entirely different personalities is not unusual. Successful individuals are always essentially themselves. This fact is brought home in Mr. Bernstein's profiles.

It would take many volumes to salute all of the leaders and innovators in this dynamic industry. Charles Bernstein's book must be viewed as the beginning of a work that really can never be completed.

The growth of the industry over the last fifteen years to become the largest retail employer with sales of nearly 5 percent of the gross national product is dramatic evidence that its leaders have accurately assessed the needs and desires generated in a period of revolutionary social change. The free market is a democratic institution where our people can and do express their individual choices with cold-blooded clarity and certainty. Success in the industry demands entrepreneurial imagination and dedication, regardless of the size of the firm.

The future of the industry will depend on our ability to attract the same qualities of character that are so well exemplified in the profiles Mr. Bernstein has selected from an abundant crop of talented leaders with which the industry has been blessed.

Robert E. Bradford
President and Chief Executive
    Officer, National Restaurant
    Association, Washington, D.C.
July 1981

SECTION I

Fast-Food Pioneers

Fast food started evolving as an industry in the mid-1950s as McDonald's under Ray Kroc and Kentucky Fried Chicken under the late Colonel Harland Sanders began their initial drives. By the late 1950s Frank Carney's Pizza Hut, Lou Fisher's Gino's, and others were in the fray. But it wasn't until the late 1960s and early 1970s that fast food evolved into a major industry, spurred by the American exodus to the suburbs and a proliferating highway network.

While McDonald's steadily widened its No. 1 position through the 1970s under Kroc and Fred Turner, a number of chains gained momentum. These included Leonard Rawls's North Carolina-based Hardee's, Warren Rosenthal's Kentucky-based Long John Silver's fish and chips, and Jack-in-the-Box out of California. Each went through its growth cycle, then suffered pains upon reaching maturity, and came back stronger than ever by 1980—Hardee's under Jack Laughery, Long John Silver's under Rosenthal, and Jack-in-the-Box under Jack Goodall. The same was true of Kentucky Fried Chicken, which faltered but then rebounded under Mike Miles's leadership.

Each of these fast-food leaders deserves recognition for his achievements. But two other individuals were chosen for this section as mavericks, intriguing personalities, and fast-food trend setters. Each suffered his own share of setbacks, and each had to overcome different types of adversity.

David Thomas, an orphan who worked in various restaurants and then with Kentucky Fried Chicken and Arthur Treacher's fish and chips, was convinced an "adult" hamburger could be created and a whole chain for young adults fashioned around it. He envisioned larger hamburgers and a simple menu of just a few items. He was a revolutionary when he opened his first Wendy's in 1969, and few thought the new-fangled idea would ever succeed. But with his own ingenuity and help from his long-time associate, Robert Barney, Wendy's succeeded beyond anyone's expectations. It grew at a breakneck pace through the 1970s, slumped briefly, but bounced back with renewed vigor and an adjusted format in 1980. Others tried to emulate Wendy's, but just couldn't come close to producing the same results as Thomas. There was only one Wendy's, and in the early 1980s Thomas was hoping to close the gap on Burger King and become the No. 2 volume burger chain. Down the road he thought that maybe some day Wendy's could overtake McDonald's in total volume, but that would have to be in the distant future.

While Thomas earned his reputation with one chain, Donald N. Smith worked wonders with three. A product of the McDonald's system, he rose to executive vice president and chief operations officer by late 1976. Just then Pillsbury, looking for someone to instill spirit, drive, and momentum in Burger King, hired him as Burger King president and chief executive officer. Over the next three years he McDonaldized Burger King—but in his own individual way so that Burger King was far from a replica of McDonald's. While the systems may have become similar, Smith utilized a Magic King character instead of a Ronald McDonald. And he unveiled a line of specialty sandwiches. Each year for three years Burger King's average per unit sales topped his original goal of a $50,000 increase.

Highly impressed with these results and with Smith, PepsiCo spirited him away in the spring of 1980, naming him president of a newly formed restaurant group for Pizza Hut and Taco Bell. PepsiCo had acquired these chains in the late 1970s and was highly optimistic since each held a wide lead in its respective market segment. But sales and earnings lagged, and Smith was brought in to perform his magic. This time he was not in his element of burgers, but the fast-food principles remained the same. It had to be his greatest challenge to arouse these two sleeping giants to their full potentials. In fact, Smith wondered aloud why pizza couldn't become America's most popular fast food, and he set his mind to this task.

Dave Thomas and Don Smith are two of the personalities who have fashioned major fast-food chains. Each has had a decisive influence on the shape of fast food in the 1980s.

1

Dave Thomas

THE "ADULT" HAMBURGER

R. David Thomas, an orphan who had to make his own way in the world, always loved hamburgers. He eventually found himself in the chicken business and then the fish and chips business, but it had to be temporary. He knew his destiny was hamburgers.

When he launched his little Wendy's hamburger restaurant, named after his third daughter, in Columbus, Ohio, in 1969, Thomas was just hoping to run a nice little business that he could enjoy. He had already become a millionaire by the age of thirty-five from earlier ventures and wasn't worried about money. It was the challenge and excitement of the hamburger business that lured him. His new-fangled operation sported Tiffany lamps and other touches that Thomas felt placed it a cut above other fast feeders.

Most of all it had a greatly simplified menu of single, double, and triple hamburgers, chili, french fries, and a frosty dessert. Portion sizes on the hamburgers were larger than those of other chains. Thomas had cleverly designed a vehicle that could attract young adults in the 18-to-39 age bracket. This was a market that hadn't been particularly tapped by other fast feeders. He felt he had a potent weapon in the burger wars but never dreamed of the eventual success and power Wendy's would wield.

By 1980 the chain was firmly ensconced in virtually every area of the country, was making entries into international markets, and managed to chalk up a $30 million net profit on $1.2 billion sales for over 2,000 units. That was heady stuff for Thomas, who started with nothing and had only a tenth grade education. But he made the long climb upward with grit, determination, and savvy in identifying and executing an available market niche. It all prompted him to say that "we can catch McDonald's in total sales in another five years." (This presupposed McDonald's would somehow stand still at its then $6 billion sales.)

MAJOR CHALLENGES

In between Wendy's first opening and its rolling over the $1 billion mark, Thomas faced serious obstacles. He always projected total confidence but still had nagging doubts about whatever he did. Perhaps it was the way his own parents abandoned him at an early age and then his foster father insisted he would never amount to anything. Yet this was a spur to push him to greater efforts. Or perhaps it was the Wall Street "experts" and various other cynics insisting that in no way could an upstart hamburger chain hope to penetrate a market dominated by McDonald's first and Burger King as a distant second.

When Wendy's faltered in 1979, the cynics raised their ever-knowing eyebrows and said "we told you so." But Wendy's bounced back the following year, expanding its product lines beyond its original constraints. For Dave Thomas, who was not inclined to gloat, this still was a time when he could say as Wendy's closed in on Burger King's No. 2 position that "yes, it could be done."

TOUGH UPBRINGING

Thomas was born in Atlantic City, New Jersey, July 2, 1932. Abandoned by his parents, he was adopted by a Kalamazoo, Michigan, family at the age of six weeks. Since his adopted mother died when he was five years old, his childhood was a turbulent one. His father, an auto mechanic in Kalamazoo, remarried a year later and remarried again a couple of years after that. The family moved to LaPorte, Indiana, when Thomas was eight, to Princeton, Indiana, when he was nine, then to Evansville, Indiana, and to Knoxville, Tennessee. Thomas lived with his father, stepmother, and three stepbrothers.

He was an enterprising young man. His first job was delivering groceries on his bicycle at the age of eleven. He spent some of his time daydreaming about one day operating a hamburger stand. After he had worked there a while, the owners said they were closing the store for two weeks and that he should take a vacation. The owners returned a week early and told Thomas to report to work. But Thomas felt he had been promised two weeks off and stayed out the full time. The owners promptly discharged him.

When he was twelve, Thomas told the manager of a Walgreen drug store in Knoxville that he was sixteen—the minimum age for getting a job as a soda jerk there. When his family wanted to take him on a vacation, he asked for time off. The manager became suspicious and asked him if he was underage. When he admitted he was, the manager dismissed him. Rather than backing young Thomas, his unsympathetic foster father scolded him, "You'll never keep a job."

That summer he started working behind the counter at the Regas restaurant in Knoxville. His shift was from 8 P.M. to 8 A.M. all summer. In the fall he went back to school and worked weekends. When the family moved again, to Oakridge, Tennessee, the determined Thomas was daily bused to work thirty miles each way. His fondest recollections of that job were working the night shift with young Bill Regas, son of the owner and later to become a powerful force in the restaurant industry. "My main challenge in this job," Thomas recalls, "was to carry four plates of food and multi-cups of coffee at the same time without dripping or spilling anything. If you could do that, you were a success." He sometimes waited on over a hundred customers a night.

The next stop was Princeton, Indiana, where at the age of thirteen in 1945 he worked in a Western Auto store as a part-time clerk. In 1948 he was off to Fort Wayne, Indiana, as a busboy at the Hobby House restaurant. He was quickly promoted to a fountain man, grill man, french fry man, short order cook, and to just about every job in the restaurant. He also met his future wife, Lorraine, who was a waitress there.

Just as he turned eighteen and as the Korean War began, Thomas joined the army. He underwent basic training at Fort Benning, Georgia, and spent most of his time in the cooks' and bakers' school. He then was stationed in Germany where he was a mess sergeant and headed the bakery and maintenance of two consolidated mess halls. He later managed an enlisted men's club for two years, possibly the youngest person ever to hold such a post.

EARLY CAREER

After the army, Thomas went back to the Hobby House restaurant in Fort Wayne with some valuable food service experience under his belt. He returned to Hobby House with the feeling that somehow barbecue restaurants would sweep the nation. His boss also had an insatiable appetite for adding new menu items and felt the barbecue idea sounded interesting. The two inquired about Mac's Barbecue restaurant in Evansville, Indiana, which had gained a reputation in the field. They were stunned to learn that the place could do as much as $2,000 in carryout business in one night. He and his boss quickly became a franchisee of Mac's Barbecue.

Thomas spent a great deal of time at the Evansville store learning techniques for cooking the ribs. He ended up calling the Fort Wayne restaurant Hobby Ranch House with Barbecue. It featured ribs, potato salad, and baked beans, served on paper plates. Business was mediocre at best, but Thomas enjoyed it.

One day in 1956 when Thomas was twenty-four years old, a man in a white suit came into the barbecue place and started talking about the chicken business. Thomas greatly enjoyed the talk and the man's wide knowledge. Thomas was impressed with this man who said he was Colonel Sanders. It wasn't long before a deal was made; Hobby House Barbecue restaurant would now also serve fried chicken and would become a franchisee of Colonel Sanders. Thomas became vice president of the expanding Hobby House restaurants in 1958 and felt proud that he had achieved this goal by the age of twenty-six.

In early 1962 Hobby House called upon Thomas to bail out four floundering Kentucky Fried Chicken stores in Columbus, Ohio. These stores actually were called "Hobby Ranch House, featuring Kentucky Fried Chicken." He promptly got rid of all the managers, sharply trimmed the menu to basic chicken and switched the name to Colonel Sanders Kentucky Fried Chicken Take Homes. Sanders never really thought these restaurants had a chance and felt the Columbus market was just hopeless.

CROSSROADS

After fifteen years with Hobby House restaurants, Vice President Thomas made a decision to leave. He was becoming frustrated by the long hours and the seeming futility of it all. He didn't mind working sixty-five to seventy hours a week, but felt he simply wasn't going anyplace. He worked many extra hours when dishwashers didn't show up. He was discouraged and exhausted by what he perceived as a lack of sophistication in the industry.

Now thirty years old, with a wife, Lorraine, and four children, Thomas decided something had to happen in his career or he would rot away. "I'd made up my mind that if something didn't break by the time I was thirty years old," he says, "I'd get out and try another thing. There was no sophistication and no real business in those days. You just hoped the dishes were washed. It was all unorganized, and I was fed up."

Thomas jumped at the opportunity to move to Columbus, Ohio, and run the Hobby House franchise. He had an agreement with his boss, Phil Clauss, to acquire ownership of the market if he made the stores profitable. He loved the work and found he could work successfully without having to spend all his nights there. He at first traded barrels of fried chicken for radio and television advertising time. Sure enough, he built up the Columbus market restaurants as sales doubled and tripled.

In 1968 he was able to sell the revitalized operation for about $1.5 million in Kentucky Fried Chicken stock. He joined Kentucky Fried Chicken as regional operations director for six months and managed some 300 Florida stores for John Y. Brown, who had acquired the chain. The two clashed on policy and style, and Thomas departed. He invested some of his $1 million-plus in three Coventry Inn restaurants. When these went public, Arthur Treacher's fish and chips units began to sprout in the Columbus area. He became Treacher's operations vice president. But the hamburger still was foremost in his mind.

Thomas liked hamburgers better than anything. He would try some of the hamburgers at the growing McDonald's, Burger King, and Burger Chef units of those days and would find them lacking in something. He clearly saw the need and niche for a quality hamburger operation. He also liked chili and thick milk shakes and didn't think anyone was doing such a great job with these either.

NEW COMBO

So it was that Dave Thomas hit upon his winning combination: hamburgers, chili and a Frosty, along with french fries and soft drinks thrown in as part of the package. He immediately established a unique priority to serve fresh meat no matter how many units he would open. Fresh meat simply was better than the frozen product being used by everyone else, he was convinced, although not everyone agreed with this. His basic quarter-pound hamburger was bigger than any of the other fast feeders of that day. This was before McDonald's established a front-running position with its quarter-pounder. As a final touch he revived the square burger. It was operationally sound because the fresh beef could be pattied by machine in the store.

Thomas lovingly opened his first Wendy's unit on November 15, 1969, in downtown Columbus. It had no drive-through window. But it did offer single, double, and triple hamburgers, and it did give customers a chance to have custom-made hamburgers with their choice of condiments. The various combinations enabled Thomas to utilize the slogan, "Hamburgers made 256 ways," although they actually were cooked just one way on the grill.

Critics scoffed at his new-fangled ideas and confidently predicted he'd never make it. He wasn't so sure himself, although in retrospect he now sees that he couldn't miss. Whatever Thomas did has to be regarded as a mini-miracle. Of a myriad of new hamburger chains that sprouted in the 1970s, only Wendy's made it. The deck was heavily stacked against success in this crowded market, and Thomas defied the odds to accomplish his objectives.

His thought processes in developing the Wendy's concept are illuminating. His objective was to give customers a luxury-type hamburger that would suit their tastes. He decided to name the operation after his red-haired, freckle-faced daughter's nickname, but also because it had a built-in identification and was easy to say. He molded the theme around "Old-Fashioned Hamburgers" in an era when nostalgia was prevalent.

Some masterful merchandising touches were unveiled. The square hamburger pattie design meant the edges of the hamburgers would stick out and emphasize what a large hamburger it really was. A triple hamburger comprised of three patties on a bun was launched even though few people would eat such a huge hamburger. But it reassured some customers to know that such a hamburger was available if they wanted it. In addition, it encouraged sales of the double hamburger, which appeared to be small in comparison with the triple.

Thomas carefully wove each ingredient into his format. His chili had about one-quarter pound of pre-cooked ground beef in it and was an ideal complement to the hamburger for the production system. The Frosty—a cross between soft ice cream and a thick milk shake—also lured customers. And french fries were served because people expected it in a hamburger place. Here frozen fries were used as a matter of practicality. The eight condiments offered were ketchup, mustard, pickle, lettuce, onion, tomato, mayonnaise, and relish. Cheese was also available.

He fervently believed in a simple, limited menu. He felt that just about everyone liked hamburgers and there was no need to mix in other items that would needlessly complicate the system. He was sure he could attract just as much family business or more than anyone else without diversifying the menu. "A family eats together in a restaurant because it wants to, not because there are all kinds of different items to eat," he declared.

Thomas's early Wendy's units sported interior decors of Tiffany lamps, bentwood chairs, carpeting, and table tops adorned with reproductions of nineteenth-century advertising. They certainly were a cut above what had been known as fast food at the time. To maintain flexibility he had only tables for four and no booths. The chairs weren't particularly comfortable as there was no need to give customers the idea they could lounge around at the tables all day. Space and the imperative for fast turns were critical, particularly during peak periods.

SIMPLE SYSTEMS

A single "snake" line rather than the multiple cash register lines of other fast feeders highlighted Wendy's system. It gave Wendy's a tightly controlled system, and hostesses could expedite orders along the line when it got too busy. The system was labor-efficient as four employees could handle the preparation and serving during peak periods, and only two were required during slack times. These units could operate with only three full-time employees—a manager, assistant manager, and trainee—and part-timers to fill in as needed. Wendy's was able to reduce its labor costs to 15 percent of sales with efficiencies and with its larger hamburgers meaning a higher sales figure. "It doesn't take any more labor to prepare a larger hamburger at a higher price," said Thomas, contrasting his strategy with that of McDonald's and Burger King.

Thomas figured a way to boost sales at both peak and slack times was to have a drive-through window in operation. McDonald's actually had tried this but hadn't done much with it. Somehow Thomas sensed a drive-through would add sales because of its convenience and would not take away sales from the interior of the unit. With a separate cooking station and crew, drive-through could account for almost half of total sales. It did just that when the second Wendy's opened in Columbus with Thomas's first drive-through.

BARNEY ENTERS PICTURE

Thomas didn't do all this innovating himself. Bob Barney had worked with him since 1964 at Kentucky Fried Chicken and then Treacher's. The two seemed to be on the same wavelength. The truth is that when Thomas opened Wendy's, he just wanted to try something on his own. He had enough experience on the operations side of the business to know he could do it. But he didn't really know if he wanted to grow into a major chain with Wendy's or just remain happily in Columbus.

Barney was the one who actually saw the full potential when he agreed to join Wendy's as a partner. "Bob Barney really forced me into Wendy's full tilt," said Thomas. "When he came over, we just had to start building more stores. He talked me into franchising stores, and I never regretted it. It was a case of either staying small or going really big. Once you start something like that, you've got to really go with it. We knew we could produce the product."

For the next decade Barney was Thomas's alter-ego. Like Thomas, Barney had worked his way up in the business at almost every operational level. Each man thought out things for himself, but in the end they seemed to agree on just about everything. "We both saw the Colonel and what he did," said Thomas, "and we felt we could succeed in a different way."

That first Wendy's in downtown Columbus managed to achieve $2,-500 sales a week. The second Wendy's, a larger version with a drive-through on Henderson Road, chalked up $6,000 sales a week or an annual $300,000 pace—heady stuff for those days.

Once Thomas and Barney clearly dedicated themselves in 1971 to a reasonable expansion rate, they decided to start selling franchises as well as continuing to open company stores. Here they made a critical decision by opting to award territorial franchises in each area. A franchisee could develop Wendy's stores in a given geographical range up to the maximum capacity that the area would take. This strategy, as opposed to individual franchising unit by unit, would enable Wendy's to blanket the entire country with strong franchisees in the next decade. It wasn't too long before hundreds were standing in line to gain a Wendy's franchise and almost all the franchise territories were taken.

SIZE AND PRICING STRATEGIES

Thomas had never particularly liked the two-ounce or smaller hamburgers that were prevalent at the time. In fact, ever since the age of fifteen he had never eaten a small burger as far as he could recall, but had always opted to find a larger burger somewhere. As he puzzled his portion and pricing strategy, he knew from the start that his basic burger would be a quarter-pound. Since it was cooked to order and fresh, he felt that if he could be competitive in his pricing per ounce it would be perceived as an excellent value.

He set the initial price at 55¢ for a single hamburger, more than double what the competition was charging for a small burger. Figuring that a number of customers would choose cheese and tomatoes too—the only condiments for which there was an extra price—this was a 75-cent hamburger and raised a lot of eyebrows in the industry. "You'll never succeed with this," was what Thomas kept hearing, but he kept pushing along to the tune of jingling cash registers.

Wendy's entire system seemed to thrive on the most limited menu imaginable for this type of operation. While competitors kept pondering new items to be added, Thomas didn't cast a glance at anything other than what he already had on the menu. His items were big enough so that he didn't have to worry about trying to gain incremental sales from other menu offerings. Most of all, the speed of service—particularly in his drive-through system—was greatly helped by the simplicity of the format. Generally, orders were delivered to the customer within a minute of being received. This was the payoff since customers didn't go there for leisurely service. An earlier drive-through tried by Thomas with numerous menu items at KFC had failed.

In the early days of Wendy's he did try a few other items, but they never rolled up enough sales to make them worthwhile. He launched a test "How Sweet It Is" sugar cream pie and punch, and sales weren't very sweet at all. Thomas also tried a breakfast menu of rolls, coffee, and hamburgers, and that wasn't terribly successful either. It would be almost a decade before he was forced to think seriously about the need for developing some strong-selling new items.

"I just got sick of seeing hamburgers abused," Thomas said of his motivation in opening his first Wendy's. "How people could precook it, put mustard and catsup on it, wrap it in paper and keep it warm under a heat lamp, I'll never know. But I did know we weren't going to do that at Wendy's."

FRESH BEEF

Thomas vowed that Wendy's would use only fresh 100 percent pure domestic beef and that it would be made into patties daily in the restaurants. Hamburgers would be served hot off the grill and never prewrapped or reheated. Adopting the motto, "Quality is our recipe," Wendy's stuck with hamburgers, chili, french fries, a frosty dairy dessert, and soft drinks.

The cynics—and there were many of them—challenged whether Thomas's fresh domestic beef really was better than anyone else's frozen beef and questioned whether a distribution system could be developed that would supply fresh beef to a wide-ranging network of restaurants. It turned out to be entirely feasible, and what really counted was not whether the fresh hamburgers were actually a better product than someone else's frozen hamburgers, but rather how the public perceived it. Generally there was a perception that the fresh hamburgers somehow were better.

By 1975, as the chain's growth and franchises spurted around the country, Barney—who lined up much of the franchising program—was so besieged by prospective franchisees at any industry convention he would attend that he simply could no longer go to conventions. This was the type of problem other franchising companies might have enjoyed.

Wendy's record was enviable—only one store closed in a business where failure and closing were often as common as success. Part of the reason for this powerful record was that Thomas made sure a daily record was maintained of the chain's lowest 10 percent of stores in sales. Immediate coupon and promotional campaigns would be triggered to revive sales at any of these lagging stores. It just wouldn't get to the point where a store had to close.

Thomas and Barney both had the advantage of having been operators for years and of knowing the individual problems of franchisees. "Bob and I learned the business from the ground up," noted Thomas, "and we knew what was required to help franchisees." They provided as much help as they possibly could for franchisees and also emphasized an intensive training program at Wendy's Management Institute in

Columbus. "No franchisee was going to fail because we didn't give him the tools," Thomas vowed.

He insisted his franchisees be involved people who were dedicated to the success of Wendy's and its hamburgers. Doctors, lawyers, and other such investors were excluded because Thomas wanted people who would work constantly to succeed only at Wendy's. Of course, he could afford to be selective in picking franchisees for remaining territories—thousands of franchisee applications were on file with Wendy's as word spread of its achievements. Franchising always has had a magical pull for investors. Considering all the failures, a proven success is bound to attract even more interest.

Thomas seemed to be proving the critics wrong every step of the way as Wendy's kept opening more and more units and grabbing a wider share of the hamburger market. By early 1979 it had 1,500 units and had just scored an average annual per unit volume of $668,000. It had jumped into the No. 3 position behind McDonald's and Burger King in the burger wars. It was proving extremely formidable competition for Burger King, which itself was moving upward.

BURGER SLUMP

But then Wendy's—more dependent on the hamburger than its competitors—was hard hit by the rising cost of ground beef, which moved from 82¢ per pound in 1978 to $1.29 per pound in 1979. Vulnerable to this fluctuation, Thomas had no choice but to raise Wendy's menu prices. Despite his philosophy of always projecting a price/value relationship, margins had to be protected. The result was a precipitous falloff in customer counts as consumer resistance stiffened against price increases. Average systemwide per unit sales dipped to $620,000 in 1979, and Thomas and Barney had to reevaluate their whole strategy.

EXECUTIVE REALIGNMENT

First, Thomas implemented a decision that he had reached before the dropoff hit. At age forty-seven he would yield the chief executive's position to Barney. Thomas would remain board chairman, but the slightly younger Barney would take full command. For a man of Thomas's ego and intensity to give up authority like this took a great deal of soul-searching. "I did it because you have to build an organization and give people a chance," he said. "It was a very tough decision for me." Thomas and Barney continued to consult on the major policy decisions, but Barney took full and complete command of the daily operations.

The first step of the plan to put Wendy's back on the track was to build a totally professional organization with more depth. Until then Thomas and Barney had been doing almost everything themselves. But the chain simply had grown too big for this. They now proceeded to mold an experienced team of top executives. Ron Fay, a former Wendy's franchisee and a veteran operations man, became executive vice president and chief operating officer. Darrough Diamond, a former McDonald's and Arby's marketing executive, was brought in as senior vice president of marketing. Joseph Madigan, a top Borden Company financial executive, came over as executive vice president and chief financial officer.

Thomas and Barney brought in others too as they repositioned Wendy's for the 1980s. The chain had gone through a classic cycle, reaching a peak and then temporarily slumping. Now all the "I told you so's" on Wall Street were having a field day. It was time for a classic comeback. While Thomas and Barney had assured everyone for years that there would be no deviation from their sharply limited menu, they had the flexibility to realize that new strategy was needed for the 1980s. They could no longer rely strictly on the hamburger and be at the mercy of wildly fluctuating prices.

MENU EXPANSION

A new three-pronged attack was launched to give Wendy's more weapons in its arsenal. Salad bars, a filet of chicken breast sandwich, and a kids' Fun Pak meal, including Wendy's first small hamburger, were tested and then launched chainwide. Breakfast was also tested, but any rollout was delayed until problems in the system could be overcome. It all seemed like treason to those who had heard Thomas and Barney repeatedly proclaim the gospel that there shall be nothing added to the menu beyond hamburger, chili, french fries, a Frosty, and soft drinks.

But circumstances changed the gospel in an effort to generate a wider base. Customers were becoming more sophisticated and demanding variety. If Wendy's wanted to draw people more than once or twice a week, they'd have to offer choices. They also were broadening their appeal to the children's market with the Fun Pak and to women with the salad bar. They were protecting their position against competitors who were pouring in with these and other items.

Wendy's was able to keep its investment costs below those of most competitors. Its average total cost for a new unit in 1980 was $529,-000—perhaps triple what it had been when Wendy's opened its initial Columbus unit in 1969 but still within reason during this inflationary period. These averages were comprised of $166,000 for land, $269,-000 for the building, and $94,000 for equipment. Thomas's tidy little package was still paying dividends in a lower investment cost and a higher return on investment. Wendy's achieved a solid 26.6 percent return on average equity for 1980.

Thomas also saw to it that Wendy's would be able to react to local market situations. Stronger regional marketing was established to give Wendy's local clout. Field supervisors stayed closer to the company and franchised units as Wendy's exercised a decentralized control over its wide-ranging system. The result was more local merchandising and local advertising identity. Wendy's still was known as a national chain but was establishing itself as the local hamburger restaurant too.

Wendy's was opening as many as 400 to 500 restaurants a year annually in the late 1970s, and the pace proved faster than the chain could effectively control. "We grew so fast that people were undertrained," observed Thomas. There were just a certain number of capable field supervisors and unit managers who could be trained to do the job. Finally, the pace of openings was slowed to a more controllable 229 in 1980 and then about 260 in 1981.

With domestic markets and prime traffic sites becoming somewhat saturated, Wendy's reached out to open units in Munich, Tokyo, London, Geneva, Lausanne, Brussels, Madrid, and Frankfurt. Agreements also were signed to develop Malaysia and Singapore. By the end of 1981 Wendy's expected to have some thirty overseas units in operation and to start truly reflecting its corporate name of Wendy's International.

CHICKEN EXPERIMENT

While Thomas was truly in love with hamburgers, he never forgot his early chicken upbringing with Colonel Sanders. He and Barney decided that what Wendy's had accomplished in the hamburger business could and should have a counterpart in chicken. The two thought of a chicken and biscuits idea and put it into action in 1979. Thomas wanted to call it Three Sisters after his daughter Wendy's three sisters, but when that didn't prove feasible he dubbed it Sisters' Chicken & Biscuits. Both men wanted to be sure that Sisters' efforts didn't dilute the main thrust of Wendy's, so a separate company was formed under the direction of Jim Near, a former Wendy's franchisee.

If one didn't know, one might have thought Sisters was a double for Wendy's. It had the drive-through window, the same production system, and the same service line for customers. But Sisters featured a semi-spicy fried chicken along with rice, baked beans, cole slaw, and corn on the cob. Four initial test units launched in Columbus achieved an average $1 million annual volume—well above the $800,000 that Wendy's was attaining on its newest units.

Wendy's acquired 100 percent control of Sisters in early 1981, but it remained a separate subsidiary and Thomas was careful to emphasize Sisters as still a test project. He was confident it could grow into a powerful national chain in its own right but was well aware of how other major chains had stumbled when they tried to diversify. Most of all, he had to ask the question of whether money being diverted to Sisters could be utilized instead to open more Wendy's units with a much higher return on investment. In any case the similarity of Sisters' physical plant to Wendy's would permit conversions if necessary.

A portly grandfather in his late forties, Thomas tried to take an objective, relaxed view of things. But he felt so strongly about Wendy's and was so confident of its future that he found it hard to accept criticism. When Wall Street was down on Wendy's in 1979, he insisted the chain was still on the right track, that this simply was part of a cycle that would require reorganization and professionalization, and that the business wasn't being run for the benefit of Wall Street. Nevertheless, he wanted Wall Street's approval. He couldn't help but smile an "I told you so" when business picked up and Wendy's was admitted to membership on the New York Stock Exchange in May 1981. This transfer from being an over-the-counter stock meant more in terms of stature than anything else.

Thomas, an acknowledged giant in the fast-food industry, has maintained for years that he's not in the fast-food business. He feels fast food is an unfortunate term connoting nonnutritious food. "We're offering food that's healthy and tastes good," he says. "Fast food really relates to something coming out of a vending machine, and it's not us at all." This feeling is a reflection of his constant striving for quality. He wants Wendy's to be ahead of everyone else.

THE McDONALD'S CHALLENGE

The Horatio Alger award winner still thinks Wendy's has a realistic shot at surpassing McDonald's in total sales. "I know we can do it," he asserts, "and we intend to do it." It does sound like a farfetched dream, with Wendy's sales at $1.2 billion in 1980 compared with $6 billion for McDonald's. But Wendy's was threatening to overtake Burger King in total sales within a few years, and Thomas's vision simply has been more farsighted than anyone else's.

Who knows, perhaps he and Barney will do it. It would be no more preposterous than someone having the audacity to think Thomas could ever grow to a $1 billion chain on that day he opened his first Wendy's in Columbus, Ohio, in 1969. Thomas has made a habit of defying logic and even surprises himself sometimes. He is an inspirational lesson in the power of positive thinking, garnished with extra food service savvy and dedication.

2

Don Smith

MIRACLE MAKER

Donald N. Smith fell in love with the fast-food business when he started working as a youth at his father's Calgary, Alberta, drive-in. Here in the late 1950s, before he had ever heard of McDonald's or Burger King or any other fast-food chain of that era, young Smith tried his hand as a grill man and at other assorted tasks at his father's place. This was a sparsely populated part of Canada by United States standards and not what one would call an ideal fast-food market, but he and his father managed to attract their share of customers.

Ketchup ran in Smith's veins from the first. Although he maintained a perspective about things, hamburgers would dominate his thinking and his very existence for many years. He literally would dream about how to make a better hamburger and a better environment in which to sell that hamburger. He would act on these dreams with remarkable success to the point where he would be labeled the Fred Silverman of the restaurant business—conjuring up the same favorable and unfavorable connotations about the television network programming "genius," depending on one's perspective. But to Don Smith, what he wrought in the burger business were not miracles but commonsense, everyday principles applied to particular situations. Just as Silverman placed his style on three major networks, Smith put his imprint on three dominant food service chain companies. But Silverman's departure from NBC in July 1981 when the network's ratings simply wouldn't come out of the doldrums contrasted with the upward surge that Smith was apparently able to generate at Pizza Hut and Taco Bell. Nevertheless, one could only hope that Silverman's sudden fall was not somehow an omen for Smith.

UNCANNY TIMING

Smith's career has been dotted with "lucky coincidences"—he always seemed to be in the right place at the right time. Whenever any semblance of an opportunity arose, he seized it. When he was twenty-five in 1965, he happened to meet Fred Turner, then McDonald's operations vice president, at a neighbor's house in a small Minnesota town. By this time Smith had most emphatically heard of McDonald's. The next thing he knew, he was an assistant manager at a McDonald's in California. Then he seemed to catapult out of a cannon, climbing rapidly from one goal to another.

He specialized in converting the worst or the mediocre into the best. California McDonald's unit sales soared 25 percent in two years when he headed that region. The Mid-Atlantic region jumped from the weakest on key criteria to close to the strongest during the three years that he was regional vice president there.

When Smith had finally risen to McDonald's senior executive vice president and chief operations officer in January 1977, he was lured away with an offer from the Pillsbury Company, which urgently wanted its Burger Kings to be more competitive with McDonald's and didn't want to be outflanked by Wendy's moving up on the outside. He became Burger King president and chief executive officer with the authority and relative autonomy he desired. Smith sometimes acted as if he were cloned from Ray Kroc, McDonald's founder and driving spiritual force, but he still managed to put his own imprint on everything.

He studied Burger King's challenges relentlessly and put in motion a series of measures designed to start closing the gap between Burger King's $565,000 average per unit sales and McDonald's $850,000.

He went for the children's market with a Magic Burger King character who could give Ronald McDonald a run for his money. He moved Burger King more into the dinner business with a series of specialty sandwiches. He sharply raised the quality of french fries and shakes. He sought to speed production and service and to upgrade decor.

By the spring of 1980 these and other actions had paid off with an average per unit sales boost to $748,000 for Burger King stores. But Burger King was still chasing McDonald's which by then had topped $1 million in average sales. Furthermore, Burger King's store pre-tax profit margin still was only 12 percent compared with 18 percent for McDonald's. The gap was closing some, and it seemed that Smith had done as much as humanly possible, given McDonald's wide original lead and inexhaustible resources. He certainly had fended off Wendy's bid to move into the No. 2 burger position.

ENTICING OFFER

It was at this juncture that Donald Kendall, chairman of PepsiCo, came in with the bid that Smith couldn't refuse. Kendall wanted this burger miracle man who had turned Burger King in the right directions to apply similar magic to the Pizza Hut and Taco Bell chains which PepsiCo had acquired in 1977 and 1978. Neither was achieving its potential although each remained the leader of its market segment.

Kendall wanted Smith to be president and chief executive officer of a new PepsiCo food service division (not to be confused with the corporation's Pepsi-Cola food service division) which would spearhead the operation of Pizza Hut and Taco Bell. Smith was enticed not only by a lucrative package but by the clear indication of autonomy to run the chains his way (providing their profits and return on investments accelerated over the next few years) and by the future possibility of acquiring still another fast-food chain under PepsiCo. Smith may have accomplished as much as he could at Burger King, and Pillsbury's other food service chains—Steak & Ale and Poppin' Fresh Pies—were under other authorities. Actually Pillsbury assured Smith he could become group director of all three chains, but he rejected this prospect. He was particularly disappointed when Pillsbury appeared less committed to invest in new Burger King company units.

In any case Smith gravitated to PepsiCo's Purchase, New York, headquarters in May 1980. When he arrived he was faced with a situation more critical than when he had assumed the reins at Burger King. He now had two problems instead of one. Frank Carney, Pizza Hut founder and president who had sold to PepsiCo with the understanding that besides making millions of dollars on the deal he would be in line for the very post that now went to Smith, predictably resigned from Pizza Hut. Carney had the loyalty and faith of franchisees, some of whom had been with him ever since he started Pizza Hut in 1958 or had joined soon afterward. Perhaps surprisingly, Smith was not pleased by Carney's resignation.

Smith had hoped to supervise changes he wanted to implement to boost Pizza Hut's lagging $235,000 average per unit sales. But he didn't relish the need to bring in a new Pizza Hut president and start totally rebuilding the franchisees' loyalty to another authority. He named Arthur Gunther, who had been McDonald's marketing vice president when Smith was there, as Pizza Hut president and set immediate goals of boosting Pizza Hut's average per unit sales $50,000 each year.

With Taco Bell, sales were not so much of a problem and the main challenge was to streamline and modernize the operation and franchisee network so that the chain could move faster. Robert McKay remained as Taco Bell president until March 1981 and then resigned. This left Smith free to take over temporarily and institute the reforms that would set Taco Bell on course. He promoted Charles Boppell to Taco Bell president in mid-1981.

By this time Pizza Hut was already turning around with new product introductions having pushed its per unit average up to a $285,000 a year pace, or the $50,000 incremental goal that Smith had set for the first year. "You simply make your goals when you work for Don Smith or you hear about it," says one associate. Smith himself never even considers the possibility that he won't make the goals, and this confidence is one reason why he consistently does achieve the goals he sets.

Smith was brought up in the mining town of Kirkland Lake, Ontario. His father worked for a large mining and oil exploration company as an accountant, and his mother was a teacher. Smith grew up doing odd jobs such as working in a grocery store when he was fourteen. The family moved to several cities, including Salt Lake City and Billings, Montana. The rise and fall of commodities markets dictated when his father would be transferred to another mining location.

BURGER BAPTISM

Smith graduated from Billings, Montana, High School in 1958 and served six months in the marine corps before moving to Calgary to work as a grill man at his father's new Burger Boy drive-in. Smith's original objective at Burger Boy was to earn money for college. The only major chain he had heard of then was the Burger Boy drive-in and coffee shop group.

After nine months at Burger Boy, he went to the University of Montana in Missoula, and graduated with a marketing degree. He also worked part-time at Henry's fast-food place there. His first job after college was as a manager trainee for Missoula's Montgomery Ward store. He learned how to sell carpeting and furniture and moved up to head the appliance department. But the food service business was in Smith's blood, and he sensed a vacuum while he was away from it.

A group which had been associated with Henry's launched a new franchise unit in Moorehead and called it Autodine to emphasize the combined drive-in and food aspects. Smith joined the operation as a manager in 1963 and became field supervisor when Autodine expanded to six units in Minnesota and North Dakota. He was fascinated with this new fast-food business, but he had nobody with whom to discuss his feelings and aspirations.

ENTER McDONALD'S

One day in 1965 a Moorehead neighbor of Smith's, an elderly lady, happened to mention that she knew someone from McDonald's and it might be interesting for Smith to meet him. Smith was delighted. About six months later the McDonald's person was on a fishing trip and passed through Moorehead. Smith's neighbor introduced them, and Smith was surprised and happy to be talking with Fred Turner, McDonald's operations vice president. Smith thirsted for knowledge and input about fast food as a business, and Turner was eager to give it to him.

"This session was the biggest treat I ever had," Smith recalls. He and Turner chatted amiably for two hours.

Turner had Smith fly to Chicago headquarters and talk with a group that had franchise rights to the McDonald's in the Salt Lake City area. The group indicated it might finance the $25,000 that Smith would need for the deal, if a deal with another interested investor fell through. The other investor came up with the money, but Smith couldn't. He lost his chance to be a franchisee but was soon to gain an even greater opportunity on the operations side.

A few months later, Smith was in a Grand Forks, North Dakota, motel near one of his Autodine units during one of the worst Great Plains blizzards. Suddenly the phone rang, and McDonald's personnel manager offered Smith a position in California with the company's new operations training program. Turner wanted to give Smith a start with McDonald's, and it took Smith all of five seconds to decide that he would accept the job as an assistant manager. He also didn't mind moving from the bitter cold climate to the California warmth.

Just a week later Smith packed all his belongings into a U-Haul trailer and moved to California where he began work at McDonald's Canoga Park unit on April 1, 1966. He had no more than six years' experience in the fast-food business until that time, but he had a flair for the business. He quickly rose from an assistant unit manager to a field consultant to the Los Angeles area operations manager. Here Smith got his first experience in how not to run a new product test program. McDonald's used its company-owned Santa Monica store near Los Angeles as a test for a new roast beef sandwich. McDonald's decided to use quality choice grade roast beef, but the shrinkage in this product gave the customer less than he expected for the price. No matter what McDonald's tried to do with the roast beef, it just wouldn't work and Smith felt powerless to do anything about it.

SOARING RESULTS

He moved up to West Coast operations manager in 1969 because he produced superior performance figures no matter what units he touched. McDonald's West Coast stores were not known for consistency in sales and profits. He changed that and stressed more productive techniques and higher margins. The sales average of the units jumped from $300,000 to $400,000 under Smith.

As word spread at McDonald's Oak Brook, Illinois, headquarters of Smith's operations prowess on the West Coast, the chain's executives were shaking their heads in dismay at the pathetic figures emanating from the Mid-Atlantic region. This was McDonald's worst region in just about every conceivable aspect of the business. Perhaps Smith could do something about it. He welcomed the challenge and took the same units with the same managers on an entirely different tack. He stuck to the basics but instilled a winning spirit in all of them. Smith would go from unit to unit preaching his positive message that "we can do it." He was in effect an equal partner with each unit manager, and together they would turn the tide.

Smith became McDonald's regional vice president for the Mid-Atlantic area based in Washington, D.C., in 1970. He analyzed the problems, and things started turning quickly. "I pushed for execution and higher standards," he recalls. "Nothing spectacular, just basics." People love to rally around a winner, and Smith projected victory in everything he did. In just three years, with some key personnel changes, he took the Mid-Atlantic region from McDonald's worst region to its best in sales and profit growth. This pattern, which would be repeated many times in Smith's career, was accomplished with essentially the same personnel.

In 1973, at the age of thirty-three, McDonald's promoted Smith to executive vice president for operations. He was also placed in charge of a special company group that headed franchising and purchasing. Smith, then the leading operations mind of the current young crop, was one of a steady stream of bright young executives that McDonald's was producing. Actually the top operations post had been held earlier by Fred Turner, then by Webb Lowe—who left to become president of the Bonanza budget steakhouse chain—and then by C. James Lynch, who had just been named president of the A&W fast-food chain. When Smith succeeded Lynch as operations head, Turner was McDonald's prime force and Edward Schmitt, later to become president, ran the field staff.

Smith made his mark as an executive vice president and officially was designated senior executive vice president and chief operations officer as of January 1977. He had actually been doing the job for nine months before receiving the official title. But just before he officially started in his new post, he was lured away to Burger King as president and chief executive officer.

"I have no regrets about leaving McDonald's," says Smith, whose successor there, Michael Quinlan, rose to president of the newly formed McDonald's USA subsidiary in 1980 but was still No. 3 in the hierarchy behind Turner and Schmitt. Smith had a high regard for Turner, who had nurtured him in the company. But each had a strong ego and strong opinions. They were starting to disagree about things, and it seemed inevitable that Smith would leave to run his own show somewhere.

When Smith arrived at Burger King in early February 1977, after taking a one-month vacation to recharge his batteries for the enormous job ahead, he faced a serious task. There was nothing radically wrong with Burger King except that it wasn't meeting its potential. It had been launched in Miami in 1954 by James McLamore and David Edgerton, the same year that McDonald's started as a company. But McDonald's had moved ahead far more aggressively and completely seized the leadership in the burger field. Pillsbury, which acquired Burger King in 1967, was not happy. By early 1977 Burger King had some 1,800 units doing $880 million total annual sales while McDonald's had over 4,000 units doing $3.75 billion. Moreover, McDonald's average per unit sales were at $850,000 while Burger King's were barely topping $500,000.

SOLUTIONS SOUGHT

Smith was charged by Pillsbury with finding solutions to the dilemma. His first impression was that Burger King basically was a solid operation but that its strategy could be sharpened. It was pushing a larger Whopper hamburger sandwich, wooing young adults and hoping to obtain family business that way. Smith actually found this attempt to establish an individual niche for Burger King a plus but felt it also would have to find other approaches to woo children and broaden its market. The chain was particularly squeezed by Wendy's large-size burger marketing approach for young adults.

Some felt that with these three major chains fighting it out for market share and burger chains of all types on every side, saturation was fast approaching. But there was still plenty of room for growth if an individual identity could be established.

As has always been his style, Smith decided to see for himself. He embarked on an extensive national tour for several months, visiting many of Burger King's company and franchised units. He might visit as many as ten units in a day, on the move from early morning to late at night. He had inexhaustible energy and enthusiasm and an indomitable will to do the job.

Smith, medium-built with alert eyes that seemed to penetrate right through a situation, cut an impressive figure as he popped into the stores. Some of the employees were pleased that the chief executive was paying so much attention to them. Others viewed the whole thing with trepidation, expecting a massive shakeup. Smith projected a friendly approach. He was there to tell the employees how important they were and to gather information as to what should be done to turn the burger wars more in favor of Burger King. "Amazingly Don Smith was the first Burger King executive we'd ever even met," said one franchisee.

NEW TEAM

As a first step Smith wanted to get his own type of team in place. Since he was taking on McDonald's in the struggle for burger supremacy and since he had the greatest respect for McDonald's people and systems, he hired some executives from McDonald's. These included Jim Lynch, who had preceded Smith as McDonald's executive vice president for operations and then had become A&W president, as international vice president; John Barnes as menu development vice president; Victor Wood as real estate vice president; and Ronald White as vice president in charge of Canada. Smith blended in some of the remaining Burger King executives with these new additions. He delegated authority wherever possible but made sure he knew exactly what was happening at every level himself.

After seven months of intensive personal observations of the stores, the product, the employees, and the customers, Smith was ready to move. He had a deliberate style of probing and thinking, but once he made up his mind he acted decisively.

BETTER TASTE

He started with two basic products where McDonald's previously had Burger King solidly beaten in quality—french fries and milk shakes. Smith knew enough customers had complained about the taste of the french fries that something had to be done. He introduced a new french fry with a different cooking oil and a different cooking process. It involved the same potato brand as McDonald's used, the same shortening, and a similar deep-frying system. At the same time the milk shake was reformulated to improve the taste. Nobody knew it for a fact, but it was suspected that these reformulations were adopted from the best of McDonald's. Smith merely smiled without committing himself when asked about it. After all, what did it matter where it came from? Assuming the specifications would be carried out at the stores, he now had superior products.

Smith's campaign to improve taste and quality was based on a premise that women and children were fussier about taste, and these were the customers where the market could be broadened. Burger King's strongest appeal had been to young adult men. Now Smith also decided to replace the chain's 1.6-ounce small burger with a 2-ounce one that would look larger on the bun and whose taste would be more attractive to women and children. He started thinking about frozen yogurt and a salad bar as possible lighter fare that would help entice the women.

Convinced that he could emulate McDonald's in some ways but do it better, Smith unveiled a Magic Burger King character who could wow children at the units. An extensive advertising and promotion campaign hailed this character as the greatest thing since Houdini. Specially trained hostesses in the stores performed magic tricks for the children. If Burger King had neglected the kids previously, Burger King was certainly making up for it now.

But if Smith expected to raise Burger King's unit sales by $50,000 a year, he would have to find a way to speed up the chain's cumbersome production system. If McDonald's could fill almost any order within thirty seconds, why did it sometimes take Burger King a minute or two? Smith quickly found that Burger King's L-shaped or T-shaped production "hospitality" system had too many built-in delays. He embarked on a modification program to streamline the operation.

He knew that any item which took extra time to prepare could bog down the whole system. Double-meat burgers were an example of how the system could be slowed, and he ordered a drastic de-emphasis of such items. Worst of all, though, was that the division of labor was out of kilter. He began converting soft drink machines and french fry bins to enable counter girls and back-of-the-house employees to prepare them. This would mean a unit no longer had to operate with the same number of employees during nonpeak hours. Equipment also had to be streamlined, and Smith introduced a new french fry machine that operated automatically at the touch of a button. He also pushed for machines that could speed the broiler loading and for more fry vats and filtering machines.

Burger King still used an old-fashioned system of having counter hostesses shout the orders over a microphone. Smith launched a new system with a printout device which could tell sandwich preparation people the items ordered when the counter hostess punched the cash register. Not only was this speedier, but it reduced the margin for error.

The backbone of the new production system would be a production manager for each unit. This person, a veteran hourly worker, would keep a careful eye on the system to be sure that customers actually were receiving prompt, courteous service. Previously the store manager had to handle all these tasks and was diverted from production supervisory tasks. Now the manager could work with counter hostesses and the rest of the operation for maximum speed. While quality still counted—and Burger King's Whopper was highly rated in this regard—the name of the game was *fast* food.

STRONGER IMAGE

Smith felt Burger King had to dress up its image if it was going to impress customers enough to gain market share. After all, McDonald's and others were pouring in hundreds of thousands of dollars in remodeling campaigns. He geared up for expenditures on new lighting, new ceilings, new seats, wall decorations, and superior landscaping. Everything was designed to make Burger King look the part of a champion without overdoing it and swinging into pretentious decor. More than any of these decor changes, though, Smith was dedicated to the idea of openness for the customer. "If there's anything I abhor," he declared, "it's walling off the customer from the food preparation. When the customer can only guess what's happening back there, he's not thrilled with it or so trusting." It wasn't long before Burger King's food preparation areas were more open to customer view.

In a sense this was one way of establishing more credibility and rapport with the customer. Another way was with a straighter pricing system. Perhaps $1.98 or 99¢ sound more appealing as price points, but Smith never believed in such gimmicks. Soon the Whopper was selling for 90¢ instead of 89¢.

Smith was convinced he had a basically solid group of franchisees to work with and that there was nothing really wrong with the company stores. But there were inconsistencies on all sides. A unit would shine in service and quality one day and slide into bad habits the next day so that a customer never knew what to expect. The way Smith saw it, a lot of this stemmed from the idea of complete central authority invested in Burger King headquarters and its executives there. At almost 2,000 units, the chain simply was too large to run entirely from a central base. Real authority was too far from the unit, too far from the customer. It meant slow reactions to regional situations and a lack of local controls.

REGIONAL STRATEGY

Smith set in motion a complete regionalization plan which would decentralize Burger King over the next one and one-half years. But this decentralization was actually the only way to maintain centralized control over the widespread Burger King empire. Smith's plan was to establish ten regions (this would grow to twelve over the next few years) with a regional director in charge of each of the offices. These regional offices would emulate the main functions of the headquarters office with operations, marketing, training, real estate, construction, and personnel managers each reporting to the regional director, who in turn would report to Burger King's operations vice president at headquarters. As this system was implemented, it gave Burger King more flexibility in reacting to local market situations such as necessary rapid competitive adjustments in pricing or merchandising strategies.

Once again Smith had taken a page right out of the McDonald's manual on how to regionalize a large chain for successful battle. With all the strategic similarities to McDonald's now appearing, some of Burger King's franchisees started asking in all seriousness whether Golden Arches would start popping up in front of Burger Kings. Smith was indeed "McDonaldizing" Burger King, but it was more a case of rational analysis of specific situations and implementation than blind copying.

Burger King soon would start to give McDonald's a run for its money, causing McDonald's executives to enter their famous "think tank" at their Oak Brook, Illinois, headquarters with reams of material on strategies to counteract Burger King's surge. One of the things which confidential McDonald's surveys had revealed was that many consumers actually preferred the Whopper to the Big Mac in terms of perceived quality but that Burger King's advertising and promotion backup hadn't come close to matching McDonald's.

Smith knew the importance of high traffic site selection from his McDonald's days. While he didn't quite subscribe to the theory that fast-food success hinged on three factors—location, location, and location—he did feel a high traffic location was very important. He opted for some innovative locations such as bus terminals, with Greyhound Food Management as the new franchisee. Greyhound started producing more $1 million to $2 million sales units than any other Burger King franchisee.

While Smith respected the franchisees and encouraged them to be innovative, there were limits. He insisted that the menu and production system be reasonably standardized while allowing room for experimentation in such matters as decor and seating arrangements. One strong-minded franchisee in particular, Horn & Hardart in New York City, clashed head-on with Smith's insistence that it be done his way. While the customer indeed could "have it your way" on some items, the franchisee couldn't. Horn & Hardart wanted to expand into geographic areas where the corporation felt they couldn't properly control and operate more Burger Kings. Smith cracked down by barring them from future franchise units.

It was essentially a clash of wills between Smith and Horn & Hardart president Barry Florescue, who earlier had been a Burger King franchisee in Florida. The result was a stalemate; both sides held their ground, filing suits and counter suits and eventually settling the matter out of court. Horn & Hardart, which had turned slow-moving, old-fashioned automats and cafeterias into profitable Burger Kings, proceeded to emphasize its future franchising with the Arby's roast beef fast-food chain.

Some called Smith's revitalization tactics "Operation Grand Slam," a term that captured the imagination of enough of the chain's employees to make a difference. His goal of minimum $50,000 annual sales increases was surpassed in 1977, 1978, and 1979. Along with this went higher dollar profits. Pillsbury was at last satisfied that its fast-food vehicle was finally starting to rise to its full potential, and Smith seemed secure in his job.

SPECIALTY PUSH

Above all else Smith's biggest contribution toward sustained sales growth was a comprehensive testing and then introduction of four sandwiches which propelled Burger King toward a new role as a specialty sandwich fast-food chain, although still buttressed by the ubiquitous hamburger. These new sandwiches enabled Burger King to widen its market and to appeal to more varied tastes. It also meant that customers no longer would feel they could frequent Burger King only once or twice a week because of the limited fare. Whatever he did, Smith made sure the new products would fit into Burger King's production capabilities.

These specialty sandwiches were primarily created to change Burger King's volume patterns. Most of Burger King's business previously was done before 5 P.M. In the evening Burger King stayed open, but the seating and service capability were underused. Smith's specialty sandwich line switched the balance so that 60 percent of the sales now came after 5 P.M. and the entire system became more productive rather than being a slave to the luncheon trade.

The backbone of the specialty sandwiches was a chopped steak sandwich. Previous Burger King tests before Smith had utilized round steak, which proved to be inconsistent from one store to the next. Furthermore, it didn't fit the fast-food image which Burger King was still projecting. Smith finally declared that Burger King would be committed to the chopped beef product, and it was rolled out nationally. He also unveiled a fried breast of white meat chicken filet as another new product. At the same time there were two products launched that were modifications of previous Burger King merchandising. A cold ham and cheese sandwich replaced a "Yumbo" sandwich, and a breaded deep-fried white fish sandwich replaced the "Whaler." These new products were soon accounting for sales rises of as much as 20 percent when they were introduced in 1979.

BREAKFAST DILEMMA

One thing that stymied Smith, though, was the complete early morning silence of Burger Kings. Productive space was being wasted because the chain couldn't devise a workable breakfast format while McDonald's for years had dominated the breakfast market. The problem was that Burger King used broilers for its burgers and that few of the units had grills that could be utilized for breakfast. Any conversion of equipment might cost more than it was worth. Naturally Smith tried to figure out a breakfast menu which wouldn't need grills. He wouldn't open for breakfast unless he felt it would be profitable. Still, he tested an egg and pancake breakfast in forty downtown units with special grills installed. Later he had broiler-type breakfast items tested which would become the forerunner of a full-fledged Burger King breakfast effort.

"Breakfast is a very tricky business," Smith observes. "It must have an extremely high sales plateau to be successful. You need an extra manager to make it work. A unit needs at least $300 sales for a few-hour breakfast period to make it pay."

He also lined up other possible items which could further expand dinner business. An individual-size pizza and a barbecued beef sandwich were items he tested for possible use. The sandwich was comprised of beef slices seasoned with barbecue sauce and served warm on a hamburger bun. The pizza was served with cheese, pepperoni, or sausage. These items were not necessarily destined for actual use but were part of Smith's strategy of preparing for any eventuality.

To maximize the sales at many suburban Burger Kings, Smith pushed the drive-through window idea. Drive-throughs weren't novel in the fast-food business then, but Burger King hadn't utilized them enough. Now they took in one-third of the total sales at many units, and much of this was comprised of incremental sales. But real estate costs were soaring and Smith had the idea that if he could find small sites, a far higher profit ratio could be achieved with a scaled-down version of Burger King. He set plans in motion for Burger Stop units which would be half the size of Burger Kings. Menu items would be sharply reduced, and drive-through and walk-up window service would be provided. No indoor seating would be included. A few test units were opened, but to Smith's eventual disappointment the plans were never carried through.

"As we looked at various areas," he recalls, "prime real estate wasn't that available. Basically bands of small lots seemed to be the best buy. I felt that if we could purchase enough small corner lots, we'd have a viable concept in addition to Burger King, a weapon to combat skyrocketing real estate costs. Unfortunately, the program didn't really jell."

Some critics of Smith maintained that all he was doing with his proliferation of menu items and ideas was to raise the average ticket beyond the point of what fast food should be. True, it had moved over the supposedly magical $2 mark and was heading toward $2.50 by early 1980. Consumer resistance toward price increases was stiffening. But the price/value relationship was still there in relation to other fast-food chains which also were moving up on the price ladder.

Burger King's biggest weakness had been on the operating side, and Smith—an operations expert—tackled this head-on. Now in 1979 he pressed for a wider marketing effort. He ordered $80 million, or more than 4 percent of Burger King's ad budget, poured into marketing.

Pressed by McDonald's lead in the children's market from one side and pressure from Wendy's on the other side, Smith geared Burger King's marketing and promotion efforts to a family approach. He hoped to capture a wider market penetration on all sides, but the prime thrust still was to young adults.

Smith must have gained some satisfaction from seeing McDonald's start to react to some of his strategies. He allowed himself a smile when McDonald's began testing a chopped steak sandwich not much different from the one Burger King was trying. When McDonald's took the unprecedented step of cutting the price of its basic 1.6-ounce hamburger by a nickel, Smith knew he was making headway with Burger King's 2-ounce burger.

As Burger King moved toward more consistency from one unit to another, Smith's goals seemed to be meshing. But he still found the chain's dependence on fresh meat responsible for too many inconsistencies. "Frozen patties are more dependable and easier to work with," he declared. "They provide a more consistent quality, are easier to cook and don't spoil." Soon Burger King was almost totally reliant on frozen patties and had virtually eliminated fresh meat. Here Smith was following McDonald's credo which said that to supply a far-flung system adequately, one had to use frozen meat exclusively. Wendy's was the exception with a total fresh meat approach in its supply, advertising, and marketing.

Smith generally succeeded in weaving together the diverse Burger King franchise system which included major franchisees such as 350-unit Chart House in the South and Midwest and 70-unit Carrols in the Northeast, with the small independent franchisees. He encouraged the franchisees' entrepreneurial spirit to drive for higher results. The franchisees were bolstered by steady sales increases they were enjoying more than by any pep talks from Smith. There still were a handful of dissidents who felt things had been better "in the good old days." But Smith's only real standards of judgment about the franchisees were performance and results. He no longer would grant franchises for an entire territory, but rather gave them individually based on a franchisee's previous results. Nor was he adverse to allowing individual franchises to operate within the territory of established franchisees.

By 1979 Smith had brought in ten new Burger King executives, eight of whom had been with McDonald's at one time or another. Ten regional offices were in operation, and two more were gearing up to open. Everything seemed to have a McDonald's stamp on it—even the real estate. McDonald's knew the profit potential in owning its sites. Smith increased the proportion of Burger King's real estate ownership from 34 percent of the units to 42 percent.

GOALS REACHED

In early 1980 Smith was on the verge of major breakthroughs. He had moved Burger King's comparative unit sales up about 12 percent each year. Total system sales were nearing the $2 billion mark. Pre-tax profits had hit $44 million, or 8 percent of the $579 million revenues for fiscal 1979. Store pre-tax operating profit margins had jumped from 7 percent to 11 percent while labor costs as a percentage of sales had dipped from 25 percent to 21 percent with the new production efficiencies. He had closed the gap on McDonald's—but there was still a pronounced gap. McDonald's was averaging over $1 million store sales and its store profit margins were at 18 percent. It was satisfying for Smith to have accomplished his own objectives but frustrating to still be lagging behind McDonald's.

It was assumed in the trade that Smith would continue with Burger King and raise his sights and goals over the next few years there. But it didn't happen that way, for reasons which are clear only in retrospect. For one thing he had accomplished his primary objective of turning around Burger King to more than respectability in his almost three and one-half years there. Any future challenges might be less rewarding since this was the No. 2 chain and was destined to stay in that slot. Furthermore, Smith wanted more freedom than he could get from the corporate hierarchy of parent Pillsbury.

ENTER PEPSICO

At about the same time, in the spring of 1980, PepsiCo chairman and chief executive Donald Kendall was wondering what should be done about the Pizza Hut chain which PepsiCo had acquired in 1977 and Taco Bell, which was acquired the following year. Each was the undisputed leader in its market segment but hadn't come close to its potential. Economic pressures and higher operating costs were making it increasingly difficult to operate these chains with the kind of return on investment that PepsiCo desired and felt it merited. Kendall was convinced he needed to create a food service division and bring in a proven food service executive to run it. This executive hopefully could shape up the two chains and put PepsiCo in the position to acquire a hamburger chain at some point in the future.

Kendall, a results-oriented executive in his own right, knew Smith from PepsiCo's dealings with Burger King. He greatly admired the job that Smith had done with Burger King. Smith in turn admired the way Kendall had built up PepsiCo through various acquisitions—and most of all how Kendall granted autonomy to each division. When Kendall offered the spot to Smith, the offer was quickly accepted. Smith wanted the challenge, increased responsibilities, and relished the autonomy. He would report to PepsiCo president and chief operating officer Andrall Pearson, but it would be Smith's show with the food service chains. The financial package, believed to be in the $500,000 annual range, was an enticement too. He would be based at the parent corporation's headquarters this time, but his real home would be at Pizza Hut's Wichita, Kansas, offices, Taco Bell's Irvine, California, offices, and in all the stores. So Smith left Burger King in May 1980 to a new four-person management team of executives he had trained.

He arrived at the campuslike corporate headquarters of PepsiCo in Purchase, New York, some thirty miles north of New York City in the midst of a crisis. Frank Carney, Pizza Hut's founder and chairman, had resigned after hearing of Smith's appointment. Carney felt he just couldn't work for Smith, who got the post that Carney assumed would be his. Smith indicates he somehow felt Carney could be convinced to stay, but there was never any real chance of this. In any case drastic changes would have to be made at Pizza Hut, and it was doubtful that the two executives could have worked together very long.

In running PepsiCo's food service division, Smith resisted the temptation to staff up with all types of executives and aides. For the first nine months there the entire executive staff consisted of himself, a research assistant, and a secretary. He finally brought in Burger King's chief financial officer, Don Christopherson, as division financial vice president. But Smith continued to operate leanly and trimly at headquarters and to place the emphasis on the chain's executive staffs themselves.

SAME STRATEGIES

He applied the same basic techniques that had worked for him at McDonald's and Burger King. He zeroed in on Pizza Hut and visited as many franchise units as possible in the first few months. "This business is a partnership between the company and the franchisee," he said. "I want to show them I care and that I respect them." He brought in Arthur Gunther, who had been McDonald's marketing director when Smith was there, as Pizza Hut president. With Smith providing the operations expertise and Gunther the marketing prowess, the two dug in to do something about Pizza Hut's soft sales. They widened the marketing thrust to emphasize pan pizza and a salad bar. They instituted a decentralized regional system of field controls. Sales shot up from a $215,000 average per unit in the spring of 1980 to $265,000 a year later.

There were those who maintained, however, that the turnaround already had been planted by Carney and that Smith was merely getting credit for it. A number of the franchisees rebelled when Smith and Gunther sought to rewrite the contracts so that franchisees would contribute co-op monies to advertising for the chain. Eventually, though, compromise plans were worked out with most of the franchisees and they became happy when sales spurted. They were also pleased when they finally received maintenance and remodeling dollars to put their units into better shape.

When Robert McKay left Taco Bell as president in the spring of 1981 to manage his own investments, Smith jumped in to start concentrating on the Mexican fast-food chain just as he had done with Pizza Hut earlier. He ran Taco Bell himself for several months "to get it into position, gear up for the number of openings, for drive-throughs, and new food items." He continued to spend much of his time in the units. "If you stay in an office enough in a corporation," he notes, "you lose sight of the values." He found Taco Bell to be "top quality" in "basic standards like cheese" but that "now we have to contemporize the standards."

BURGER RUMORS FLY

Smith was ambitious to acquire a hamburger chain, but not until Pizza Hut and Taco Bell were sailing on a completely upward straight course. Rumors flew about Smith's and PepsiCo's intentions anyway. One day in June 1980 not long after Smith had started with PepsiCo, he and Kendall went to Columbus, Ohio, for a social game of golf with Wendy's chairman Dave Thomas and president Bob Barney. Kendall and Thomas had been business and personal friends for years. Within a day word had spread throughout the country of top-level meetings and a pending merger. There was no truth in it.

Then in March 1981, Don Smith addressed a company convention of Carl's Jr. fast-food people in California. Rumors quickly flew all the way to the East Coast that PepsiCo was about to acquire the privately held and successful Carl's Jr. But it turned out that this was a different Don Smith, director of the Michigan State School of Hotel and Restaurant Management, and that there were no merger plans.

PERSONAL PHILOSOPHY

Smith doesn't let problems fester. He is direct and immediately goes to the source of a problem, searching for a solution. His work days vary from eighteen-hour ones on the road in the beginning of new fact-finding cycles to eight- or ten-hour days. He has learned how to be super-efficient and obtain maximum productivity. His mind is active around the clock, and he might wake up at 3 A.M. and scribble down some brainstorming thoughts as they occur. He is demanding with his associates, his secretaries, and himself, driving for the maximum in a work day.

He doesn't believe long hours are really necessary for success, but feels that smart, well-organized thinking is essential. He is actually on the road only a few weekends a year, tries to be home weekends, and takes regular vacations. He is family and sports minded as well as business minded. Skiing, golf, tennis, and scuba diving are very much in his repertoire. Extremely competitive, he nevertheless plays sports for fun. He is in his second marriage and sees the three children from his first marriage, ages ten to fifteen, in Miami as often as feasible. But his favorite has to be the son who was born in early 1981 and given the name of Donald N. Smith 2nd.

Smith heads over $1 billion in front-running sales with Taco Bell and Pizza Hut and is confident this volume can be doubled in the next five years. "Taco Bell has a great deal more potential even though it already has a wide lead as No. 1 in its market segment," he declares. But perhaps his secret ambition is for pizza to overtake hamburgers as the nation's most popular food somewhere down the road. "Why not?" he asks. "Nobody has done research on how big the pizza market really can be. There's no reason why it can't be No. 1 led by Pizza Hut." Obviously Smith no longer has complete loyalty to the hamburger.

"I want to get satisfaction from my job," says Smith. "I want to exercise my independence and entrepreneurial instincts. I want it to be right."

Don Smith was right on target with McDonald's and Burger King. There's no particular reason to doubt that he will do it again at Pizza Hut, Taco Bell, or anyone else that PepsiCo acquires. Don Smith has an instinctive way of finding the right combination.

SECTION II

Conglomerate
Food Service Leaders

As food service has evolved into a powerful force, large corporations have become increasingly intrigued with the investment potential. At the same time independent chains that want to expand rapidly have found themselves cash-shy in the face of high interest rates and soaring costs. The results: much the same merger mania as has afflicted other segments of the economy.

It seems as if everyone wants to get into the act—often with multiple entries. A partial lineup in 1981 showed Quaker Oats with Magic Pan creperies and Engine House pizza units; General Foods with Burger Chef and GuadalaHarry's Mexican dinner houses; Ralston Purina with Jack-in-the-Box and the diversified Continental Restaurants; Pillsbury with Burger King, Steak&Ale, and its self-developed Poppin' Fresh Pies; PepsiCo with Pizza Hut and Taco Bell; and W. R. Grace with Far West Services (Coco's coffee shops and dinner houses such as Reuben's and Plankhouse), Jojo's coffee shops, Del Taco Mexican fast-food units, El Torito Mexican dinner houses, Gilbert/Robinson (Houlihan's), the Buena Vista Cafe in San Francisco, and the self-developed Jenny's healthy food restaurants. Grace epitomized the trend with at least six separate chains among its diversified holdings.

Despite the prevalence of acquisitions and diversifications, food service executives themselves rarely emerged with major corporate roles. Two who did through perseverance and innovation were Joe Lee and John Teets. A third, Charles Lynch, played a reverse role, coming from a conglomerate then basically outside the food service industry and taking command of a diversified food service corporation.

Lee, brought up as a cotton farmer, learned the business from the ground up, sweeping floors, working in the back room, doing every conceivable job. He managed the first Red Lobster restaurant in Florida and grew up with that chain, taking increasing executive responsibilities. After Red Lobster was acquired by General Mills in the early 1970s and received the capital for rapid growth, Lee moved up to become the chain's president. Then he became restaurant group president as General Mills acquired Ohio-based York family steak-houses. By 1980—when the General Mills restaurant group had purchased a Casa Gallardo Mexican restaurant in St. Louis, Darryl's theme restaurants based in North Carolina, and the Good Earth healthy food restaurants in Southern California—General Mills was a conglomerate food service leader and Lee had risen to a corporate executive vice president while still heading the vastly expanded restaurant group.

Meanwhile, Teets—a food service executive—had become vice chairman and chief executive officer of the highly diversified Phoenix-based Greyhound Corporation in the fall of 1981. He also headed its Greyhound Food Management group as well as Support Services and the entire Armour division. Teets came to this station via a circuitous route, having worked with Greyhound restaurants in New York in the mid-1960s and then heading the Canteen Corporation restaurant division. He subsequently was executive vice president of Bonanza before being recalled to Greyhound as president of then troubled Greyhound Food Management, a mixture of Prophet contract feeding and Post House restaurants. He straightened these out and kept moving up the Greyhound corporate ladder.

Lynch, with a wide business and organizational background, headed the W. R. Grace consumer service group, which included Far

West Services (before Grace's massive food service acquisition drive). He was selected by California-based Saga Corporation as president and chief executive to get its diversified food service house in order. This consisted of widespread contract feeding divisions and chains which had been acquired. He brought corporate and strategic planning expertise to the task and in three years set Saga on a fast-moving course, becoming a food service person in the process.

Lee, Teets, and Lynch were likely to have immense impact on food service in the 1980s within their corporate frameworks.

3

Joe Lee

FARMER TO PRESIDENT

One day in the fall of 1980 patrons at the Good Earth restaurant in San Diego noticed a round-faced, determined-looking man of about forty sitting at a table near the cash register. As he ordered various selections but only sampled the food with small bites throughout the evening, the customers noticed that this mysterious man seemed far more intent on eyeing the cash register than in eating his food. They would have been most surprised to learn who he was and what he was doing there.

He was Joe R. Lee, president of the General Mills restaurant group and one of seven group executive vice presidents in the corporation. He presided over a mini-restaurant empire of over 400 units totaling $700 million annual sales. They were Red Lobster Inns, York Steak Houses, Darryl's theme restaurants, and Casa Gallardo Mexican restaurants, as well as the SigmaCon design, construction, and equipment company and the Aqua Finca de Camerones experimental shrimp farming project in Honduras. He was best known for helping to develop Red Lobster into the unquestioned leader in the family seafood market. He and his team had perfected a purchasing system in the early 1970s that was the envy of the industry and the key to Red Lobster's emergence well ahead of anyone else in its market segment.

On this particular evening Lee was trying to figure out whether General Mills should proceed with its projected acquisition of the Good Earth restaurant chain, a Southern California regional operation that could provide a potential national wedge in the "healthy" restaurants field with General Mills's financial backing. Lee had heard dazzling accounts of the Good Earth's sales figures, but he never left crucial details to chance or to someone else's general opinion. He wanted to see for himself what the sales count was on a particular evening before he would give the green light for General Mills to finalize the acquisition.

To Lee's amazement and pleasure, the sales that he estimated closely from observing the cash register actually exceeded the pace that the Good Earth's management had indicated. Thus Good Earth became the second chain bought by acquisition-minded General Mills within six months, the previous one having been North Carolina-based Darryl's. York had been acquired in 1977 and Casa Gallardo in 1979.

Those who know Lee realize that in his totally unpretentious way he is always thinking five steps ahead of anyone else. He has a knack for applying everything he's ever learned to future planning three and five years down the road, invariably hitting the target almost perfectly. His attention to detail and his interpretation of it are mind-boggling. When he eats at a competitor's restaurant—even when his wife, Dale, accompanies him—he not only observes the customers and the cash register, but he keeps a pocket thermometer handy to test the temperature of each item. "Joe manages to absorb every aspect and detail of a restaurant while having an enjoyable dinner," noted one associate.

It might be added that he still gets a big kick out of every aspect of the restaurant business. In the various steps of his career, from a cotton/tobacco farmer to a highly successful president in a most complex business, Lee has always had a positive outlook on everything he tackles.

INSATIABLE CURIOSITY

Lee doesn't waste time in small talk though he can more than hold his own in it. When he travels to a convention or conference anywhere in the country, he'll find the time to explore almost every significant restaurant in that market area. Or if he is driving around looking at some of the Red Lobster restaurants and hears of a new type of dishwasher somewhere, he'll go miles out of his way to see that dishwasher for himself. "Lee understands the systems and makes them function," said one restaurant manager who has observed his work habits. He likes to talk with the employees in the various units and see how they feel about things. But he makes his own judgments about the various challenges of a restaurant—sanitation standards, training, staffing, and systems development.

When he returns on weekends to home base at Orlando from his travels, Lee makes it a point to visit numerous restaurants around the area—his restaurants and others. He has an inexhaustible appetite for finding out what the competition is doing. What better way to spend Friday and Saturday evenings than on a busman's holiday in restaurants? He'll marvel at and admire a competitor's handiwork, and he'll learn from it.

Joe R. Lee certainly has come a long way from his childhood days when he picked cotton and tobacco on farms near Blackshear, Georgia. But he has never lost those old-fashioned virtues of hard work, dedication, and modesty. He doesn't hesitate to put in fourteen-hour days or to schedule a meeting at 10:30 P.M. when it is necessary to discuss something. "Joe Lee even tried to devise an eighteen-hour day or to decree one," remarked one associate.

UPGRADING CHAIN

As president of Red Lobster in the late 1970s, he led an upgrading of the chain from one designed to appeal to blue collar people to a broader market base. Decor was spiffed up so that consumers would find menu price increases more palatable. But there still was consumer resistance to the prices, and it took Red Lobster until 1980 to totally adjust its new format for a wider customer base. Lee still faced the problem of an industry slowdown and the impact it would have on each of his five diverse food service chains.

Red Lobster continued as his No. 1 asset even with the diversification to other chains. He had the advantage of having gone through every aspect of the operation and knowing the intricacies of each challenge. He and Red Lobster president William Hattaway plotted the chain's new strategies for the 1980s. They tested new floor plans and color schemes, added seats to some units and brought the seating capacity to the 150-to-350-seat range, made cocktail lounges definite adjuncts to restaurants, and kept portion sizes the same or bigger rather than reducing them.

They also insisted on no more than three or four Red Lobster restaurants per field supervisor, permitting close controls on the units. This was in contrast to comparable chains which might cut corners and have as many as eight or ten units under one supervisor. Actually Red Lobster's main competition came from the local seafood restaurant that knew its market. This was formidable competition in many metropolitan areas, and he never allowed anyone at Red Lobster to let up for a minute.

Lee's temper flares occasionally, but generally he is calm, low-keyed, and operates at a far higher energy level than anyone else no matter what the hour. When in the office, he keeps a tight schedule, hammering away at the main points and quickly moving from one appointment to another. He'll usually grab a snack at his desk and keep going. For exercise he'll dash away for half an hour of fast-paced racquetball at the YMCA. "You never really know what Joe will do," observes a fellow corporate executive, "but you do know that whatever it is, it will be something productive."

FARMING AND FOOD SERVICE

He was born December 18, 1940, in the south Georgia town of Blackshear, the only child of a farming family. His father owned a 200-acre farm, and Lee learned from the farm at a young age. He also picked crops on other farms in the surrounding rural areas. He was an industrious young man and tackled each task with a vengeance. He took speed-reading courses and encouraged others at his school to do likewise. When he played with the other children, he was always the leader. He was president of his junior and senior class in high school.

At Blackshear High School, Lee worked in the news and sales departments of various radio stations. His first direct exposure to food service was as a part-time carhop in a Marriott Hot Shoppe drive-in while he was stationed in the air force in Virginia. The government appointed him to the Air Force Academy. He later attended Valdosta State College in Valdosta, Georgia. By then he had married his childhood sweetheart and was becoming more ambitious. While attending college, he worked part-time as a night manager at the Ramada Inn and later with Darden Enterprises of Waycross, Georgia. Darden was shortly to become the significant force in Lee's career.

While going to Valdosta College, he had met Darden, owner of other restaurants and the Green Frog restaurant in Waycross. Lee was highly impressed with Bill Darden and his operations. One day he went to Darden's office and told him, "I want to learn the restaurant business." Darden agreed to train him at the Green Frog and at a Howard Johnson's, and the young man quickly showed a remarkable aptitude for the business.

Darden also had purchased a place in Orlando, Florida, called Gary's Duck Inn seafood restaurant, whose slogan was "waddle out." He now decided it was time for a popularly priced seafood house. When the first Red Lobster Inn opened in Lakeland, Florida, on January 2, 1968, Lee was co-manager. Lee, Darden, and the opening management team jumped into the project with great fervor. Within two weeks they decided they could do better, pulled out all the equipment and installed more efficient equipment. They also promptly established a price-value relationship for the fledgling operation. It featured a steak and lobster combo for $2.95, and large offerings of shrimp, which were to become the chain's mainstay, for $1.35. These prices quadrupled in the next thirteen years.

Lee often worked through the night at the restaurant and practically lived there. He thrived on the pace as volume far surpassed a $500,000 goal and hit $900,000 the first year. When his wife and two young children wanted to see him, they would visit the restaurant and spend as much time as they could there. They understood, and so did he.

RED LOBSTER GROWTH

It wasn't long before Darden opened a second Red Lobster in Daytona Beach and then units in St. Petersburg, Orlando, and Tampa. Lee put in twenty-hour days as the regional chain started to sprout across Florida. He was promoted from a manager to operations supervisor for the five restaurants. General Mills took a hard look at the fledgling chain in 1970 and saw potential. Acting on the theory that it takes at least five restaurants to know whether a concept is really "chainable" on more than a regional basis, General Mills acquired Red Lobster, paving the way for the rapid expansion that followed.

Gene Woolley was General Mills's corporate executive in charge of the Betty Crocker pie shops and Tree House restaurants. He was also responsible for Red Lobster when that was acquired. "Gene gave us the freedom to do our own thing, yet maintained a degree of control for the corporation," recalls Lee. General Mills, which had encountered rough going with the pie shops and Tree Houses, now strengthened its commitment to the restaurant business with Red Lobster's apparent winning combination. Once again the extreme difficulty of a corporation starting its own restaurant chain from scratch and the desirability of acquiring a thriving operation with all the systems in place were demonstrated.

Lee modestly credits Woolley with challenging and motivating Red Lobster's management. "He kept us excited about being with General Mills and encouraged us to grow personally," Lee says. "He enhanced our own entrepreneurial spirit rather than letting the corporation thwart it. He helped us develop our training schools, our marketing, and our purchasing systems." Woolley was the ideal executive to guide Red Lobster through the transition from complete entrepreneurs to part of a corporation. In this sense Red Lobster and Lee were fortunate since they were treated entirely differently than one of General Mills's multiplicity of cereal divisions. Woolley recognized that restaurants were a personal service business and could not be treated with the same overall marketing approach as cereal. Restaurants required personal attention and tender loving care, and he encouraged Darden, Lee, and their team to provide all these ingredients.

General Mills decided quickly that Red Lobster's headquarters would remain in Orlando and that any other restaurant operations also would be based there. This may have seemed a natural decision, but it was significant since it indicated a desire to give autonomy to the restaurants and not to put them under a corporate marketing umbrella—as other conglomerates did, much to their later regret. This was a personal service business, and General Mills knew it could not be run like one of its cereal divisions. "Since the highest level of expertise in our restaurants was in Orlando," said a corporate spokesman, "we always kept the restaurant group headquarters there." The distance between General Mills's Minneapolis corporate headquarters and Orlando actually would prove a great benefit to the restaurants as they developed in their own way.

PURCHASING STRUGGLE

Establishing a viable purchasing network for Red Lobster would determine whether the chain could grow out of its regional status and prosper, Lee realized instinctively. As operations director and then operations vice president, he traveled extensively in the early 1970s to help establish a supply, purchasing, and quality control system that could enable the chain to grow as fast and prosperously as he visualized. Darden and Lee brainstormed how they wanted to set up the purchasing network but got off to a couple of false starts in this complex process. They finally brought in George Gross, who had been fisheries attaché to Latin America and Africa and had worked closely with the State Department in dealing with fisheries. He had the worldwide contacts to establish a purchasing foundation. Gross selected William Hattaway, who would become Red Lobster president after Lee, to help set up the system.

Lee was responsible for operations, personnel, and training as well as purchasing where he focused on Mexico, Brazil, and Iceland while Hattaway set up the West Coast, Canada, Alaska, and Europe. "We all were involved because it was so critical to our success to have a consistent supply of high quality products," recalls Lee. Persistent to the nth degree, he flew back and forth to Brazil for two years to convince a leading supplier to work with Red Lobster. The supplier had insisted they could not sell to restaurants, but Lee persuaded them otherwise. (A decade later the supplier and Red Lobster were completely delighted with the relationship.)

These early purchasing days were not without their adventures. One day Lee, Hattaway, and several others were on a mission to Newfoundland searching for a new supply source. Lee felt he had to see all major prospective suppliers personally. Their hired bush pilot was a stickler on conserving fuel and never carried more than he needed. The door on the small plane kept popping open, but that was the least of their worries. It ended up with the pilot crash-landing the plane during a snowstorm at the top of a mountain on his last gallon of fuel.

Lee and his cohorts, who escaped uninjured, arrived late for their appointment with the supplier, but it was a miracle that they arrived at all. They were hailed as heroes by local villagers in this remote area. No other outsiders had landed there for over twenty years. It was all in a day's work for the Red Lobster team, and they continued with their priorities to build up the supply-purchasing system.

QUALITY CONTROL

Lee saw the need for an extensive quality control program to insure that the highest quality products were served. This ranged from ingredients inspections to management sanitation training to the authorization of a microbiological lab at an $80,000 cost. A system of certified quality control audits also was implemented. Auditors would check each restaurant and consult with management on a regular basis. Under Lee's and Hattaway's direction, meticulous floor plans were drafted of each Red Lobster restaurant, and hazard analyses were launched. High-risk items were emphasized in the search for quality control problems and solutions. For example, if there were flies in the kitchen, the dump site and other key points would be checked. This same hygiene-quality control system was extended to other General Mills's restaurant chains.

Lee stresses simple approaches that work. He tries to boil down problems to their simplest elements rather than making them more complex. David Hetterly, who became Red Lobster quality control vice president, recalls that when he was a trainee at the Lakeland, Florida, restaurant, he felt the task was overwhelming. But Lee simplified it and made employees in the restaurant feel comfortable. "I know you have a lot of questions," Lee would tell the trainees. "Just put a notebook in your pocket and write down the questions. Once a week we will sit down and work out the answers." Invariably Lee did have all the answers and presented them in a constructive manner. He was excellent in training and motivating employees.

With General Mills bankrolling the operation, Lee devised the systems to put Red Lobster into consolidated distribution and bulk purchasing—systems that enabled the chain to save hundreds of thousands of dollars annually. Red Lobster's ability to overcome the bulk purchasing obstacles inherent in any seafood chain and to develop specialized equipment to cut costs paved the way for rapid growth. Lee and Darden selected and motivated the key people to develop these innovative approaches though they modestly maintain that "it was strictly a team effort."

Lee also helped integrate other support systems which became crucial to his group's multi-chain approach. These are SigmaCon, the General Mills company that designs and builds Red Lobster units and restaurants for other company chains; the Pinellas Seafood Company, a procurement and processing firm; and an experimental shrimp farm designed to supply Red Lobster and protect it from shortages of its best-selling item. The latter division represents some of Lee's most innovative thinking, and in 1980-81 he made a number of flights to Honduras to deal with the political structure there and set up a farm to raise huge supplies of freshwater shrimp. This was an experiment being closely watched in the industry.

He also promoted the idea of a strong consumer research arm. Extensive consumer research programs enabled Red Lobster and General Mills's restaurant group to anticipate many of the trends well in advance of their occurrence. The types of trends spotted and changes made in different markets were consumer preferences for broiled items, a desire for garlic bread instead of hush puppies, and other localized menu offerings. Intense local marketing and merchandising programs were launched by Red Lobster under Lee, who emphasized a decentralized system. He felt a chain must be able to act on local trends in each area. "Let the people out there on the line make these choices," is his philosophy.

AUTONOMY STRESSED

Lee gives the presidents of each of his five chains as much authority as feasible. He personally meets with each of them quarterly and asks for only monthly progress reports. As long as there is progress, the presidents don't have to worry about interference from their group head. "Once Joe Lee approves a plan, he lets the presidents do whatever they need to implement it," a company source said. He is results-oriented and won't stand in the way of a forward-moving plan. Nor will he stand still if he sees a lack of progress.

"I'm a decentralist," Lee emphasizes. While in most chains a field supervisor is responsible for anywhere from five to ten units, it's only three or four units per supervisor at Red Lobster. Part of the reason is that each restaurant generates an average $1.7 million annual sales, representing a big chunk for any supervisor or manager to control. But mainly it's General Mills's and Lee's philosophy to place the maximum controls and autonomy close to the restaurant. Red Lobster's steady expansion to over 300 units was made possible by the careful controls.

Red Lobster's annual total sales growth rate exceeded 100 percent in its first three years. Then sales and earnings for the whole restaurant group maintained an annual pace of over 25 percent growth for the next decade through 1981. Meanwhile, Red Lobster's annual per unit sales doubled in that decade, and its total annual volume topped the $500 million mark. Red Lobster is the group's prime growth vehicle, with York Steak Houses second. The entire restaurant group's pre-tax return on average invested assets was 22.3 percent in 1980—an enviable figure in a demanding industry. This return is highly creditable in view of total initial land, building, and equipment costs for a Red Lobster restaurant soaring to about $1.5 million, compared with $400,-000 when the chain first started.

Lee has thrived under General Mills's policy of "the freedom to fail." This means it's perfectly acceptable to try new things and not always to feel everything must succeed. Two of the most notable examples were the Betty Crocker pie shops and Tree House restaurants of the early 1970s and the more recent Hannahan's test, a sort of speedier-service, more steak-oriented version of Red Lobster. Neither concept worked, but Lee notes that "all were profitable. It's just that they didn't meet the minimum corporate return-on-investment goals. Therefore, the money could be better invested on expansion of higher return chains."

Interestingly, all of General Mills's five restaurant chains were acquired. Whatever new concepts were launched within the company just didn't measure up to standards. This is not an unusual phenomenon in the restaurant business where the odds become greater against new entries making it as the field becomes more crowded. "It's extremely difficult to develop your own concept in a corporate environment," a General Mills spokesman noted. "We're still trying and may come up with a formula. We must expect a high failure rate, but we're willing to risk it. The only way to develop winners is to take chances." Actually if their acquisitions produce a real winner half the time, they're surpassing most of the industry.

General Mills's own corporate philosophy, particularly as applied to its restaurants, reads: "With the dramatic growth we anticipate by 1985, we remain committed to a decentralized organization that can move quickly ahead of changing trends. Innovative, risk-oriented managers in each of our business areas, who have highly satisfying careers with General Mills, are one of the keys to our long-term success." As corny and old-fashioned as this may sound, it works to a surprising degree and is indicative of Lee's own personal approach.

He sees the rapid restaurant expansion as beneficial in providing diversity and a sharing of information among the various chains. It also provides a series of controls and financial cross-checks. But most of all, each of the five chains concentrates on a different customer segment. Even with some overlap, the total customer base is greatly widened. A cross-fertilization of talent within the company's various divisions is another advantage.

SEAFOOD CRISIS

Lee and his team faced a serious crisis in 1978 when Red Lobster's growth slowed. Seafood prices had tripled, and there was no doubt menu prices would have to keep rising to balance profit margins. But customers were reluctant to accept these price hikes. As traffic in the restaurants started to drop, Lee and Hattaway concluded that customers wanted something more for their money in finer atmosphere now that they were paying more for their food. Sensing customer expectations, the two executives and operations vice president Ron Magruder drastically curtailed Red Lobster's expansion while rushing through a one-year crash program of complete remodeling and sharper decors. Traffic started to rebound in 1980 as customers became more accepting of the higher prices now that the atmosphere felt more comfortable.

As group head, Lee's prime strategy was to remerchandise Red Lobster in appearance and a wider menu so that it would be able to branch out beyond its blue collar base. Once this was accomplished by late 1980, Lee and Hattaway pondered some recommendations that portions should be reduced so that prices could be lowered. They categorically rejected such strategy, refusing to do anything that might cheapen the product in the short term or long term. Red Lobster held the line on prices and portion sizes and was subsequently vindicated with gradually higher traffic counts. Meanwhile, table service was upgraded, desserts were added, and a new system was launched whereby customers who had drinks in the cocktail lounge could pay for them with dinner rather than separately. "It was infuriating to a customer to have to pay two separate times," Lee recalls, "and defeated our purpose of pleasing the customer."

A born leader, Lee is still regarded as a team player with an intensely analytical mind. He works all hours, from dawn to dusk and well beyond, both in the office and on the road. He somehow never looks or feels tired. While others are wilting, he's as fresh and energetic at a 9:30 P.M. meeting as first thing in the morning. He simply loves the business and finds it fun rather than work. He is a no-nonsense executive who settles problems directly with dispatch so they don't fester and cause frustrations.

WIDE ACTIVITIES

Lee believes he has a responsibility to the industry that has meant so much to him. He plays an active role in industry work and in promoting industry causes. "We can't stay on the sidelines and expect to get friendly legislation passed," he declares. "We have to stand up for what we believe in Washington and our state capitals." In 1981 he served on the National Restaurant Association's Board of Directors and was chairman of the National Restaurant Association's Political Education Committee and of its Food Legislation Committee. He encourages Red Lobster executives and those of his other chains to speak out on issues and take an active role in lobbying efforts. He also frequently talks to other restaurateurs and to industry groups about major issues.

In his home city of Orlando, Lee is a member of the Sun First National Bank Board of Directors as well as of the John Young Museum board, the Loch Haven Art Center, and the Orlando Chamber of Commerce. He formerly was a member of the Department of Commerce's Marine Fisheries Advisory Board. He was initial co-chairman of the Fisheries Committee which reclassified all fish species. He not only keeps his restaurant managers actively involved in their local communities but gives unstintingly of himself to his home community.

Lee has a wide variety of interests and is a voracious reader of all types of books. "He is a great conversationalist about almost any topic under the sun," observes his wife, Dale. "He surprises people with his detailed knowledge of so many things outside of business." He has as much of an insatiable curiosity outside of business as in it. He is a self-made man who has continued his education throughout his working career.

General Mills's Woolley encouraged him to attend seminars and summer courses at Dartmouth College in the early 1970s. But Lee kept pushing his own education with night school, summer school, and extensive reading. He has a wide-ranging library at home with books of almost every major business author and of many other authors and philosophers. He has devoured virtually every book on these shelves. He is self-educated with exceptional concentration and discipline. He was never handed anything on a silver platter and knew how to make his own breaks.

ACQUISITIONS INTEGRATED

Lee has gradually put together the pieces of the General Mills restaurant puzzle. He became president of Red Lobster in 1975, president of General Mills's newly formed restaurant group in 1979, and also a corporate executive vice president in 1980. Ohio-based York Steak Houses, a regional Midwest leader in the budget steakhouse market, was General Mills's first acquisition in 1977 at the start of a four-year spurt from the Red Lobster base. York had forty-eight restaurants in eighteen states when it joined General Mills. Four years later it had some 150 restaurants in forty states as it greatly expanded its scope under Lee's and General Mills's guidance. York seemed the ideal vehicle to balance steak with Red Lobster's seafood success. "We're looking for diversity and balance in our various chains," says Lee. But York itself has widened it market with expansions into chicken and seafood entrees.

Casa Gallardo, designed in the style of a classic Mexican manor, joined the General Mills family in 1979. It had just one restaurant in St. Louis specializing in authentic Mexican food. But Lee saw in that one unit a prototype for a chain. Four more Casa Gallardos soon opened near St. Louis and in the Southeast, and plans were in motion for a multi-market Mexican restaurant chain although that segment was becoming a bit saturated. Everyone seemed to think they could open endless Mexican restaurants. Lee himself conceded that perhaps plans for nationwide expansion of Casa Gallardo would have to be somewhat curtailed.

Next aboard the General Mills express was Darryl's, a North Carolina showplace for authentic antiques, architectural artifacts, curiosities, and a casual, diverse menu. Customers in these surroundings had their choice of dining suspended from the ceiling in a ferris wheel, in an antique elevator or a London taxi cab, a fire truck, or a double-decker bus. The menu in this casual setting included prime rib, lobster, barbecue beef, pork ribs, soups, salads, sandwiches, quiches, and pastas. Thad Eure, owner and president of Darryl's parent Creative Dining Systems, agreed to the acquisition of Darryl's in the spring of 1980 only with the stipulation that he still would run the operation. Lee was glad to assure him of this and to carry out the pledge. Meanwhile, the eleven Darryl's units were to be doubled and tripled over the next few years in a race to gain a casual-restaurant foothold in the South. Lee felt that Darryl's acquisition illustrated another General Mills principle in such deals. The idea was to acquire talent and creativity such as Eure possessed, as well as the actual chain.

That fall General Mills concluded a deal to purchase San Diego-based Good Earth restaurants and their unique "natural foods" menu. Among the highlights of this potential growth concept were fresh-baked desserts and breads, three-egg omelets, fresh fruit, Malaysian shrimp, Zhivago's beef stroganoff, country-style lasagna, and specially seasoned fresh vegetables sautéed in Chinese woks. Most significantly, refined sugar, flour, and preservatives were nowhere to be found.

VARIED MARKETS

Each of General Mills's five chains serves a different market, but there is the common ingredient of a popularly priced operation that attracts families. The point is not that the prices are necessarily so low but that within a given market segment they tend to be lower than other chains. For example, Red Lobster's $8 or $9 average per person ticket may not seem low for a "family" restaurant, but it comes in well below other limited menu dinner houses which tend to range from $10 to $15 average tickets. This makes Red Lobster a strong entry to attract middle income people. The same is true of each of General Mills's other entries. "We must avoid the temptation to constantly raise menu prices," says Lee, "and find ways of operating more efficiently. Otherwise, we will simply drive away the customers."

Will General Mills opt for a sixth, seventh, and eighth restaurant chain acquisition? Possibly some time in the future, but for the early 1980s Lee charted a course of taking time out to catch the group's collective breath and of building each of the five chains toward its maximum rather than looking for still more purchases. "I think we have enough for a while," observes Lee, while not ruling out a special acquisition "if the right opportunity does come along." In any case his goal is to double the group's 400 restaurants to 800 by 1985 and to do it in a fashion that will promote the growth of unit sales and profits too.

FAMILY DEVOTION

Lee works hard at his family responsibilities and takes them as seriously as he does business. He is able to separate each segment completely and focus on that entirely. He and his wife reside in the Orlando suburb of Gotha not far from Disney World, but their world is a real and happy one remote from the make-believe. "I try to give my children the benefit of my experience," he says of Mike, nineteen, and Keena, seventeen. Neither works in restaurants but at other jobs, and Lee is perfectly content to let them find their place in whatever field interests them.

He finds the time to be with his family for camping trips, picnics, riding dirt bikes together, and puttering around the house. They spend frequent weekends at their beachfront condominium in New Smyrna near Daytona Beach, Florida. When Lee was up for a major national award in the restaurant industry in 1980, his daughter Keena sent her own nomination (unknown to Lee). She told the judges that "my father is the most devoted, the best family man, has the best sense of humor, and is the best in the business. He is so much fun to be around, and we are all happy when we are with him. He deserves to win this award."

Lee maintains his priorities very much in focus. He keeps a packed suitcase and travels all over at a moment's notice to the diverse General Mills restaurants. "I've got to have the feel of the business myself," he says. "I can't get that in an office. I want to see what is actually happening in the restaurants and with the customers." He evaluates everything he observes and hears. What emerges inevitably is a battle plan in Lee's mind to excel in each segment and stay well ahead of the competition.

However, he is able to see things in human terms and has a sensitivity toward others. He gets the job done effectively—but not at anyone else's expense. He succeeds in a corporate environment by being his own person. He is proof that sometimes nice guys do finish first.

4

John Teets

"GO JOHN GO"

As the tall, lean man with finely cropped hair, streaked with silver, surveyed the scene at Greyhound Corporation's Phoenix headquarters that day in early 1976, he knew he faced a great challenge. He had assumed the responsibility of chairman, president, and chief executive officer of its wholly owned subsidiary, Greyhound Food Management.

While Greyhound Corporation was known for its intercity buses and bus manufacturing, food processing, consumer products, and financial services, it was by no means known for its food service group. In fact, Greyhound Food Management had little to recommend it. Morale was at a low ebb; earnings were a lackluster $3.6 million; and an appallingly high percentage of its accounts were jostling each other in the race to see which one could lose the most money in a single year. The group simply hadn't measured up to its potential even in its best years.

Small wonder that the management of Greyhound Corporation was anticipating with genuine relish a future without Greyhound Food Management among its subsidiaries. The decision to retain Greyhound Food Management was essentially made when chairman Gerald H. Trautman decided to give it one more shot by naming new management and by bringing in to head the organization the one man he felt could turn it around.

In January 1976 at age forty-two, John Teets took over the helm of Greyhound Food Management. Today the Greyhound company boasts a reputation as a pacesetter in the industry and a leading name in food service.

CHIEF EXECUTIVE

Teets's career reached a pinnacle at age forty-eight in August 1981 when he was named chief executive officer of the entire $5 billion Greyhound Corporation. This gave him overall responsibility for widely diversified holdings including Armour meats and Armour-Dial consumer products, Greyhound bus lines, bus manufacturing, financial and computer services, convention services and a rent-a-car operation as well as Greyhound Food Management. But his prime challenge now was to pump more life into the Armour group, which accounted for over half of corporate revenues but only a small portion of profit.

He already had attained the titles of a corporate vice chairman, ceo of Armour, group vice president of the services group, and chairman of Greyhound Food Management. He was slated to become corporate chairman in August 1982 upon Trautman's scheduled retirement. But as corporate ceo, Teets had achieved a position that very few food service executives ever have reached as head of a diversified corporation. This appointment as ceo surprised some industry observers who simply didn't visualize a food service executive running a wide-ranging $5 billion corporation. Yet Teets in effect had been training for this position for over thirty years in developing and fine-tuning his ability to motivate, inspire, and organize people to overcome all obstacles.

FIRST JOB

Born in Elgin, Illinois, in 1933, Teets began his career at the age of fourteen in Dundee, near Chicago. The way he recalls it, one day he rode his bike to the Milk Pail restaurant, gathered together all his courage, parked his bike outside the restaurant, walked in, and asked the owner for a job. He was hired as a dessert boy and—as is the style of John Teets—immediately went to work. He was quickly introduced to three different-sized ice cream scoops and fifteen different flavors. Then he was on his own.

When a waitress handed him an order for five different pies, each with a different ice cream, and another waitress came along with a similarly complex order, the lanky youngster decided this wasn't for him. He discarded his apron and headed for the door. But the manager stopped him in his tracks and told the waitresses, "This is the third dessert boy we've had in a week. It's got to stop. You will train this one properly."

Thus reprieved, Teets started in the restaurant business. Throughout the rest of his career, he made his own luck. He had a knack for sensing when he had achieved maximum growth from a job and then moving to something more challenging.

Teets's initial contact with Greyhound dates back to Jan. 1, 1964, when at age thirty he managed the only two successful restaurants at the New York World's Fair, grossing more than $1 million a month. When the fair was closed, Greyhound promoted Teets to vice president of the company's Post House division, which operates restaurants in Greyhound bus terminals across the country. The next year, at age thirty-two, John Teets was offered the position of Post House president, making him one of the youngest company presidents.

In 1968, he left Greyhound for an even larger challenge. He accepted a post as president and chief operating officer of the John R. Thompson Company (later acquired by Green Giant), which until that time had been a family-operated company. Here he was responsible for all financial and operational areas in the $33 million company which owned Henrici's restaurants, Holloway House cafeterias, Red Balloon restaurants, and Holloway House Frozen Entrees. This is where Teets conceived and developed the idea for Henrici's Steak and Lobster Houses.

Opportunity knocked on Teets's door again in 1971 when he joined Canteen Corporation as vice president of the public restaurant division and chief operating officer of the Jacques restaurant group. But Canteen wasn't as committed to public restaurants as Teets would have liked.

In early 1975, he moved to Dallas as executive vice president of Bonanza International, where he was responsible for total profit, planning, expanding, and operation of 225 company-owned restaurants. He was also coordinator of the field efforts for 350 licensee restaurants. This was his first introduction to franchises.

RETURN TO GREYHOUND

During these years Teets did not lose contact with the Greyhound executives as they closely watched their former Post House president's career progress. When he accepted the chairmanship of Greyhound Food Management, they were confident that it would only be a matter of time before the company would be profitable again. He was given almost complete autonomy to turn around Greyhound Food Management.

The two main divisions of Greyhound Food Management were Prophet Foods and Post Houses. Both were hemorrhaging from economic circumstances. Prophet, which operates food facilities in plants, hospitals, schools, and institutions, was being hard-hit by the automotive plant layoffs that took place in 1975—a critical area where it was dependent for much of its business. At the same time Post Houses, which operates restaurants and snack bars in Greyhound bus terminals, was struck by a decline in bus traffic.

Greyhound had started in the food service business in 1937 when it formed Post Houses. When the company acquired Prophet Foods in 1964, Greyhound Food Management was formed to umbrella both operations. Greyhound chairman Gerald Trautman had hoped the Prophet Foods operations would help diversify and balance the Post House commercial operations. But the balance hadn't worked as well as anticipated. Meanwhile, Greyhound acquired the profitable Faber Enterprises, which had some twenty food service operations in Chicago. It also formed another division to go under the Greyhound Food Management umbrella, Greyhound Support Services, which won the contract to feed some 6,000 workers along the Trans-Alaska pipeline. Today this company is active in the Middle East as well as being the major support service company still operating along the Alaskan pipeline.

One of Teets's toughest tasks was to motivate employees being sent to Saudi Arabia when Support Services won a contract to provide food service and other services along the huge oil pipeline construction project there. Typically, an employee would take one look at the primitive setup in the desert and want to jump on the next plane back home. But they had to sign a two-year contract and were given exceptionally high pay to try to keep them happy. They also received considerable time off at the project to recuperate from the desert heat.

REVAMPED DIVISIONS

Teets's plan was to first focus on the two large-volume divisions—Prophet Foods and Post Houses. Both divisions lacked direction, pride, and morale. His first order of business was to move Prophet's Detroit headquarters to Phoenix to have a centralized main office. Those who balked at the move, or couldn't make up their minds, were quickly phased out of the picture. Teets is a no-nonsense executive who surrounds himself only with "winners." Switching Prophet headquarters to Phoenix was construed by some as a move to more attractive surroundings, but the bottom line was that it gave Teets an opportunity to reorganize the group his way. Trautman backed him fully.

TURNAROUND YEARS

Each of the four turnaround years has its unique personality; 1976 was the year of backbreaking, mind-boggling restructuring, of slogging through waist-high problems and attempting to stop as rapidly as possible the financial hemorrhaging. Within the first few months of 1976, Teets developed a plan to halt the drain of profits and resources of the Prophet Foods division. He and his management team began by taking the ten poorest performing accounts and establishing a target date and goal: either turn them around or resign the account. Then on to the next ten poorest and the next. The process may have hurt some feelings, but this single action resulted in a savings of over $1.5 million.

The next order of business was new business. A system by which one executive made the cost bids and pricing decisions on a potential account was disbanded in favor of a specialized "team approach," a task force of three or four key individuals—each an expert in his own field including cost accounting, operations, quality assurance, and nutrition. Each would visit a prospective account and draft full proposals within twenty-four hours. This new approach paid off by indicating to prospective clients an unusually conscientious and professional approach. It also helped curb a natural tendency to overbid or underprice a project.

Yet there were still complaints that Prophet was not servicing its accounts closely enough once they were obtained. To overcome this, Teets insisted that as soon as a new account was signed, one individual from Prophet would be personally assigned as a "troubleshooter" and would be available twenty-four hours a day, seven days a week, to solve any problems. The troubleshooter, in effect, lived on the client's premises. Better feelings about Prophet began to generate throughout the trade.

To avoid being subject to the cyclical fluctuations of industrial plants, Teets pressed for more of an effort to gain added food service accounts in stable businesses such as schools, colleges, business institutions, and convention centers. Today Prophet Foods has contracts in thirty-eight states and feeds over 220 accounts ranging from opera houses to universities to industrial plants to business institutions.

Teets then turned his attention to Greyhound Food Management's other major operation, the feeding of bus passengers in Greyhound terminals. The Post House restaurants relied on the traffic in the Greyhound bus terminals. These restaurants mirrored the fortunes of the bus industry—up when bus travel was good, languishing when bus travel was down. He concluded that stability in the bus terminal facilities lay in converting them to operations that would attract not only bus passengers but off-street traffic as well—office workers, shoppers, tourists.

BURGER KING CONVERSIONS

Among his most notable accomplishments in saving this division was the conversion of many Post Houses into Burger King franchises.

In early 1976 Greyhound Food Management opened its first Burger King restaurant in Philadelphia. It was a success. In 1975, the Post House restaurant located in the same space had suffered a $6,820 net loss on $216,000 sales. A year later, as a Burger King, the operation showed a $200,000 net profit on $1.39 million sales. Today the company operates over twenty Burger King restaurants, each representing an investment of over $500,000 in renovation and decor, and each grossing between 70 percent and 90 percent of its customers from off-the-street business.

For those units not converted to fast-food operations, Teets implemented a different type of renovation. Each restaurant was redesigned to reflect the environment or history of the town it was located in, transforming them from old-fashioned dull operations to brighter, more vibrant ones. In addition, menus were changed to appeal to the people from local areas as well as passengers. Today no two Greyhound Food Management Burger King restaurants or Post House restaurants look alike; each is designed with its own individual theme. In the Savannah Burger King, for example, one is taken back to the past to eat in an antebellum Southern mansion, and in the Eugene, Oregon, restaurant, one is eating in the environment of an old lumber town.

At the close of 1976, initial returns were starting to reflect Teets's whirlwind changes. Net profit for Greyhound Corporation's food service group had jumped to $4.5 million on a modest 13 percent sales rise. With operations in place, as well as his executive team, Teets's next step would be to improve quality control, human relations, personnel programs, and sales and marketing approaches. "The biggest mistake any executive can make," he said, "is to be away from the office too much and suddenly find out things are deteriorating. A good executive is in the home office as well as the field and knows what's happening every step of the way."

He initiated monthly operational review meetings with Greyhound Food Management's district managers, costing the company almost $25,000 each time he and his management team left headquarters. Teets maintains these meetings are effective learning experiences, providing managers the opportunity to discuss with one another their successes, problems, and solutions. "These managers have as much right to be involved in the decision-making process as I do," said Teets.

"I see managers every four months. I want to know what's going on out there, and I depend on my district managers to inform me totally. If you think I can learn all this by sitting behind my desk, you're mistaken."

MOTIVATION

Teets believes there are four factors that motivate employees: recognition, security, challenge, and money. "Each employee at Greyhound Food Management, from top management to lowest echelon, has a hand in setting realistic goals for himself and his job. Each employee knows his role in the company, and no one is able to don the cloak of invisibility," said Teets.

The Human Resources department would be responsible for establishing programs that would attract, develop, and motivate people. Training programs, management development programs, and motivational programs would all be included in the package.

Teets believes in career development and doesn't try to hold back any individual. He wants his employees to be able to grow within the company to maximum potential. For this reason he insists each individual receive an annual comprehensive performance evaluation so there are never any surprises. "Each employee knows exactly where he or she stands in this company," he says. "Basically, I find the best kind of review is one that builds up the employee by praising strengths, but also is constructive in suggesting how improvements can be made in weaker areas. We're trying to build our people up, not knock them down. That's why I think turnover is less than minimum at Greyhound. Our people know we care about them."

At the same time he feels the company has developed a comprehensive set of programs giving employees every opportunity to grow. He believes in career development and encourages his people to reach full potential. Training programs, seminars, and tuition reimbursements are included in the Greyhound Food Management package for all employees. Performance standards were established and performance measurements were installed for each employee. For Teets this was a way of reassuring employees they they were considered to be an important piece of the Greyhound Food Management puzzle.

WIDE KNOWLEDGE

Teets enjoys chatting with the unit employees and district managers whenever possible. When he arrives at a unit he greets the manager and all of the other employees, usually by first name. He spends much of his time in the field boosting morale and soaking up important information on each unit. He has a photographic mind and can recall invaluable details about specific units and employees. They know him as "big good John," not "big bad John."

District managers are constantly overwhelmed by the array of facts and figures at Teets's fingertips about every aspect of an operation. He has numerous types of graphs, charts, and projections prepared by a battery of top financial analysts in the company. He doesn't walk into a meeting with a district manager and say, "How are we doin'?" He asks a series of pointed questions about why each figure is up or down, what can be expected, and what can be done to improve the situation.

It is his unique way of knowing just when to put pressure on his employees that keeps the high activity level at Greyhound Food Management. "Yes, he's tough," said one employee, "but he would never ask anything of one of us he wouldn't ask of himself." At Greyhound Food Management one never asks *whether or not* a problem can be solved, but rather *when* and *how* it can be solved.

A quality assurance department was also established. Food service specialists, reporting to the Greyhound Food Management Quality Assurance Board, were trained to inspect, evaluate, and report daily on the degree to which assigned branches were adhering to established company policies, procedures, techniques, service, and standards of quality. This department has its own evaluation kitchen in headquarters. Here, new and old recipes would be tested and updated. In addition, before purchasing any new product, quality assurance would test the product.

Purchasing would no longer be simply on the basis of price alone but also on the basis of the quality and service offered.

In a matter of four years, Greyhound Food Management had been revitalized in every aspect of its operations, reporting a net income of $9.1 million at the end of 1979. However, the true test of turnaround comes when a company meets and conquers challenges of a difficult economy. In 1980 Greyhound Food Management was faced with these challenges which not too long ago would have spawned substantial losses for the company. For example, the automotive industry, where many of Greyhound Food Management's feeding accounts are concentrated, was in total disarray, with well over a quarter of a million auto workers laid off. Needless to say, this triggered almost overnight cutbacks in many of Greyhound Food Management's food service contracts and a consequent abrupt falloff in income.

"EATIN'S EASY"

Late in 1979, however, Teets and his management team had anticipated this occurrence and devised a number of contingency plans aimed at minimizing the adverse impact. For one thing the moment an automotive feeding contract was reduced Greyhound Food Management simultaneously cut back a broad range of predetermined areas of internal costs. In addition, rather than simply walk away from the auto industry Greyhound Food Management devised new ways to feed automotive workers that reduced expense and fed them more efficiently. One such innovative program was the introduction at two General Motors plants of the Eatin's Easy concept—a highly creative way of combining the benefits of fast-food feeding with a limited hot entree line. Not only does the Eatin's Easy concept move workers through the feeding line faster, but for Greyhound Food Management the setup is less labor intensive, allowing improved profit margins.

Finally, and most significantly, Greyhound Food Management added over $19 million of new accounts in 1980, almost $14 million of which are in nonautomotive areas so as to lessen Greyhound Food Management's dependence on that one industry.

At the end of 1980 John Teets's management techniques proved successful as Greyhound Food Management was able to endure and weather a lean year. His ability to pick the right people for the right spots was crucial for Greyhound Food Management's rise, as was seen when the company reported 1980 earnings of $4.3 million and was heading for considerably higher earnings in 1981.

INDIVIDUALITY

While being businesslike and professional, Teets also feels that "human" qualities are essential. He acknowledges he cannot devote 100 percent of his time and energy to business, nor does he want that from his employees. "If a motor runs all the time," he said, "there's no question it will wear out." He encourages his people to spend as much time as feasible with their families and not to give so much to business that they ignore their personal lives. He encourages them to stay in top physical condition. "I find that a happy, well-balanced person can produce more and contribute more to himself, his family, and his job," he says.

Teets follows this philosophy himself. He keeps himself in excellent physical condition, running five miles every morning and exercising extensively in the evening hours. He enjoys reading and spending as much time as possible at his Paradise Valley home with his wife, Nancy, and four children.

He has intense pride in his accomplishments, but is still modest about it all. Some credit his wife, Nancy, for giving him the encouragement to excel. Upon receiving the International Foodservice Manufacturers Association's Golden Plate Award as food service operator of the year in May 1980 Teets said, "I accept this award for my family and all the people at Greyhound who have done so much to help me."

John Teets is a self-made man who did it on his own. He has the capacity to learn from others and to grow through adversity and success. When one of his earlier bosses, ITT president Howard Miller (ITT owned Canteen when Teets was there in the early 1970s), congratulated him on the award, both agreed that "we've learned a lot from each other." Certainly Teets has adoped many of the management techniques that Miller advocated. "I give someone the authority to do the job," is Miller's credo, "and they do it. I don't believe in interfering as long as the desired results are achieved." (That sounds like Teets.)

His ambitions may seem far-fetched to some, but it must be remembered that Teets has always achieved his goals, no matter how long it takes. He simply doesn't give up, and he somehow finds a way to eventually cross the finish line first.

5

Charles Lynch

STRATEGIC PLANNER

Charles A. Lynch, who became president and chief executive officer of the diversified Saga Corporation in mid-1978 at age fifty, always seemed to be in the right place at the right time. He had an intuitive knack for timing and knew how to take advantage of opportunities. He had a ceaseless drive to succeed, was extremely well-organized, and analyzed every situation backwards and forwards. Although flexible, he left nothing to chance.

Lynch could, at a moment's notice, pull out figures and charts on everything a division or company had achieved or not achieved for the last ten years and everything it potentially could achieve in the next five or ten years. He could also refer to evaluations and dates compiled at his direction on hundreds of people working within his organization—on their job records, their personal aspirations, their growth potential. He had the people themselves fill out their own career-planning charts showing where they wanted to go and how. He mapped goals for his company the same way. In short, he was the epitome of a total strategic planner.

Lynch recalls that when he was starting his career in a Detroit sales office, one of his early mentors would demand absolute promptness. He therefore set his own watch five minutes ahead at all times. Lynch adopted this habit and made promptness a virtue for himself and his people. But it always seemed that Lynch's agile mind was running hours, days, weeks, months, and even years ahead. Yet despite the utter seriousness of his approach, he always knew how to tell a good joke and how to enjoy one. He never took himself or the executives around him so seriously that he couldn't enjoy the job.

SAGA'S CHALLENGES

It was quite natural that Lynch would tackle the major challenges of Saga Corporation head-on in the late 1970s and early 1980s and apply all the strategic managerial precepts he had learned from extensive corporate life. He had applied the same steady principles from his earliest days into the restaurant and food service management company—but this time the stakes were much higher as he was running the entire organization and the results were his total responsibility.

Three college youths—Harry Anderson, W. Price Laughlin, and William Scandling—launched Saga on the Hobart College campus in upper New York State in 1948. Instead of just complaining about "boring" college food, as so many students did, their goal was to take constructive action to remedy the situation. The trio convinced Hobart administrators that they could succeed at running the campus food service operation, and they did.

From this small beginning, the founders of Saga branched into food service operations at numerous college campuses. Their first diversification came with service to health care facilities in the early 1960s and to business and industry clients in 1969. The acquisition of two pizza companies that same year formed the base for the Straw Hat Pizza chain and was their first venture into public restaurant service. In 1971 the Velvet Turtle dinner-house chain was acquired, and in the two following years, Stuart Anderson's Black Angus steakhouses and The Refectory restaurants.

SEARCH CRITERIA

In late 1977 the three founders decided to step down from the daily operating responsibilities for the company. They began a search for a new chairman and for one person who would be both president and chief executive officer. In early 1978, Ernest C. Arbuckle joined Saga's board and, effective April 1, became chairman. Arbuckle's main mission at that time was to assist the founders in seeking a highly qualified chief executive officer. Some of the criteria they set for this mythical miracle person were most illuminating in view of the final choice:

The person should have a firm independent personality, strong discipline, and balanced judgment; be ready to undertake a major reorganization and reassignment job; understand the value and limitations of professional and support staffs; and have the self-discipline to delegate in situations where he is not needed in a direct role.

Although the "perfect" person who could fulfill all these expectations did not exist, Lynch came the closest. He had in effect trained throughout his career for this very challenge. He could take the accumulated managerial expertise of over twenty-five years in varied business situations and apply it to a food service corporation just as he had applied it to conglomerates.

Lynch's story is not one of rags to riches. Rather it is one of a solid upbringing and a steady upward curve. He grew steadily at each juncture and was always ready for the next challenge.

Lynch was born in 1927 in Denver. His family moved to Beverly Hills and then to Bronxville, New York. He attended the Hill School in Pottstown, Pennsylvania, for four years and graduated in 1945. He then served a stint in the navy and became a quartermaster third class.

He always had a Harvard Business School approach although he never went there. He attended Yale in the late 1940s and graduated with a B.S. in industrial administration. By then he was confident enough to resist pressures to go to the Harvard Business School, in favor of direct business experience. He still thought he might go there one day, but he never found it compelling as his business career progressed.

FAST SERVE

Given his ability in the sport and his athletic prowess, Lynch probably could have been a top-ranking tennis champion. But he chose instead to build a solid career. He was a rising young tennis star in 1950—an era that bestowed neither the prestige, glamour, nor money that eventually would handsomely reward many of the players on the tennis circuit. But he was a fierce competitor who didn't want to lose— the same trait he later showed in business.

He had classic strokes and a powerful serve which made him one of the most feared players of his day when he was team captain at Yale and afterwards. He was a top-ranking Eastern junior player and upon graduation participated in the Prentice Cup matches in England with what many considered the best all-around strokes of any young player at the time.

His demeanor on the tennis court was the same as it would later be as a leading executive. He displayed none of the temper tantrums and angry bouts that marked some of his colleagues. He was calm with a supreme will to win, and he sometimes bested other gifted but temperamental players on this basis. Charlie Lynch was always first at anything he did. He demanded nothing but the best from himself and his people.

Despite his prep school and Ivy League upbringing and his drive for perfection, he did recognize and accept some imperfections as long as the person was heading for a specific goal. Nor was he snobbish, but rather a down-to-earth and a natural person. He hated phonies, though he did want to make the best possible impression.

BUSINESS CAREER

Lynch started in business at age twenty-three shortly after his graduation from Yale in 1950, finding the challenge of business more appealing than the challenge of a less-than-lucrative tennis career. He joined E. I. duPont de Nemours as a sales trainee, which led to a sales position in bookbinding. When a sales spot developed in the automotive industry, Lynch grasped the opportunity. The trail led to Detroit where he trained under the late "Red" Williams, who was of the old school: "Get the job done no matter what, and the customer is supreme."

Lynch stayed with the company nineteen years and moved into positions of steadily increasing responsibility in footwear, automotive trim, industrial rubber, luggage, and upholstery. His most glittering accomplishment was as director of marketing for the introduction of Corfam. He learned every aspect of fabrics and was able to fill walls with the publicity he generated in the national press and consumer magazines with the exclusive articles he leaked to them about Corfam. Lynch also recalls how duPont sent him to "umpteen management courses until it was coming out of my ears. But I must have absorbed some of it."

His next stop was Columbus, Ohio, where in 1969 he became president of Shoe Corporation of America's manufacturing group of five companies. He headed men's, women's, and children's footwear and an importing division. He moved to W. R. Grace & Co. in New York in 1972 at a time when Grace was reevaluating its major diversification program to move away from its designation as a "steamship company."

GRACE EXECUTIVE

He started as group executive of the footwear group of five companies and in 1973 also took charge of the recreational vehicles group of two companies. He kept acquiring more responsibility for numerous consumer services companies until early 1976 when he was named corporate executive vice president for all consumer services. This group was composed of some twenty companies, including Herman's World of Sporting Goods stores, Jacques Borel of France, and Far West Services restaurants. Subsequently he added to his sphere Shepler's western leisure apparel, Handy City, Channel, and Orchard Supply Home Centers when Grace acquired these.

It was at Grace that Lynch developed complete trend lines for all his companies and curve slopes on expenses, sales, return on assets, and every conceivable thing anyone ever wanted to know about anything. It was then that his philosophy became firmly entrenched: One has to understand the last five years before mapping plans for the next five years and even the next ten years. He scanned every industry statistic for the diversified consumer holdings, and projected goals and ideal target acquisitions. He would check all the data and decide which companies were worth considering. It was because of this thorough approach that Grace looked at hundreds of companies as potential acquisitions over the next several years.

Lynch's criterion for a potential acquisition was that it must either be the leader of a growth market segment or have the potential to be the leader. An absolute key was to have strong management in place. His home center acquisitions proved to be particularly profitable, so that his painstaking research and preparation paid off. In the food service field it wasn't that easy because the road map of which segments would prosper and which chains would lead these segments wasn't as clear. Lynch was instrumental in seeing that over 500 food-service chains were scouted in varying degrees until the list was scientifically reduced to a handful of chosen ones.

RESTAURANT ACQUISITIONS

The results of his careful spadework were realized between 1976 and 1978 when his group acquired the California-based El Torito Mexican dinner houses and the Kansas City-based Gilbert/Robinson, sparked by its Houlihan's casual restaurants. El Torito and Houlihan's were leaders in their respective fields and grew even more rapidly once they got Grace's financial power behind them.

But all the science and potential in the world can't guarantee success. One of Grace's acquisitions which had been on Lynch's target list, Del Taco (at least the national expansion rights for this California Mexican fast-food chain) faltered in 1979 after he left the company as it tried to expand too rapidly to Georgia and Texas markets. At the same time Grace's original food service acquisition, Far West Services, started showing chinks in its armor. Its dinner houses such as Reuben's and Plankhouse—once the envy of the industry—found themselves in a bitter battle with newer competition. Far West's Coco's coffee shops also encountered tougher times. Management changes and adjustments were set in motion for these operations.

Despite temporary setbacks, Grace maintained a high batting average on its consumer service acquisitions. The man who was instrumental in boosting this average, Charlie Lynch, would soon find himself in a reverse situation at Saga; he would have to apply the same business principles to reorganizing, pruning, and divesting judiciously.

When Lynch arrived at Saga Corporation's campus-like headquarters at Menlo Park, California, in mid-1978, the situation wasn't desperate but the company wasn't making anything near its profit goals. Margins were extra tight—particularly on the contract feeding side.

With his usual confidence, Lynch was sure he could turn things around. He received a three-year contract when Saga lured him from his Princeton, New Jersey, and New York surroundings. But he said he would gladly settle for one-year or no contract. "Either I'm going to do the job or not," he declared at the outset, "and that's how I'll be judged." (He simply assumed he would succeed as he always had in the past.)

CAREFUL ANALYSIS

Rather than jumping to any conclusions or solutions, Lynch spent six full months carefully studying what should be done. He insisted on a complete review of everything that had transpired in the company's thirty-year history, particularly the last ten years and five years. Just as when he was a rising executive at duPont de Nemours and Grace, Lynch couldn't make a move without analyzing detailed background. Management development and corporate strategies revolved around his penchant for a complete conceptual analysis of every department and division for the last five years and of its potential direction for the next five years.

After his extensive analysis of the data, Lynch decided to revamp Saga's entire system of financial values. He felt that Saga's traditional focus on profit margins, after food and labor costs were subtracted, was not effective in meeting the current inflationary environment. It was far more crucial to understand the whole picture and concentrate more on return on assets.

"We must look at all the figures and their interrelationships, rather than just profit margins," he proclaimed. He did feel that the contract feeding divisions' failure to come close to reaching an appropriate net profit was a result of not evaluating all aspects of the business.

Saga's contract feeding traditionally had thin pre-tax margins that had been declining, but provided a cash flow in contrast to Saga's restaurant chains which enjoyed higher profit margin and a smaller cash flow. Lynch sought to raise the contract feeding margins to a more respectable level. Yet he was saddled with a number of contracts whose terms were severe and could not easily be amended.

REEVALUATION

Shortly after arriving at Saga, Lynch formed a committee of senior executives. For the next year he and his team focused on conceptual and strategic planning covering a ten-year horizon. The first thing he concluded was that Saga should reevaluate what the company did as a service organization and should not identify itself as Saga Food Service, the name under which the contract group operated. Lynch developed a business definition that excluded the word *food:* "Saga is a consumer service organization with a retail orientation committed to profitable growth through excellent service, high value/quality products, and dedicated people."

By defining Saga as a "consumer service" company, Lynch opened the way for future opportunities. But he also reoriented the thinking of others at Saga so that they saw a company that could serve the consumer in a variety of ways, including restaurants and food service management. This was the philosophy he had developed at W. R. Grace.

Lynch had painstakingly reviewed Saga's previous five-year period to chart future growth plans. He found that where the company had obtained 77 percent of its $295 million net revenues in contract food service and 23 percent in restaurants in 1974, the balance had shifted to 70 percent and 30 percent respectively by 1979. He also noted that while the contract divisions were contributing 66 percent of operating income in 1974, that ratio dropped to less than half of the profits starting in 1977 and to 19 percent in 1979. Furthermore, compound annual operating income growth (1974-1978) was 32 percent for the restaurants against only 8 percent for the contract division.

The apparent conclusion would be to put more emphasis on and build up revenues for the higher margin, more profitable restaurant divisions. Yet things weren't quite that simple. The contract side contributed heavily to cash flow—an element urgently needed by the corporation. Perhaps the real challenge was to find ways of reversing the contract group's erosion of margins.

Lynch also traced some of the company's problems to expenses that had gotten out of control for the amount of profits being produced. General and administrative expenses from 1974 to 1978 had compounded at 21 percent annually, contrasted with a 17 percent compounded revenues growth. This was a deteriorating factor in Saga's performance, Lynch concluded. General and administrative expenses had risen 28 percent between 1978 and 1979 while interest expenses were soaring by 75 percent. Saga faced a serious dilemma.

TIGHTER ORGANIZATION

By mid-1979, after a full year of study, Lynch was ready to take action. First, the organizational structure was changed to a more functional setup. For years Saga had operated with a system of three groups—a "core" group composed of corporate management, a restaurant group called Saga Enterprises, and a contract group called Saga Food Service. Each of the two operating groups had their own staffs and support functions, many of which duplicated the functions of corporate management. This overlap led to higher expenses and less efficiency. Lynch himself had some twenty executives reporting to him at first.

He merged the contract food service and restaurant groups to eliminate financial distinctions. The new single operating group was organized into seven separate divisions: Education, Business and Industry, Health Care, and Canadian divisions for the contract side; and Stuart Anderson's Black Angus/Cattle Company, Velvet Turtle, and Straw Hat Pizza chains as the restaurant divisions. Division heads all reported to executive vice president and chief operating officer Jim Morrell, and Lynch now had only five executives reporting to him. He believed in a simple, streamlined setup and was able to implement it. Now the staff support functions worked directly with the divisions.

A number of advantages were obvious from the new organization. It provided one specific strategic direction with complete management commitment, tighter controls of all of Saga's available resources, opportunities for cross-fertilization of management talent, and quicker promotions within the company. In any case decentralization made controls stronger at each level and resulted in more accountability and wider management participation.

OUTLOOK IMPROVES

Besides strengthening the entire organization, Lynch's actions paid immediate dividends. For the first half of fiscal 1980, general and administrative expenses rose only 8 percent while sales jumped 14 percent—a welcome change. Lynch faced the problem squarely and reduced the overhead partly by dropping a number of employees. Some found this to be ruthless, and Lynch himself got no pleasure from it. But this was the job he had to do.

Another decision he reached was to sell The Refectory restaurants. The customer segment targeted for this chain was adequately covered by Saga's Velvet Turtle dinner houses and Stuart Anderson's Black Angus steakhouses. As a result of long-range planning, he determined that The Refectory no longer fit the company's strategic direction. Most of all, Lynch felt that The Refectory, with only ten units, did not offer viable expansion opportunities. This type of operation could be better handled by individual investors.

As he looked to the 1980s, he formulated a strategy of keeping each of the newly created divisions as, in effect, an independent corporation. Profit improvement and overall performance ratios—without sacrificing quality—would be the main areas of concentration. If an acquisition opportunity arose, Lynch might look at it. But he preferred to wait until everything was as he wanted it at Saga and until the necessary capital was readily available.

Lynch set specific financial ratio goals to attain in the early 1980s: a higher return on assets of at least 12 percent; a debt to total capital ratio of under 50 percent; and capital commitments within cash flow capabilities, which meant a drastic reduction in the $47 million spent in fiscal 1979. The latter dropped to $28 million the following year and stayed in that range as the company moved to a more solid financial footing. Shooting for a goal of at least a 2 percent net profit to sales ratio by 1985, he also set priorities for compound earnings growth of 20 percent annually.

REALIGNMENT

Lynch took a hard-nosed look at businesses. That was the basis on which he decided The Refectory would have to go and that a pilot Wild Strawberries "healthy food" restaurant just didn't fit into the company's plans. "We have to look at our business in a businesslike manner," he declared. "If we determine that any business cannot contribute at established threshold levels over the long term, you can be certain we will very carefully find a way of working out of that business."

He is convinced that site selection is the most crucial decision any operation must make. Once a site is chosen and built on, a company usually has to stick with this decision for many years, for better or for worse. "Improper site selection can hurt a business more than anything else," says Lynch, "and we are trying to address that very aggressively."

Ever a realist, he feels the price/value relationship is the most crucial thing affecting operators. He was extremely concerned when by 1980 the price/value relationship for pizza had dropped because of inflation and its impact on disposable income along with price rises for raw materials. Forced to raise prices to offset rising costs, Lynch nonetheless made sure that increases to customers were kept as low as possible.

Lynch put a high priority on training and encouraging managers to grow from within the ranks. He made it a point to visit college campuses and observe the performances of student managers that Saga had assigned to help run food service on campus. The ones who were most successful in managing the "hash lines" were gradually moved up within the Saga system.

He provided clear-cut parameters for all his managers, and they knew what was required to reach goals. "I am convinced we will improve our performance over time," he said, "and believe we are already starting to demonstrate our ability to handle our businesses effectively even in difficult inflationary periods."

MANAGERS UPGRADED

After reviewing hundreds and hundreds of pages of reports, Lynch set about solving the situation. For one thing, the managers of each individual unit had to be clearer on their tasks. He set out on a course of "training, training, training" everyone right down the lines. If an employee of a major business went to one of Saga's food-service installations, each person working there had to be completely trained to produce the desired results.

"This is a people business," Lynch emphasizes. "We've gone to extremes to interview the right people and to hire the best ones." To take care of Saga's growth needs over a five-year period, Lynch figured an average of ten applicants daily would have to be interviewed. That would yield an average of one actually hired each day and would meet the needs. "It sounded incredible to my staff," he recalls, "but it had to be done that way."

Lynch likes to show his managers a large picture frame. "There are certain goals on this frame," he says, "but how you paint this picture and achieve these goals is entirely up to you." He also decentralized authority down to the lowest feasible level. This means more power lies with regions and regional controls.

Lynch also was looking to the day when he would have the cash available to exercise his acquisition magic and acquire another chain. "We're looking for a quality acquisition in a service-oriented business. It doesn't have to be in food as long as the mentality is the same."

Lynch believes in anticipating consumer shifts. "It's the 'me' generation," he says, "and we have to know how they will affect our restaurant." He doesn't hesitate to challenge any strategy. "There's always a better way, and it pays to be prepared for all eventualities. What if red meat is no longer popular? Sounds far out, but we'd have to be prepared with a concept to replace the steakhouses, or at least to refine them to a related format. You have to be prepared to modify things so you don't get trapped."

He is totally organized in his approach to the operating groups. With the chief operating officer, he makes sure that the president of each division has a specific idea of the goals, challenges, and objectives that must be achieved. Each of his managers knows, for example, the relationship between the cost of capital and a division's performance ratio.

His feelings about the problems of Straw Hat Pizza are that "fast food is not a saturated segment of the market but is maturing and, as a result, we'll have to accept slower real growth trends." The situation with The Refectory was different. Although marginally profitable, it simply did not meet corporate objectives. The way Lynch saw it, The Refectory failed to help Saga with its goal of "improving our competitive position in the market and, hence, the financial community."

EXPENSES CONTROLLED

Lynch's management principles seemed to pay off as results surged for fiscal 1980. Saga was on the way to achieving some of its objectives although it still had quite a way to go. Net profit jumped sharply from the depressed earnings of $1.5 million in fiscal 1979 to $7.2 million in 1980.

With his economy measures, Lynch managed to hold the growth of general and administrative expenses to 2 percent for 1980—an excellent figure in comparison with the 12 percent revenues increase for the year. Strict guidelines to control and evaluate every aspect of the business contributed to the improved results. Most importantly, every division had higher revenues and all had higher operating profits except Straw Hat Pizza.

The actual performance resulted in a substantial operating income rise from the previous fiscal year's $9.7 million to $16.8 million on a 14 percent revenues hike to $226 million for the restaurant chains—Stuart Anderson's Black Angus, Velvet Turtle, and Straw Hat. On the contract side of the business, operating income soared from $2.3 million to $8.5 million while revenues jumped 11 percent to $507 million.

To boost the stature of each of his division heads, Lynch in 1980 named four general managers as division presidents—Thomas Dillon for Velvet Turtle restaurants; Ralph Pica for the business and industry division; Carl Randall for the education division; and Robert Van Horn for the health care and Canadian divisions. Stuart Anderson continued as president of his Black Angus steakhouses, as he had since Saga acquired the chain. (Anderson moved to chairman in 1981.) Howard Berkowitz was brought in as president of Straw Hat in 1979.

In each division, Lynch worked with the chief operating officer to target the problem and work toward a solution. For the education division the strategy was to pinpoint new accounts to develop, boost the management and profitability of existing accounts, and develop marketing capacities to tackle new opportunities.

If an account could not be properly developed within a reasonable period of time, it was agreed that the contract was to be terminated since a quality product could not be developed. Thus the number of accounts in the education division had been reduced from 393 to 373 by the end of fiscal 1980. In addition, operating overhead was sharply cut and special campus marketing programs to improve the volume and revenues mix at each account were implemented. New product-line concepts were introduced.

NEW MARKETS

Saga's business and industry division pushed in the direction of the white collar market since it was less penetrated by food service operators and was less vulnerable to layoffs which often occurred in factories and other blue collar plants. To provide better individual services, the division was divided into six geographic regions with teams of executives in each region. At the same time lighter menu items became the order of the day. Sandwich bars, salad areas, and grills were launched at several installations.

Lynch took advantage of the fact that with health care costs soaring, a number of health care facilities chose to turn to professional contract food service management to help them. Saga was a specialist in dietary service, giving particular emphasis to administration, safety, and dietary therapeutics in handling its accounts. It pulled in twenty-two new accounts in fiscal 1980.

Saga's final contract food service division is Saga Canadian Management Services Ltd. Colleges and universities were the prime target for

Saga in Canada, but the division also began stepping up its sales efforts to acquire health care and business accounts as well.

RESTAURANT CONCEPTS

On the restaurant side Saga launched new generation Velvet Turtles. The first two were built in Woodland Hills and Thousand Oaks, California. Then two more were opened in Puente Hills, California, and Phoenix to give the division a total of twenty-two restaurants, all company owned. Remodelings and a "new look" were planned for all the restaurants.

One of the best marketing gimmicks launched by the Velvet Turtle was "Sunset Suppers"—4 to 6 P.M. weekday specials at lower prices during a time when the restaurants normally would not be crowded. New items were added, including fresh fish in crust on the dinner menu and tournedos Rossini. Luncheon salads were augmented with fresh spinach and seafood and papaya. Lynch continued to insist that the Velvet Turtle retain its "top-of-the-line" dinner house reputation with high quality food.

Straw Hat Pizza, with 230 units, used fiscal 1980 to consolidate its operations. It introduced pan pizza and implemented an advanced labor management system considered a leading model for the industry. A new incentive program was also launched for the restaurant managers with spurs to build sales and profits at each unit. The restaurants continued to feature Hot Hats and submarine sandwiches and a salad bar in addition to a variety of pizzas. Straw Hat closed twenty-three unprofitable units while it opened twenty-two new restaurants during the year. Average per unit sales of Straw Hat's company-owned units dipped from $350,000 to $345,000, and Straw Hat faced the imperative of raising this figure.

QUALITY GOALS

As a result of the strategic planning process, a "quality combination" theme was introduced throughout the company. Lynch set *quality* at every level as a priority for the 1980s. "We must make quality a way of life," he declared. "All of us must be committed to excellence in everything we do, from hiring and keeping exceptional employees to striving for effective communication." Among his other priorities were to assure a sharing of ideas through participative management and to set clear guidelines of authority and responsibility. His philosophy also emphasizes "minimizing duplication of effort, maximizing the speed and efficiency of decision-making, and analyzing how to serve our customers best."

He set as goals for his five-year program an improvement in profitability and return on investment for shareholders, consistent earnings growth, and maintaining a competitive advantage. To meet these objectives, he said, "we must be committed to profitable growth through excellent service, high value/quality products and dedicated people."

Lynch sees Saga as a consumer service organization. "We are not a food service organization," he declared. "Food is merely the vehicle by which we serve our customers." He is extremely positive and confident at all times. "We have an unbelievable profit opportunity in front of us if we effectively use the tools we have," he asserted. "We can and will make quality a way of life at Saga." Lynch is convinced that dedication and quality can solve any problem. It sounds old-fashioned, but so far his methods have worked.

SECTION III

The Entrepreneurs

Even in an age of bigness, the restaurant business is still dominated by entrepreneurs, for it is entrepreneurial by its very nature. Thousands start off in this business with dreams to build one restaurant into the best or perhaps to become a leading chain. In most cases these dreams are never realized. They often end in bitter frustration with a bankruptcy or closing. The pace is just too tough and demanding today to reward anything less than an absolute professional effort.

But some defy the odds and do make it in varying degrees. Three of the more fascinating entrepreneurs who have steadily grown in scope and dimension are portrayed in this section: Stuart Anderson, Norman Brinker, and Alex Schoenbaum.

Anderson, a cattleman with an early interest in hotels and restaurants, overcame the odds in the rigorous steakhouse market. Through a combination of promotional efforts and market positioning, his Seattle-based Black Angus restaurants have sprouted to a formidable chain. More than anything else, his individuality and courage to do it his way have carried Black Angus ahead of other operations. He prides himself on being the true cowboy-restaurateur—and being so successful at both within Saga's corporate framework. He is not the corporate man in any sense.

Brinker seemed destined for mediocrity in his early career at Jack-in-the-Box and then while running an unhappy place called Brink's restaurant. But with his own foresight and indomitable belief in a concept, he made Dallas-based Steak&Ale the No. 1 volume steakhouse chain. He and his wife, the late Maureen Connolly, together believed that an eating place based on the film *Tom Jones* could become a leading restaurant and a highly profitable chain. They were right. Even after Pillsbury acquired the chain, Brinker retained his entrepreneurial spirit.

Schoenbaum, hard-nosed All-American football tackle who tried many businesses early in his career and then ran bowling alleys in Charleston, West Virginia, was a leader in the coffee shop field. He started with a Parkette drive-in and gradually built an empire of Shoney's Big Boy coffee shops and Captain D's fish and chips units. Along the way he got considerable help from Dave Frisch, Bob Wian, and Ray Danner. But it was Schoenbaum's ingenuity and spirit that propelled Shoney's into such a wide-ranging force. He felt the Big Boys were for the middle class and the masses. He stuck to his guns and resisted the frills that others were adding. As a result Shoney's sales and earnings increased every quarter over the same quarter the previous year, for twenty-two consecutive years through 1981.

6

Stuart Anderson

COWBOY BUSINESSMAN

By the time Stuart Anderson was ten years old, he was convinced he wanted to be a rancher. He frequently visited his uncle's ranch-farm on Orcas Island outside Seattle and was fascinated with the animals, the open spaces, and the sounds of the outdoors. This fascination for working with animals would stay with him through his career and lead directly to his success in the restaurant business.

Actually he was brought up in an exclusive area of Seattle in the late 1920s and 1930s and attended the finest schools. His father, an orthopedic surgeon, made sure that Anderson, a brother, and a sister received the finest education. They went through the Depression years without any great want. In fact, they had two cars in the garage and a maid almost always in the house.

Perhaps young Anderson got his penchant for ranching from a family tradition. His grandparents in Sweden had been farmers, and his uncle was a rancher. He decided that by being a rancher he could continue the high standard of living his father provided. But while he loved to help his uncle round up the cattle and appreciated the open spaces, he also relished those occasions when his parents would take him to

95

restaurants. They would try different types of restaurants whenever possible, and he was getting an early exposure to this aspect of life which many of his peers were unable to afford.

With no practical experience in ranching but a real desire for it, young Anderson was inclined to pursue a career in this direction. Yet his family wanted him to receive the broadest possible education. He went through a series of phases that had no direct influence on his real ambition.

Anderson attended Dartmouth College in New Hampshire starting in 1940. Pearl Harbor struck in late 1941, and students went their separate ways. He transferred to the University of California and then joined the army where his education continued in an engineering-type program. But the program was dismantled in 1943 when things were tough on the war front, and he became a tank corps driver. He fought in France and Germany in 1944 and 1945.

Shortly after the war was over he graduated from the University of Washington with a degree in Business Administration. More interested then in making a decent living than in breaking new ground in ranching or restaurants, he took an office building management opportunity in Iowa. His first business experience was managing his grand-father's building there. This spurred an interest in both office building management and hotel management.

HOTEL JOBS

He moved back to Seattle in 1950 to look for a job in the hotel business. He applied to a major hotel chain, but they rejected him on the grounds that he had no practical hotel experience. He told them he wanted to use his wartime savings to lease a small old hotel but they warned him, "Never go into your own business. That's the way to go broke." (This advice turned out to be only partly true.)

Anderson gathered together his savings in 1950 and leased the old Caledonia Hotel in Seattle. "In a way," he recalls, "this was how I could buy a job." In any case the timing was fortuitous. The state of Washington had just liberalized its liquor laws, and cocktail lounges were now permitted in hotels. With the Korean War in the early 1950s, Seattle became a booming port city and the hotel prospered.

While operating the hotel on a leasing agreement, Anderson subleased its restaurant facilities on an annual basis. These facilities seemed to lose money perpetually, and he decided in 1957 to take over the facilities and operate them in conjunction with the hotel. He called the operation the Caledonia Grill. Within three years he exercised his entrepreneurial spirit to convert the massive, unproductive lobby of the hotel into dining room facilities while switching the grill into a cocktail lounge called the Downbeat. This exposure to the potential of entertainment was to play a crucial role in Anderson's later restaurant experiences.

He featured stereo music in the cocktail lounge and drew crowds to what was considered a trendy place at the time. A combination of "beautiful people" and stereo music made the place prosper. But while he was concentrating on the glamorous lounge, the dining room moved toward collapse. There were evenings when all the customers congregated in the lounge, and only four or five dinners would be served in the dining room.

FRENCH RESTAURANT

Obviously something had to be done. Later in 1960 Stuart sold the hotel and leased back the restaurant to raise capital for an extensive remodeling which could give his restaurant some uniqueness. This time he called it the French Quarter and emphasized French food. But the restaurant again failed, although it served perhaps ten dinners a night instead of five. The lounge continued to prosper.

Not easily discouraged, Anderson researched the entire problem. He found that an exclusive French restaurant was overshooting the mark and that he'd be better off with a well-presented basic mass concept. He latched onto a 96-cent-per-pound imported Australian beef, which finally did pull in the customers—at a reasonable profit. He stuck with this low-cost item as his staple in the French Quarter restaurant for the next few years and later utilized it to launch a revolutionary one-price steak concept. But the reputation of "low-cost" beef bothered him, and he vowed to find a way to upgrade this image. Capitalizing on the inexpensive beef, he switched the French Quarter restaurant in 1962 to a "Gay '90s" theme and renamed it the Gold Coast. This setup jelled for a while when the World's Fair was at Seattle and there was no lack of customers.

RANCHING

Meanwhile, Anderson had been dabbling with his first love— ranching. In 1955 he had purchased a small 160-acre ranch on the outskirts of Seattle in what is now the city of Redmond. Anderson and a partner raised peas and operated a dairy. He sold the ranch at a healthy profit when the city sprawl overran the area, and resumed ranching in the Columbia Basin further from Seattle. It was then that he started raising Black Angus cattle, which he steadfastly believed were the best breed.

He commuted between the ranch and his hotel-restaurant but spent more time with the latter and still made no connection between the two businesses. In 1963 he noticed serious changes taking place in the landscape and felt that the hotel business no longer would be profitable. Besides, he wanted to strike new ground on his own. He sold the hotel-restaurant and planned to use the proceeds to open his own operation which would be supplied with beef from his ranch.

Anderson thought over his interests and concepts before he settled on a specific format. By 1964 the World's Fair had closed in Seattle, and the bloom was off the restaurant market. Everyone expected tough times, and not surprisingly many restaurants were up for sale. In this atmosphere, as he saw it, there were no true steakhouses with pleasant atmosphere and choice steak. A few research trips he made through the West convinced him to get away from imported "cheap" beef and emphasize quality U.S. choice grade beef. He still could keep the price low through his own cattle ranch. At the same time he hit upon a new idea to simplify the entire process for the customer and for the benefit of his own cost structure. It was a general nuisance for customers to have to figure out a hodgepodge of prices on menus. Why not just have one across-the-board price, period?

BLACK ANGUS

Thus in April 1964 the original Stuart Anderson's Black Angus restaurant opened in Seattle. For what now seems an incredibly low price of $2.95, customers were given a choice of six different cuts of steak along with a potato, salad, and bread. Exceptional value on a quality steak meal and a push for rapid turns of customer business proved an unbeatable combination. With almost no advertising but considerable hoopla from customers, volume reached a stunning $750,000 in the first year alone. Considering the low ticket format, customer counts had to be running at record levels for those days.

When Anderson thought with pride of fast turnover, the last thing on his mind was "fast food." He insisted from the first on accommodating the customer with a high level of waiter and waitress service. His original Black Angus was so successful that it never has spent even a single day in a "loss" position.

This was in sharp contrast with previous restaurants on the same site. Anderson had known the restaurant there called Skipper's in his boyhood. It had been successful for years but had fallen on hard times. Three different owners tried to make it work with various formats, but couldn't. He was told he would have to be crazy to buy the location and that it could never be profitable. This only whetted his appetite for the challenge. He located his corporate headquarters across the street from this original Stuart Anderson's Black Angus restaurant—always his personal favorite.

As he saw his new format becoming very successful and opened more of the same type of restaurants, Anderson began buying more cattle acreage. He thought that some day he might be operating numerous Black Angus restaurants and would have to raise enough beef to supply all of them. Eventually his little ranch—through gradual additions— would become a sprawling 2,500 acres and yet still wouldn't be nearly big enough to supply all the Black Angus restaurants.

UNCONVENTIONAL APPROACHES

From the start Anderson remained the individual who defied convention. He reversed the usual industry formula and made his food costs higher than his labor costs. He was willing to risk pushing his food costs to over 50 percent of sales initially on the theory that customers would want the best possible quality meat within the context of the operation. He tried to reduce the food cost ratio by pushing for higher volume and became one of the first to emphasize liquor sales. Liquor would not only bring in more traffic but would also balance the high food costs and yield a higher profit margin. He felt the strategy would work as long as he maintained quality food. Early in the game he offered live entertainment with live bands. He frequently traveled to Europe to find new ideas, and he adopted European-type stainless steel dance floors for his Black Angus restaurants. Cocktail lounges were a feature of Anderson's restaurants from the early days.

By 1972 Anderson had opened twelve units, established a winning basic format, and knew that if he were to continue growing in his combined cattle ranching-restaurant business, he would need financing and support. When Saga Corporation, a food service management company based in Menlo Park south of San Francisco, came along with an attractive offer, he jumped at the opportunity. It was also desirable to Saga, which needed to balance its contract feeding business with a fast-producing restaurant chain.

Anderson knew instinctively that as successful as his twelve restaurants were, he could not expand at the pace he wanted on his own. "There was no way I could generate that much cash flow from those restaurants," he notes. "I needed financing to really run with the formula I felt could be successful and had been tested in other states. I was anxious and ambitious to put myself in a position of directing a strong expansion."

SAGA ACQUISITION

While Saga's financial backing was crucial to Anderson, he was now very much the individualistic Western entrepreneur and was reluctant to yield his leadership or autonomy to a corporation. Saga agreed to let him continue managing his organization to grow at whatever speed he wanted. That speed has been steady every year—a rapid pace, but not one that soared out of control as happened with many chains. As long as Anderson's chain has consistently been by far the most profitable of all of Saga's chain holdings, he has continued to enjoy virtually complete autonomy and Saga's financial backing. He is not in the corporate mold but does fit comfortably into corporate goals for a healthy profit.

Anderson was able to carve out a distinct market niche and stick to it under Saga. His target was primarily the blue collar and middle income adults—not those in the higher executive ranks. He was not only an astute rancher and promoter, but he knew his marketing. Perhaps he intuitively sensed that he needed to find his own niche at slightly lower price points than the competition. He was able to find a gap in the market somewhere between the other limited menu dinner houses and the coffee shops and family restaurants. His objective was to provide basic family dining with quality steak at the lowest possible price. This price couldn't stay at $2.95, but the idea of a full dinner with one basic price did prevail in some form through the years. Prices and variations kept climbing toward the $6 mark but remained a good value. Finally, the idea of "one price only" had to be scrapped as more choices appeared on the menu in an effort to broaden the market.

Anderson built in a wider mass appeal than most of the other steakhouse chains. He consistently has attracted more of the "average folks" with consequent higher traffic counts and higher volumes. He has stuck with an extremely casual Western-style decor—certainly not an overbearing atmosphere. But country-Western music is seldom if ever heard there, and in no sense is Black Angus a country-Western place.

SAME FORMAT

Perhaps the great thing about Black Angus restaurants and Stuart Anderson is that both have remained basically the same since the first opening in 1964. It is certainly the flagship of Saga's chains—well ahead of Saga's Velvet Turtle dinner houses and Straw Hat Pizza units in bottom line performance and sales averages. Black Angus's annual sales were averaging over $2 million by 1981, and some were even hitting $3 million. The price that Saga paid for Black Angus in 1972 has multiplied many times over.

During all this time Anderson continued as president and chief executive of a chain which by early 1981 had proliferated to seventy-eight restaurants in the West, Midwest, and Southwest and was making motions toward expanding to other areas. He remained the premier promoter-salesman for the company and its leading rancher. Since the demand for all these high volume units had outstripped the supply, he found himself having to deal with many local sources. An expert Black Angus cattle breeder, Anderson purchases from three major packers who in turn buy from 500 ranchers. He also remains dedicated to only company-owned units, maintaining direct controls and avoiding the pitfalls of franchising.

The real Stuart Anderson—the one that he is most comfortable with and that the public adores—is the Stuart Anderson of the television commercials. During one commercial a helicopter swirls in for a dust-spilling landing. A tall fellow dressed as a rancher and with a movie-star look steps out. He walks over to a nearby jeep and drives off to look at his herd of prize cattle. Next the viewer sees a restaurant kitchen where the rancher watches a chef making juicy-looking steaks. Then the rancher sees a waitress serving the order to the most happy customers. Suddenly the rancher's voice sounds loudly over the speakers, "If you don't think ranching knowledge gives us the edge, then talk to Stuart Anderson."

Anderson is recognized by some as the "Colonel" of the steakhouse business. Yet he takes it all in his stride. One would never know from talking with Stuart Anderson that he was any sort of a star. But in his own way he is a star of the restaurant world, for he is an innovator who seems always to get the best results. He is considered "one of the old adventurers," and he loves to be in the limelight. But Stuart Anderson, who projects a simple image, is a brilliant operator who knows exactly the right impression to make on customers and exactly how to relate to his company, his restaurants, and his employees at headquarters and in the field. Most of all, he knows how to create a maximum value package.

There's no doubt that Anderson and his restaurants have been very cleverly packaged to the public. But he is totally respected by everyone who works for him. "Thanks to Stuart," says one of his executives, "we're really a group of entrepreneurs." Anderson himself has a management philosophy of not choosing "pegs to fit into slots." He prefers to "find very highly motivated, talented people and build the jobs around them. Shelter them and guide them, and they will be your salvation." He believes in downplaying authority whenever possible and giving maximum freedom. This way each employee seems to feel an important part of the chain's success.

As the chain has grown, Anderson has found it more difficult to maintain close contact with the restaurant employees. But he still delights in being on a first-name basis with many, and he is an inspiration to the employees.

EXECUTIVE TEAM

Anderson, who once could handle much of the operation himself, has gradually molded together a team to handle all the restaurants and position the chain for further expansion. But many of the executives date back to earlier days. The one person who has been with him longest is senior vice president Bruce Attebery, who started working in Anderson's Seattle hotel restaurant in 1960 as a bartender and cook and later became manager. He is Black Angus operations vice president and supervises its northern sector including Alaska, Washington, Oregon, Idaho, Colorado, New Mexico, Iowa, Nebraska, and Missouri. Tom Lee, who is operations vice president for the southern sector, started with Anderson as a moonlighting bartender and became manager of the first Black Angus in 1964.

Ron Stephenson, development vice president, joined the chain in 1969 after serving as divisional manager for a leading coffee company. He has been the force behind Black Angus's site selection and construction. Roberta "Bobbi" Loughrin, operations services vice president, started with the company in 1971 and has responsibilities for environmental health and safety and field accounting. Haig Cartozian, marketing vice president, began with Anderson in 1971 as advertising director. Having run his own public relations and marketing consultant business, he is the real professional, specializing in the restaurant industry. Cartozian is a prime mover behind the packaging of Anderson and the positioning of the chain.

Parent Saga Corporation moved over two executives to strengthen Anderson's team. In 1980 Saga vice president and controller Dan Sharpley became Black Angus's financial vice president and controller. Then in mid-1981 Saga's food service business and industry division president Ralph Pica was named president of the chain. Anderson gave up the presidency but took the new post of chairman. It was still his chain even if Saga was utilizing professionals to help him.

He was still giving customers choice cuts with salad, potatoes, and bread for $6.95 in 1980. When liquor, which accounts for 30 percent of the sales mix, and other items were added in, the average per person check was up to almost $10, causing some concern that he was starting to price himself out of his target blue collar and middle class market.

He has clustered units and gradually expanded to new markets rather than leapfrogging suddenly. His goal is to keep five-unit clusters for each field supervisor and thereby gain maximum controls. In addition, with the clusters, the distribution and television advertising are more efficient. However, by 1980 Anderson was gradually moving into the Midwest with units in Iowa and Missouri without slackening his controls.

ADJUSTMENTS NEEDED

Despite the continued basic format, there have been modifications. As costs have risen, so have the population requirements for locations. Early Black Angus restaurants could afford to open in markets with a 50,000 population within five miles. But by 1980 a 250,000 population was required to provide the necessary volume base which could offset land, building, and equipment costs that had soared to an average $1.8 million for new units.

In the tough 1979-80 economic climate, Anderson's customer counts softened a bit. With beef costs also rising, he launched some light lunches and added seafood and chicken entrees to the dinner menu. Daily specials were widened for variety, and omelettes and a number of egg-based dishes were introduced. Many of these strategies were aimed at offsetting high labor costs—which ran to 25 percent of sales—as well as the high beef costs. To keep costs in line, he emphasized a one-plate dinner approach and steered away from a salad bar. He even bought some beef frozen or in the futures market as a hedge against adverse price fluctuations.

With the economic climate softening, Anderson cut his expansion rate to only five new restaurants for 1980. In the old days this $9 million investment for new restaurants would have been considered astronomical. But now it is modest.

Beef will continue as Black Angus's trademark even with some diversification of the menu. Anderson won't soon forget an experiment in the mid-1970s when he tried to merchandise a gourmet seafood restaurant called Stuart's in Seattle. This upscale ego-oriented project simply didn't work. It wasn't Stuart Anderson at all. The fancy menu and a strict dress code were completely out of character. The physical plant was enormous and was usually half empty. (Later, Anderson's new baby did turn around when the menu reverted to basics and the dress code was dropped.)

ENTERTAINMENT MIX

Anderson incorporates some form of entertainment in 70 percent of his restaurants, looking for the extra pizzaz and traffic it can add. But he packages this entertainment carefully. In California and Arizona, discos predominate. In other areas of the country, it is live bands. His marketing savvy enabled him to target his customers and work out a formula for two separate audiences and maximum utilization of space at his restaurants with recorded music. From 5 to 10 P.M. an adult audience would hold sway for dinner. Then for the next few hours a younger group would populate the cocktail lounge, and liquor sales would jump. Of course, there was some overlap in the two "groups," and diners at times would feel that the noise from the disco was an intrusion. But generally Anderson's plan seemed to work.

At no point did he want to become involved in the so-called budget steakhouse market of cafeteria-style self-service. He kept to the idea of table service. Volume climbed each year at the restaurants—even in soft times. Customers generally have voted an endorsement of Anderson's price-value relationship. He has kept a market niche somewhere between Ponderosa's $3.50 average ticket and Victoria Station's $13. Anderson has created a form of "ranch" restaurants, with the necessary embellishments. He looks like a rancher and comes across like a rancher in his personal advertising appearances.

Anderson sees quality control and consistency of product as the main challenges of the 1980s. Other chains have relaxed their controls as they have expanded around the country. But Anderson has no intention of compromising on quality and insists that every customer suggestion or complaint be completely followed through.

Some feel he is too slow at making decisions. "He procrastinates," says one associate. "He gets too much input and then sits on things." Actually Anderson is a deliberate thinker and tends to underplay his shrewdness. Outwardly he may seem to be a cowboy, but underneath it all is a hard-nosed businessman.

Anderson enjoys sailing and playing squash or tennis in his spare time. But he is happiest when selling beef as he does in numerous television commercials and while smiling from billboards and covers. He signifies nonchalant elegance: the gentleman rancher, gentleman restaurateur, and beef expert. He loves his ranch and utilizes the newest techniques on his registered 800-head herd of cattle. He also delights in showing off the ranch to large groups for steak feeds, hayrides, and barn dances. He has predicated his career on a love of beef. "We expect to remain in the same popular steakhouse niche," he vows. "With the nutritional value of beef getting more attention, we are nowhere near our peak." His customers are a diverse mix but have one thing in common: a continuing desire for quality choice beef.

It is the marketing of this desire that has given Anderson his niche and his opportunities. But it is his own ingeniousness at capitalizing on the desire which has propelled him so far. He is America's true cowboy-restaurateur.

7

Norman Brinker

TOM JONES TAMED

The intense man of thirty-three and his wife, former world tennis champion Maureen Connolly, peered at the movie screen with unusual curiosity. What had started as simply an entertaining outing to see *Tom Jones* turned into a reality destined to change their lives.

The sensual eating scenes portrayed in the movie haunted both Maureen and Norman Brinker. A close couple, they shared similar ideas and aspirations. They had been disappointed in their attempts to revitalize a little coffee shop they had opened just a year ago. The lusty old English inn portrayed in the movie was so alive and exciting. Could they recreate that same atmosphere in Dallas, Texas, in 1965?

It was with great anticipation that Brinker had decided in 1964 to leave Jack-in-the-Box, the San Diego-based fast-food chain, where he was Southwest regional manager and partner. He had obtained a relatively low rental deal on a coffee shop at Gaston and Carol Streets in an older section of Dallas. Yet despite a major redesign and backbreaking eighteen-hour work days, "Brink's" was scarcely at the break-even point. A projected refurbishing of the lower income area surrounding the restaurant did not materialize. Brinker wasn't ready to give up on the restaurant business, but he was beginning to think he was in the wrong place at the wrong time. What he needed, he thought, was a whole new approach and a fresh start.

While the Brinkers were sitting in that movie theater transfixed at the way chicken legs were being eaten with such gusto and huge succulent fruits were being devoured with equal fervor, an idea which had been germinating began to flower. "Why can't we do something like this?" they thought. They visualized a limited menu steakhouse based on the legs and joints they had seen devoured in the movie. It fit!

Fast food, coffee shop, now what? He was thinking of a further upgrade in his concept, status, and—most of all—in his bottom line. She was thinking that with all his effort and talent, he should achieve a much better return. Most of all, he realized that even if the area around his coffee shop somehow could be revitalized and business should pick up for him, a coffee shop motif did not fit his ambitions. He wanted to expand to a wider-ranging chain and saw too many problems inherent in a coffee shop format. His intuition and ability to anticipate future consumer thinking like this would prove indispensible to his future success.

Without thinking about it too much longer and with his wife's encouragement, Brinker leased a site at Lemon and Oak Lawn Avenues in Dallas. He vowed not to repeat the same mistake he had made at the coffee shop and to open in a reasonably prosperous area with strong traffic flow potential. He decided to call the new place Steak&Ale, with food to predominate and a healthy mix of spirits to be included. This concept eventually would become the leader of its market segment though he could not have foreseen such immense success at first.

INTENSE COMPETITION

Brinker tended to excel at whatever he tackled. He was born in 1931 in Denver and brought up in Roswell, New Mexico, where he attended school. He went to San Diego State University and graduated with honors and a B.A. degree in marketing. He was president of the student body. A well-conditioned athlete with intense competitive drive, he was outstanding in horseback riding and related events. He represented the United States on the 1949 Equestrian jumping team and in the 1952 Helsinki Summer Olympics. His greatest athletic challenge was in the modern Pentathlon world championships at Budapest in 1954. The five-event competition combined horseback riding, épée fencing, pistol shooting, a 300-meter swim, and a cross-country run. Brinker managed to stand up to the pace of these grueling events until breaking a shoulder while riding a horse. He had to withdraw—a bitter disappointment after all his efforts.

Perhaps it was predestined that two such highly tuned competitors would meet and marry. He met world champion tennis player Maureen Connolly (Little Mo) in 1952 when he was in San Diego and she, at eighteen, had swept every conceivable world and U.S. tennis championship. As a sports writer for the *San Diego Union*, she first met Brinker when she interviewed him about his riding achievements—a pleasant turnabout from the constant press interviews to which she was subjected. This was one interview that both enjoyed immensely. They started dating and were married three years later, after Brinker finished his navy service. Both always retained a close interest in sports and in helping young people.

They shared common interests and a close relationship with each other and with their two daughters. Maureen Connolly Brinker died in 1969 at the age of thirty-four after a heroic struggle against cancer. She captured the hearts of many throughout the country with her courage and optimistic spirit to the very end. The loss had a profound impact on Brinker and made him even more sensitive to the needs of others personally and in business.

NEW FORMAT

When formulating the first Steak&Ale restaurant in 1965, Brinker called in Frank Lutkus, who had designed his coffee shop. Visualizing the *Tom Jones* movie and utilizing their own instincts, they adopted an old English inn motif which they felt would provide a special niche in the market for the initial restaurant and for the chain that was foreseen. Individual rooms with fireplaces were designed to give a warm and comfortable feeling to the place. Old English uniforms from the movie were adapted for the waiters and waitresses. Seating capacity was kept at a modest 106. The basic menu was limited to five cuts of steak along with corn on the cob, baked potato, and mushrooms—a far cry from today's diverse selections, but ample for those days.

Brinker and Lutkus managed to get the first Steak&Ale into action quickly, and it opened in early 1966. Brinker fervently hoped that his second venture as an entrepreneur would be a happier experience and yield a better return. His strategy was to emphasize a limited menu, a well-controlled steakhouse several notches above the "budget steakhouse" category but not at the gourmet level. Until that time this market had been largely unexplored. Brinker's theory was that by keeping the operation simple and with a minimum of overhead, a reasonable profit could be achieved. High volume and minimum expenses were the formula. Despite the basic nature of his operation, he insisted on the best cuts of steak. He wanted to give a feeling of quality and of a real dining experience. He was also finally running the type of restaurant he enjoyed.

EARLY SUCCESS

For the first year he projected that Steak&Ale could attain total sales of $250,000—with a little bit of luck and a great deal of care. He operated out of a tiny office at his Brink's coffee shop, which he intended to sell. He worked eighteen-hour days at Steak&Ale—just as he had when Brink's was his only operation. But now there was a big difference. Steak&Ale's cash register jingled well beyond even the most optimistic expectations. Brinker had thought it would take time to gain recognition for his new format. But in its first year Steak&Ale's one restaurant achieved almost a $400,000 volume—an impressive figure in those days for a limited menu operation with no bar. In contrast to Brink's coffee shop, which could barely do $300,000 with a far more complex menu and higher expenses, it was profitable from the beginning.

Brinker and his original operations partner, Harold Deem, never took a day off for the first two years of his Steak&Ale operation. But

Brinker certainly didn't need any vacation—he was having the time of his life! He opened a second Dallas Steak&Ale restaurant in 1967 at Northwest Highway and Shady Brook Street. It had a similar format to the first one. After all, why change a winning combination? The foundation was now in place, and Brinker would develop each market—starting with Dallas—before expanding to another market. He retained many of the elements of the early format, only gradually expanding the menu and making other adjustments for better service. There have been no radical changes.

Finally in 1968 Brinker—by now totally committed to Steak&Ale—sold Brink's. He then indulged in the luxury of opening his own office—even hiring a secretary—and being able to take an occasional day off. The concept of Steak&Ale, relatively new for its day, took hold. Customers appreciated the warm atmosphere, courteous service, and basic value they were receiving. With just five items on the menu, Brinker and Deem had complete control of the operation. With competition rather sparse, they could gain a wider portion of any given market. Among the few early limited menu steakhouse contenders in those days were Chuck's Steakhouses and Denver-based Cork 'n Cleaver.

Now the challenge was to expand into a viable chain operation. Brinker knew instinctively he had to have more units to support his cost structures and to attain his goal of any sort of reasonable entrepreneurial success. To help with plans for new units Lutkus, by trade a theater designer, entered the picture full time in 1968. It was altogether natural that he would join the chain. After all, as Brinker and others saw it, a restaurant was in many ways a theater. Customers came not only for the food but for an evening of entertainment—and that meant a pleasant environment and atmosphere. As customers were becoming more sophisticated, it was necessary to upgrade the decor gradually without overdoing it. Lutkus recalls those days when everything was so simple: "We could put the entire five-item menu on a cleaver neatly packaged and easy for everyone to see. It fit in perfectly." In many ways Lutkus and Brinker regret they eventually grew to a point where the menu would no longer fit on a cleaver and they had to switch to a fancy leather-folder menu.

One incident when Brinker and Lutkus were putting the final touches on upgrading the initial Steak&Ale unit on Lemon Avenue illustrates the thoroughness with which Brinker handled things down to the last detail. Regulations required that all wood used in the restaurant had to be fireproof. Lutkus assured Brinker as they completed the project that the wood was fully and unquestionably fireproofed. But just to make sure, Brinker took samples home to try to burn in his fireplace. When it simply wouldn't burn, he felt confident that the building was in fact completely fireproof.

The second Steak&Ale did even better than the first, and now more and more Steak&Ales would gradually be added, starting from a base in Texas, branching through the Southwest, and then to other parts of the country.

STRENGTH OF CHARACTER

Besides his acute sense of the marketplace, Brinker in those early days established himself as a trustworthy man whose word was as good as gold. This—more than all his astuteness—was largely responsible for his success in his dealings with suppliers, employees, and customers. "It was a pleasure to do business with Norm Brinker, as well as mutually profitable," observed one supplier from those days who has remained faithful to Brinker and continued the relationship as a major supplier through the growth years. When it came time for Brinker to sign his first $1 million contract with a supplier. Brinker's signature wasn't needed. "His word was plenty good enough," said the supplier, "and it has always been for multimillion dollar deals."

His modesty also helped. Instead of taking credit himself, he would praise his executives, employees, and suppliers. At Christmas parties he would give leading suppliers engraved plaques expressing his appreciation of their efforts. At stockholder meetings he would publicly praise his top executives for the success that Steak&Ale was enjoying. He demanded the best from himself and everyone who worked for him, but when a job was well done he lavished praise on the individual both publicly and privately. He knew how to motivate people.

CRITICAL DECISIONS

In any chief executive's career, there are a handful of critical decisions he must tackle. These decisions—usually no more than one every two years—set the entire direction of the company. Once a strategy and course of action are decided upon, it is hard to reverse the direction. A company's entire future literally can ride on a decision which only the chief executive officer must make, regardless of all the recommendations of committees and advisers. Brinker thrived on these critical decisions and had a decided knack of making the right ones.

The first major decision occurred in the late 1960s when it was fashionable in the dinner-house business to open a restaurant in one city and then another city without any scientific way of connecting the two. Brinker had the foresight to commit Steak&Ale to a new strategy of clustering units in major markets. Rather than opening restaurants in a haphazard manner whenever the site and the urge came, he decided to develop one market first as much as feasible before moving on to another one. His thinking was that newspaper advertising and future TV advertising would progress with far more impact and lower per unit costs by clustering.

This strategy seems obvious in retrospect. Yet other dinner-house chains kept opening separate units without common identities. They wanted to establish the individual identity of each one and avoid the stigma of being regarded by customers as a chain. Brinker's courage in bucking the trend paid off with the huge growth of television advertising. He was able to capitalize to the fullest on a metropolitan area and new regional TV advertising packages. The marketing strategy was well ahead of other chains which were caught short and years later had to start pouring in more units to their existing markets to gain headway through clustering.

In the second critical decision—the type of beef used—Brinker again proved farsighted. He committed the chain in 1973 to utilize only fresh beef and to stay away from frozen beef. His strategy was to strive for quality and expect the customer to be willing to pay for it. Brinker entered the cattle futures market as purchasing director Marvin Braddock established a program which later enabled Steak&Ale to forestall heavy beef price rises and maintain profit margins at a time when others were stumbling on this problem.

The third critical decision involved not doing something which may have appeared attractive at the time. Brinker was pressed on all sides to devise a central production commissary and distribution system. He saw the inherent problem of putting money into the supplier-distribution business and insisted on putting the money into restaurants. This gave him the flexibility and distribution advantage of being able to purchase and distribute from regional and local sources closer to the market. General standards were set from central headquarters.

A fourth critical decision point was reached in the early 1970s as the chain grew to twelve units doing $10 million total sales. Average per unit sales had been raised to almost $1 million, and a growth pattern was established. Yet more capital was required to promote a faster growth pace if Brinker wanted to step up expansion. He could use just so much of his own and of the company's capital. Many friends cautioned him against going public. As a private company he had many advantages, they noted, and going public could increase scrutiny and a need to report all figures publicly. But Brinker didn't see any problem. The company had always been operated as if it were public. He made the decision as much by instinct as anything else. "Let's go public now while things are going well for us," said Brinker, who always felt timing was crucial to the success of any endeavor. "Do it now and don't procrastinate," was his philosophy.

PRICING DILEMMA

Of all the major decisions, one that stands out was not made at a conscious level at any particular point. Brinker inherently knew that consumer resistance would surface in direct proportion to rapid price rises. He kept the increases to a minimum whenever possible and managed to maintain an average per person ticket no higher than $12, including drinks, as late as 1980. This was a time when some of his competitors had raised their average ticket over $15 with resulting substantial losses in customer counts. Although Steak&Ale did suffer slight dropoffs in customer counts during a difficult economic period, the reductions weren't as drastic as those of some other limited menu dinner-house chains which had opted for higher ticket averages. In 1981 Steak&Ale showed substantial customer count and real sales gains. Cost-cutting measures were enacted to avoid menu price rises. Field supervision controls were cut back with one supervisor now delegated responsibility over eight stores instead of four. (This might keep the return on investment over the 20 percent goal, but it left observers wondering whether it was too much of a cutback in supervision and perhaps a rare strategic error for Brinker.)

As profit margins were squeezed by higher beef costs, Brinker vowed that higher prices could not be passed along to the consumer. He reduced headquarters and field expenses by tightening up wherever feasible. He also decided to brighten the old English inn decor in line with new customer desires. Some considered the older restaurants too bleak, and something had to be done if customer counts were to be raised.

MENU EXPANSION

Another key to his success was that he remained true to the origins of the chain. He built off the original base, making adjustments but never anything that was drastic. For example, the menu gradually grew from five to some twenty entree items between 1966 and 1980. Yet this was achieved without diluting the limited menu concept or losing the relative simplicity and low production costs of the operation. Groups of related items enabled Steak&Ale to keep adding to the menu while utilizing existing equipment for multipurposes.

By 1980 Steak&Ale's menu had proliferated to include four cuts of steak; three cuts of prime rib; one- and two-tail lobster dinners; combinations of lobster and steak, or steak and crab, and steak with baked potato; and a five-crab-leg feast. Beyond these main choices were a "poacher's platter" of marinated chickens or chicken and steak; desserts of carrot cake, cheesecake, and pie, tumbleweed (ice cream with liqueur) and plain ice cream, and coffee and tea. Side orders of mushrooms and corn on the cob were also being offered. This was a far cry from the first Steak&Ale menu of 1966. But the expansion of items over the years was a necessity in view of consumer desires for more diversity. Brinker managed the transition by just adding an item or two each year and emphasizing promotionally priced specials.

STAFF BUILDUP

Brinker had a fine-tuned ability to concentrate closely on each of a myriad of tasks. But he realized he could not do it all himself and knew how to delegate authority. From a basically two-man operation of himself and Deem, Steak&Ale blossomed into a well-oiled organization. Lutkus had joined in 1968 as design and special projects director. Then came John Titus, a real estate expert, who came aboard in 1970. He started as real estate and construction director and later became corporate development vice president. Next were Alan May, named executive vice president in early 1970; Carl Hays as vice president in 1971; and Braddock, another Jack-in-the-Box alumnus, as purchasing director in 1972.

When Brinker wanted a particular level of expertise he tried to find the best he could anywhere in a particular category. Lou Neeb was assistant to the Wage and Price Commission chief in Washington in the early 1970s. He had a promising career there and might have risen through the governmental hierarchy. However, Brinker pursued him and hired him as operations vice president in 1973. Neeb eventually took over as president and chief operating officer for day-to-day matters with Brinker becoming chairman and remaining chief executive officer and the policy maker. Brinker's plan from the first was to move Neeb toward president at a steady pace. Until then Brinker had been chairman and president.

Marketing received more emphasis in Steak&Ale's plans as the chain kept expanding. Ron McDougall, a marketing executive with Procter & Gamble and then Pillsbury, was named Steak&Ale marketing director in 1974. To reinforce financial strength—with Alan May taking more responsibilities as executive vice president—Brinker named Cece Smith financial director in 1975. She had just been selected as one of the ten top professional women in business. Brinker

Dave Thomas, center, celebrates the opening of a Long Island Wendy's.

Dave Thomas loves to pitch in whenever he gets the chance.

Dave Thomas expounds on his favorite subject—Wendy's.

Don Smith tries to devise a better pizza topping.

Whether it's burgers, tacos, or pizza, Don Smith searches endlessly for the best way to prepare them.

Joe Lee.

The Lee family dining at Casa Gallardo: wife, Dale; daughter, Keena, and son, Mike.

Mr. Lee with a Red Lobster manager discussing business.

Joe Lee receiving a citation from the Honduran government.

John W. Teets, chief executive officer of The Greyhound Corp.

John Teets participating in the Annual Phoenix Corporate Challenge 10K race sponsored by The Greyhound Corporation.

The executive committee of Saga Corporation. From left (seated) vice president and chief marketing and administrative officer John G. Hollingsworth; president and chief executive officer Charles A. Lynch; vice president and controller Jeffrey O. Henley; vice president and treasurer David B. Shipley; from left (standing) executive vice president and chief operating officer James W. Morrell, vice president of human resources Earl C. Royse.

Mr. Teets at a taste-testing evaluation.

Charles Lynch's ferocious backhand is as formidable as his totally organized approach to business.

Lynch at a stockholders' meeting.

Charles A. Lynch.

Stuart Anderson,
promoter extraordinaire.

Stuart Anderson, the cowboy-restaurateur, is equally at home on the range or in the restaurant.

Stuart Anderson relaxes on his ranch.

Norman Brinker at one of his Bennigan's restaurants.

Norman Brinker . . .

and a Steak & Ale restaurant.

Alex Schoenbaum, right, proudly displays his 1981 National Institute for the Foodservice Industry award presented by former Illinois governor William Stratton, NIFI president.

Alex Schoenbaum.

Mr. Schoenbaum enjoys a toast with Betty, his wife, at a surpirse birthday party.

Warner LeRoy's flamboyant costume at Tavern on the Green, New York.

LeRoy at home on his Long Island estate.

LeRoy at Maxwell's Plum,
San Francisco.

Mr. Morton in the garden
area of Arnie's.

Arnold Morton at Arnie's restaurant.

Lavish decor.

Mr. Baum tasting with Jacques Pepin.

Joe Baum

Mr. Baum with the original working model of The Big Kitchen, Market Bar, and Dining Rooms.

George Lang.

George Lang with Craig Claiborne.

George Lang at The Market in Citicorp Center.

Lang with one of his cats, Escoffier.

went the Washington route again in 1976 to put a polished touch on his team when recruiting, motivating, and training had become a paramount need. Rick Berman, a labor expert at the U.S. Chamber of Commerce, became human resources director.

PILLSBURY ENTERS

In 1976 Steak&Ale numbered 100 units doing over $100 million. It was an attractive acquisition candidate. The real question was not whether but rather from whom, when, and how much an offer might be forthcoming and whether Brinker could accept a deal that might reduce the authority and autonomy that were so dear to him. As it turned out, the offer came in the fall of 1976 from the Minneapolis-based Pillsbury Company, which already owned Burger King, had developed a Poppin' Fresh Pies chain, and was a powerful supplier of products primarily for supermarkets. Pillsbury bid just over $100 million—a price that some of Brinker's advisers thought rather low. "Hold out for more either from Pillsbury or from someone else," they urged.

"No," Brinker persisted, "this is the right company and the right price for us. It's the right time and the right match. We shall proceed with the deal." He has never regretted this decision. Not only did he emerge as Pillsbury's largest stockholder, but Pillsbury kept its word and gave Steak&Ale almost complete autonomy as long as it produced the desired bottom line results.

The strength of Brinker's character was illustrated one day in the early fall of 1976 when he pondered a dilemma: he was the scheduled keynote speaker at a major industry conference of 600 leading executives. If he went through with his commitment—just as the Pillsbury negotiations were at their most delicate stage—the entire deal conceivably could be snafued. Inevitably someone in the audience would ask the logical question: are you planning to be acquired and are any deals pending? How could he answer that truthfully without giving away the secret deal? He didn't ponder the dilemma too long. Any commitment was sacred, and he would go through with it. He managed to sweat out a twenty-five-minute talk on an inside view of Steak&Ale with an outwardly calm appearance. He breathed a huge sigh of relief when somehow no questions arose about any acquisition.

The only defection from his executive ranks occurred shortly after Pillsbury completed the acquisition. May left to go into his own business. May, who was executive vice president, sensed he would not be named president and that his role of dealing with the financial community would be substantially reduced now that Pillsbury was in the picture. But the rest of the team stayed and continued to grow almost exactly as they had prior to the acquisition. As Neeb, who moved into his predesignated slot as president in 1977, sees it, "Norm Brinker is goal-oriented every step of the way. He's willing to experiment, but he knows precisely where he and his company are going at each juncture."

Although a well-honed team at the top management level is essential, the war is most frequently won or lost in the trenches on the front lines at unit level. Field supervisors and restaurant managers foster winning esprit de corps at the direct sales level where it counts most or they can set back an operation drastically. In Steak&Ale's case, middle management field staff turnover continued at a moderate rate through 1976, but since then Brinker and other executives apparently were able to transfer more stability down to the field and restaurant levels and such turnover was curbed.

ALTERNATE CONCEPTS

Never one to rest on laurels, Brinker began developing a string of new concept restaurants in the late 1970s. The strategy was that to gain a maximum share of market in any given area, a mix of different concepts was highly desirable. Different names, contrasting styles, and varied price ranges could attract different customers. It would not be practical to have two Steak&Ales within a mile of each other, but it would be feasible to package two or three different-type restaurants nearby. That way the company could attract a typical customer perhaps three times a week instead of once. If that customer didn't spend his money at one of the Steak&Ale restaurants, he'd spend it somewhere else.

Furthermore, Brinker anticipated the continually developing, more casual lifestyle and felt that some of the operations should be geared to extreme informality. Thus were born Bennigan's, Orville Bean's Flying Machine restaurants, and a pilot Juan 'n Only Mexican restaurant. These were the "casual" entries in the growing arsenal. Just to be sure, the company also went in the other direction, launching a Rafter's restaurant a notch above Steak&Ale in menu and decor, with a $15 average ticket. Brinker is convinced that "we must constantly vary our restaurants to meet changing lifestyles and fluctuating consumer preferences now and in the future."

Of all the new concepts, Bennigan's seemed the one most likely to break out as another full-scale chain. It had the advantage of a lower investment cost and lower menu prices but higher customer counts yielding almost the same return as Steak&Ale. Bennigan's, considerably larger at 260 seats than Steak&Ale, was yielding an average ticket of $7.50 on a more diverse menu of forty items. Its menu features a bevy of items: a 10-ounce New York strip steak, a Bennigan's "Super Chopper" hamburger steak topped with sautéed onions and mushrooms, "smothered steak" (sirloin with provolone cheese), and fried shrimp, or a steak and shrimp combination. Finger snacks are emphasized with fried vegetables, side orders of corn on the cob, potatoes, mushrooms, and onion soup; a choice of five salads; varieties of nachos, quiches, and soups, and sandwiches including Reuben, chicken, and burgers. A number of desserts also are featured.

To Brinker, Bennigan's is another approach to the same objective. "There is no one absolute way to do it," he says. "I like to try different methods. Today's customer wants a really personal experience whether it's fast food, a train station, a salad bar, or live entertainment."

VARIED DIRECTIONS

Steak&Ale assumed control of Pillsbury's highly profitable forty-five-unit Le Chateau steakhouse chain in the Southeast in 1980. Since the format was somewhat the same, there would be some consolidation. Meanwhile, Steak&Ale's own expansion was curbed while Le Chateau was integrated into the system. But total capital expenditures were expected to remain at $50 million to $60 million annually, and an aggressive remodeling program was slated to continue on many of the older Steak&Ale restaurants. Anywhere from twenty-five to thirty new restaurants were slated to open in all divisions, depending on the economy and the availability of sites. The company's some 300 restaurants in 1981 were yielding an average of $1.1 million annual sales, with Bennigan's somewhat higher. Together they were pulling in a pre-tax profit of well over $25 million for the company and for parent Pillsbury.

Brinker always opted for company-owned units with complete control in the company's hands. But in 1980 and 1981 he was planning possible franchise units in a few selected markets. He felt there were situations in medium and small markets where Steak&Ale wouldn't have full company supervision and that "perhaps in those instances a local franchisee would know the market better." As for franchisees helping with financing in difficult times, Brinker feels that Pillsbury and Steak&Ale have more than enough capital.

Brinker is a straight shooter who really hates "gimmicks" although he has allowed his people to try them, based on purported consumer desires. He much prefers to present customers with a clear picture of what they are buying without frills. Thus it was with considerable trepidation that he allowed live entertainment in Steak&Ale. When it didn't attract more customers to the restaurants, he breathed a sigh of relief. Entertainment actually blurred the chain's image between a dinner house known for quality and a place for entertainment. Customers wanted to know exactly what they were getting for their money.

COMMUNITY SERVICE

Active involvement in the local community is an absolute for Brinker and for the restaurant managers. Even more significantly, he has not shied away from standing up for the food service industry against government regulation attempts. He, Neeb, and Berman put together possibly the strongest Political Action Committee in the industry. "We must be active in politics and government affairs," Brinker says. "Otherwise, we will simply lose to a government insensitive to the free enterprise system."

Brinker remains active in numerous community, civic, and charitable programs. He devotes considerable time and effort as a trustee of the Maureen Connolly Brinker Tennis Foundation, which sponsors tennis clinics for youngsters throughout the country. He still enjoys playing polo and has been chairman of the U.S. Polo Association for several years.

He has consistently been able to meet personal and business adversity or success with calmness and courage. He keeps his emotions inward but expresses himself clearly on how he really feels about a situation. As an individual he projects warmth and charisma. "When Norm inspires a group of people and then leaves the room," says one of his regional directors, "everyone just wants to follow him." Brinker gets the job done without being ostentatious. He is modest and works well with peers and subordinates alike. But he also knows how to be a hard-nosed businessman when the situation requires it.

An example of how astutely Brinker handles his executives occurred in 1980 when Pillsbury was looking for a new chief executive for its Burger King chain after Donald Smith had left to become president of PepsiCo's new food service chain division. Brinker recommended Neeb as a possibility for the post even though he knew what a fine job Neeb was doing as Pillsbury's Steak&Ale president and chief operating officer. It was Neeb's chance to become a chief executive, and Brinker did not want to block him. Neeb finally decided to take the position as Burger King chairman and chief executive officer. Brinker then surprised observers by naming Hal Smith, thirty-four, a Steak&Ale regional vice president based in Washington, D.C., as president to succeed Neeb. While some top executives at the chain's Dallas headquarters wondered why this was done, it seems clear that with the expansion and necessary decentralization, regional vice presidents had assumed presidential-type powers over their entire areas. Thus it could be said they were in training for a chain presidency—a type of transition that has occurred at a number of large chains.

With Neeb's departure for Burger King and Hal Smith's becoming Steak&Ale president, executive changes inevitably occurred. One of the key moves saw Michael Woodhouse, a Pillsbury executive for twelve years, move to Steak&Ale as financial vice president. He succeeded Cece Smith, who left to join an industrial concern. Changes in regional management also were carried out by Hal Smith under Brinker's direction.

Brinker is well-set financially and careerwise as the largest individual stockholder in Pillsbury. He serves on the boards of Pillsbury and of its Steak&Ale, Burger King and Poppin' Fresh Pies subsidiaries, as well as of the First National Bank in Dallas. He also is a Pillsbury corporate executive vice president. His influence is great with all of Pillsbury's restaurant operations.

His trademark has been progress without radical change. He has kept Steak&Ale on course by remaining true to the original principles and making gradual modifications in presentation, pricing, and perceived value. He is always eyeing the next challenge and trying to stay one step ahead of rapidly changing consumer trends. Whatever he plans for the future, it promises to be something innovative that will unveil a new market niche and make others wonder why they didn't think of this idea first.

8

Alex Schoenbaum

THE WILL TO WIN

The solidly built man with the determined look visited one restaurant after another that month and created a stir wherever he went. He was fifty-nine and had merged his Shoney's drive-ins and restaurants into a corporation. He had turned over a good deal of the leadership and responsibility to younger men. But he was far from ready to retire.

When the company designated a "Founders' Month" in 1974, Alex Schoenbaum promptly embarked on a travel odyssey that took him to every Shoney's restaurant—well over a hundred of them. It would have been an exhausting schedule for a younger man, but for Schoenbaum this nonstop tour was a highly enjoyable experience. He personally shook the hands of almost every employee in these restaurants, thanking each of them for keeping the momentum going. He regretted that with the growth of the company it was no longer possible to be on a first-name basis with everyone. But he still retained his entrepreneurial drive, radiated a personal warmth, and inspired everyone he saw. He was proud of what he and Shoney's had accomplished.

Schoenbaum's extraordinary willpower and accomplishments prompted one associate to say, "Hell, Alex wasn't born. He's a legend.

They made him up." He is one of these rare individuals who seem to have been born a winner, successful in every undertaking. He was an All-American football player, forsaking a professional gridiron career for business. Today he is known for his food service achievements but is equally acclaimed for his philanthropy and service.

SMALL START

It was Schoenbaum who opened a small cinder block building in Charleston, West Virginia, in 1947, outfitted it with 50 drive-in stalls and watched it grow. Today he is senior chairman of Shoney's, Inc., a multi-faceted food service company featuring Big Boy coffee shops and Captain D's fish and chip units. That one tiny cinder block building has grown beyond belief. Along the way Schoenbaum has helped more people start their food service careers with his plentiful advice and franchises than anyone could imagine.

He takes great pride in Shoney's as a leading coffee shop chain, and he takes equal pride in what he has done for the community. "Always give back to the community something of what it has given you," is his favorite axiom. He is widely known as a generous man, endowing hospitals and colleges and even underwriting educational and youth programs for his native West Virginia. He also is a strong supporter of his Jewish faith and has contributed and raised many millions. "Without Shoney's I couldn't have done any of these things," he says, "and without my basic philosophy Shoney's may not have become what it is today."

Shoney's in 1981 was far more than drive-ins and more than coffee shops. Captain D's, with accelerating growth as one of the leading fish and chips chains, has plans to widen its thrust from the South to a national scope. Also under the Shoney's banner are full-service specialty restaurants such as the Fifth Quarter, Sailmakers, and Town and Country. But the anchor remains Shoney's itself—Shoney's Big Boy, a dominant force in the Southeast and expanding into Missouri and Arkansas. (In late 1981 Shoney's agreed to acquire the Famous Recipe chicken chain and to sell its own 22 Kentucky Fried Chicken units.)

One of Schoenbaum's earliest ads proclaimed, "Dine for one dollar in a five-dollar atmosphere." He has maintained the same principles for Shoney's although the numbers are far larger. Shoney's stuck with its value package concept and in 1981 still had an average per person ticket of about $2.25—a notch under the competition.

FIRM CHARACTER

Let's take a closer look at this man—this solidly built, rugged, imaginative, paradoxical man. He is an extremely generous, devoted family man and yet possessed of drive, determination, and willfulness to get the job done. He is a fighter, a no-holds-barred type of guy; he has a street fighter image and yet is thoughtful and considerate.

His father, Emil "Pop" Schoenbaum, was the greatest influence on his career. At the age of fourteen Emil packed all his belongings into a solitary knapsack and emigrated from Russia to New York to study music in the hope of becoming a concert violinist. Instead, he was alternately a trolley motorman, banana salesman, musician in a pit orchestra providing audio dramatics for silent movies, and for eleven years ran a billiards and supply parlor in Petersburg, Virginia. Emil married Goldie Masinter, and the couple had four sons. Alex was born August 8, 1915, as the third child. He felt challenged to compete at everything with his brothers and his friends even as a youngster.

Young Alex was athletically inclined from the first. He would often stay out in the evening playing baseball, football, basketball, or track, whatever the season happened to be. He got lickings from his father for staying out past suppertime. Later Alex remembered with fondness his father's iron discipline and other attributes. He created an award in 1964 to go to a Shoney's franchisee "most exemplifying the philosophy of 'Pop,' who spent a great deal of his time helping the underprivileged and making people's lives better or more comfortable." Pop was a compassionate man who cared, and Alex learned from him and also from his mother Goldie's examples of charity.

FOOTBALL STAR

It was as a football player that Alex, always big for his age, made his mark early. He learned to take his hard knocks from tough sandlot play in a rugged neighborhood and played on the Cammack Junior High

School team. He was so good at the game he loved as a ninth-grader that he worked out with the high school team. To the dismay of his junior high coach, he made the high school varsity. But he had to cut his last-period class to ride the bus to high school practice, and the junior high failed him for cutting a class, making him ineligible for high school competition. He returned to junior high, his grades improved, and he became Cammack's star performer.

At Huntington High School he quickly established his football prowess and was named to the West Virginia all-state team as a tackle. But Schoenbaum was dissatisfied. He knew there was more to life than football and felt he was falling behind in the learning process. A young friend, Lucian Smith, had watched him grow up and knew that as football players go, Schoenbaum was someone special. Smith began to sing the praises of a Pennsylvania prep school he was attending. "The University of Pittsburgh will pay your way to go to Kiski," Smith told Schoenbaum. "You'll get a scholarship, board, and tuition, and you'll be playing with guys who can really play this game." One visit to Kiski and Schoenbaum was sold.

The first day he walked onto the practice field in his senior year at Kiski, he counted seven big tackles. At 215 pounds he was the smallest of the bunch. But he quickly earned a first-string berth and received invaluable experience playing against top college freshmen teams rather than prep schools.

At the same time Schoenbaum became chief of the working boys at Kiski and began his restaurant experience by personally serving the dean's table. He really began to appreciate the importance of positioning oneself in the market, of having the right product at the right time. Alert to opportunities, he realized growing boys had enormous appetites and would buy additional food if it were available. As hall proctor, he had a free rein to leave the school while other students were confined. Each evening he would go to the grocery store to buy loaves of bread and sandwich ingredients. He later would assemble the sandwiches and sell them throughout the dormitories, earning extra spending money.

Although Schoenbaum was ticketed to play football for the University of Pittsburgh, he decided upon Ohio State instead—probably because it was closer to his Huntington, West Virginia, home. He alternated between right and left tackle for the Buckeyes, playing sixty minutes a game for coach Francis Schmidt so well that he was named to Grantland Rice's All-American team three consecutive years. He was once even named the nation's "player of the week," an honor usually reserved for running backs.

Just as important as his playing prowess were the inspiration and lift he gave the team through his winning attitude. One day shortly before a particularly big game, he was nowhere to be seen in the dressing room. His Ohio State teammates were poised to race out onto their home turf and rip apart the opposing team as they often did. Suddenly Coach Schmidt, who was Ohio State coach before the legendary Woody Hayes, interrupted, "Hold everything. We can't go out on that field without Schoenbaum. Where the hell is he?"

Schoenbaum, very much in control of events, was outside the stadium selling tickets for the big game until the very last minute. The timing was almost perfect that day for the enterprising young man—as it would be throughout his career. He raced into the dressing room just in time to lead his teammates onto the field and to another victory.

He was a "jock" on the campus, radiating power and authority wherever he went, whatever he did. But he kept his feet on the ground and felt football was a game—an important game but not his final objective by any means. Nothing could stop him from attaining his goals and reaching for the next ones.

In the late 1930s football was played in the trenches, and linemen earned their reputation the hard way. "That kind of competition helped me become mentally and physically tough," says Schoenbaum. "It certainly helped in my approach to the business world." He was well-known in Columbus in those days—a more familiar figure than all the backs on the team. When he would visit Columbus in later years, many people greeted him as the former football hero even though he had achieved fame in the business world.

CAMPUS LIFE

But Schoenbaum's very first day at Ohio State in 1935 was probably the most important one. He went to a dormitory to pick up his date for a welcoming dance and there by chance encountered a girl named Betty Frank. In typical Schoenbaum fashion he said to her, "You're the most beautiful girl I've ever seen. Are you Jewish?" She was, and she was the answer to his prayers, but laughingly says that dating Schoenbaum was difficult. "We went to dances all right," she recalled, "but we didn't dance. We were too busy selling drinks and food." Schoenbaum quickly learned on the Ohio State campus that food-related efforts were profitable. He had no qualms about forsaking personal pleasures to handle the concessions at school dances and other activities. While his classmates were doing the Charleston and the Swing, Schoenbaum and his wife-to-be (he married her after graduation in 1939) were pumping soft drinks and snacks.

The ambitious young man developed a calendar filled with advertising and sold the franchise rights to another student. Schoenbaum also worked at the Lazarus department store in downtown Columbus as a salesman. He studied customer traffic flow carefully and made this the subject of an extensive research paper. (Later he would fall back on this scholastic experience to study and chart customer traffic flows in fast-food restaurants.)

He applied himself to his studies at Ohio State and decided, despite his gridiron success, that his future would be in business rather than football. Professional football salaries were low in those days, and he had made some strong contacts in the business world. He played in the 1939 college all-star game in Chicago against the New York Giants and in other all-star games against professional teams. Among the players on the college all-stars that year were All-American Marshall (Biggie) Goldberg and Sid Luckman, who later starred as a quarterback with the Chicago Bears. Schoenbaum was drafted by the old Brooklyn Dodgers pro football team but turned down a contract offer. With a wife to support, he wanted to get serious about business.

(He would return to football in the mid-1960s as owner of the champion Charleston Rockets of the ill-fated Continental Football League. He also was board chairman of the league's executive committee and was largely responsible for the CFL holding on for even a few years.)

Schoenbaum had his heart set on a business deal in Columbus after graduation. He saw marvelous potential in a large ice-skating rink. His plan was to rent it to Ohio State University for ice hockey games and ice skating classes, and open it to the public too. He took his ideas to invest in this venture to John Galbreath, a leading local businessman who later became owner of the Pittsburgh Pirates baseball team. He also told Galbreath of unlimited opportunities in drive-in fast food, a relatively new concept. Drive-ins, as Schoenbaum saw them, had a built-in advantage of low labor costs. Carhops were being paid only $1 daily because tips supplied most of their income.

Galbreath was impressed with young Schoenbaum and with both these business concepts. Schoenbaum had an option on a drive-in at Olentangy Boulevard in Columbus. The interest was there, but so was some concern. Hitler had invaded the lowlands, and World War II was around the corner. It did not seem to be an auspicious time to open any new business.

CAREER VENTURES

So in the summer of 1939 Alex Schoenbaum went to work as a salesman with the same enthusiasm he would have put into his favorite drive-in or ice-skating rink. He merchandised hair tonics which cost 8¢ each to manufacture and sold them to barber shops for 67¢ each. Thanks to his sales efforts, this product went on thousands of shelves, and he urged the supplier to advertise to consumers. "I wanted him to take half his profits and plow them back in," Schoenbaum recalls. "We had a good product for the general public. Now we needed acceptance." But all his powers of persuasion couldn't convince the supplier. Reluctantly he turned his back on the customers he had sold in Kentucky, Ohio, Pennsylvania, and West Virginia and looked for other means of support.

The next spot for Schoenbaum was as a salesman for a Pontiac agency in Columbus. Here he showed his usual talent for sales and promotion. He was drawing $100 a month and living in a $40-a-month apartment with his wife, but he somehow managed to make a $75 contribution to charity.

Car sales weren't particularly fantastic in those days, and with his boss's encouragement to get out of the auto field, Schoenbaum gravitated to the insurance business, starting as a salesman with Pacific Mutual Life. "I think I could have been as financially successful with insurance as I have been with the restaurant business," he says. "I liked it and really feel I had a knack for helping people with their problems and making them see the value of life insurance. I really didn't want to get out of the insurance business, but it somehow just happened."

BOWLING ALLEYS

Schoenbaum's older brother, Raymond, had been slated to return from World War II and work with his dad operating the family businesses, billiards and bowling. But Raymond was killed in action in 1945 and, as oldest surviving son, it was up to Schoenbaum to assume those responsibilities. He felt an obligation to his father and started by running the small bowling alleys at the Ritter Arcade in Huntington while "Pop" continued to run the large Boulevard Recreation Center in Charleston, West Virginia. Having suffered a heart attack, "Pop" had been limited in his activity. One day he called and said, "We're going to change jobs. I'm going back to Huntington. You're coming up here and run this tiger. I can't handle it."

"When?"

"Today. Right now."

So off Schoenbaum went to the big Charleston bowling alleys. His main experience for the new post consisted of his father's handing him the keys and saying, "Go to it." Initially there were backbreaking hours of setting ten-pins, and it began to look as if the bowling business might end up as Schoenbaum's career. Automation had not yet come to bowling, and when any of the help didn't show up for work, he personally would become the pin boy. He once set the pins for 240 games in a single day!

Schoenbaum practically lived in the bowling alleys, working sixteen to eighteen hours a day, but he showed keen business acumen as well as incredible endurance. He professionalized and automated the bowling business. His advice was sought throughout the bowling industry, but the dream of a drive-in restaurant such as the one he had envisioned in Columbus was never far from his mind.

As it was, the bowling alleys had their own in-house snack bars, and these gave Schoenbaum some exposure to the food business. But it wasn't enough to satisfy him. Intuitively he knew the postwar years would see a nation on wheels with people moving, and he wanted a restaurant accessible to this new mobility. He was open-minded and willing to learn from others, yet unswerving once convinced his decision was right. He outlined his plan for a drive-in to an architect friend and came away with a cardboard model, complete with pieces of movable equipment.

Late at night, when the bowling business slowed somewhat, Schoenbaum and "Pop" would visit other Charleston restaurants. Sometimes they would discuss Schoenbaum's dreams and listen to other operators discuss equipment and its proper location for the best possible flow of food to the customer. One friend remembers such an occasion vividly. "Alex and Pop would come in for a late dinner and stop to talk," he recalls. "One night Alex came in with a big box under his arm. He opened it up and showed a big model with moving parts. 'What's that?' I asked him. 'It's a drive-in restaurant,' Alex responded. 'I want to show it to you.'" The friend was impressed with Schoenbaum's determination but couldn't muster much enthusiasm for a drive-in, explaining, "It was honky-tonk to our way of thinking in those days."

DRIVE-IN LAUNCHED

A big break occurred for Schoenbaum when a major oil company came to Charleston and wanted to lease property adjacent to the bowling alleys for $300 a month. Since his associates were so anxious to accept this offer for their land, he topped the oil company and agreed to pay $400 a month for the land. He eagerly had a twenty-square-foot building constructed and called it the Parkette (Park and Eat) drive-in. The building had no inside service—just an outside area and carhops. The only employee was a kitchen manager who managed the entire unit.

Schoenbaum excitedly called his friend who had seen the model.

"We're going to open that drive-in today," Schoenbaum told him. "Why don't you come down and take a look at it?" His friend did just that and later remarked, "I had agreed with Alex it was a good location, but couldn't believe what I was seeing. There were people everywhere. You would think it was a brand-new invention, that people were getting something for nothing. They were really busy. But that building didn't look a bit like the model Alex had shown me. He had built a square cinder block building. It couldn't have been more than eighteen or twenty square feet. The model he showed me had been round and much bigger."

A round building actually would arise two years later, but for now Schoenbaum was on his way. He had spent only $10,000 for the building and equipment and had guessed perceptively about the new postwar automobile trend. The Parkette quickly became so popular that he hired twelve carhops to service the fifty-four car stalls. He also hired three employees just to hand-dip milk shakes made from ice milk. Hand-dipped milk shakes and hamburgers each sold for 15¢. He also offered low-priced cheeseburgers and chicken. Within a year he added shrimp, oysters, and barbecued ribs. "It got so we were selling more oysters than the railway express guys," he recalls.

Annual sales for the drive-in soared to almost $400,000 in 1948, making it one of the country's highest volume drive-in restaurants. (This was before the days of McDonald's.) Schoenbaum's biggest problem was not a lack of business, but control of the huge crowds which thronged his drive-in. "There were a lot of young bucks champing at the bit," he recalls. "We had to have discipline, but we still let these people know we loved them and wanted them. We were constantly forced to run people out from under the canopy. It took four of us just to police the lot and direct traffic. We had to see a turnover in the drive-in stalls to manage our business properly."

One of Schoenbaum's great strengths has been his ability to develop people. The four men policing that first drive-in were to become very successful in their own right. Schoenbaum, with his physical bulk a deterrent to would-be troublemakers, was everywhere, flanked by his four lieutenants: Ray Staab, a rough and ready ex-Florida State football star who would become head of his own Shoney's division in Knoxville; Bob Phillips, later a successful restaurant entrepreneur in Charleston, West Virginia; Jim Prentiss, future chairman of Shoney's South, Inc., and the late Bill Arbogast, who built a successful food service career.

With business booming, Schoenbaum began to search for a second location that he figured could do $1 million sales. After all, when he and his father, brothers, and ten carhops would take orders, the rapid volume increases achieved with just a little suggestive salesmanship were amazing.

REMODELING SHORTCUT

It didn't take long for the original unit to become obsolete, and Schoenbaum knew it should be remodeled to achieve higher potential sales. He found a quick solution when the employees went on strike. He didn't bother negotiating with them, but simply snapped pictures of every aspect of the drive-in, tore it down, showed the pictures to a contractor and asked how it could be improved. An architect mulled possible plans for a modernized building. But by the time he had drafted real plans, Schoenbaum had already completed the new build-ing. It took just four months, as fast as possible with the construction methods then available. The glittering new unit had a voice box in front where cars pulled in, curb glass in front, and a marquee overhang. It was a round building, just as he had originally contemplated. When complete remodeling of this new drive-through and drive-in unit was completed, it also had eight counter stools for inside dining. Far more elaborate than its predecessor, the new Parkette had custom-made special equipment to dispense the food faster and cost $200,000, twenty times the amount spent on the original venture. Hot dogs were added to the menu, and sales climbed to $500,000.

"We had to build other restaurants in Charleston just to relieve the pressure from that unit," recalls Schoenbaum. "We opened in Kan-awha City near Charleston just a few months after remodeling the Parkette." Another prime reason for expansion was to enhance his bulk purchasing power. Always conscious of the need for a steady cash flow,

Schoenbaum established a system of paying purveyors on credit. They knew they could rely on the hardworking young man, and his credit line became as good as gold.

WHAT'S IN A NAME?

Still, there were problems. A major one was the name of his drive-in restaurant. Other park and eat places were springing up all over the country, some even bearing the name "Parkette" as restaurateurs discovered drive-ins were here to stay. Schoenbaum knew he had to find something unique. He needed a merchandising tool and started traveling all over the country looking at every type of restaurant operation for ideas, determined to capitalize on the rapid growth of the restaurant industry. "I had heard about the fabulous success of Frisch's in Cincinnati," Schoenbaum says. "Since I had met Dave Frisch when we served together on a restaurant panel for drive-in operators at the National Restaurant Show in Chicago, I decided to spend some time looking at his operation."

Each time Schoenbaum's travels took him to Cincinnati, he marveled at the constant crowds in Frisch's Big Boy, which was actually more of a coffee shop than a fast-food place. Frisch's was capitalizing fully on a relatively new medium called television. "The announcer was really good," recalls Schoenbaum, "and his secret was simple. He made the food look appealing. He just smiled at the camera, picked up a Big Boy and began eating it. The sandwich looked scrumptious on television, and people flocked to the restaurant."

Frisch got the idea for a double-deck burger from Bob Wian, an operator from Glendale, California. He had named it after an oversized young man who ate the sandwich in Wian's restaurant every day. This young man became a permanent symbol for the new Big Boy sandwich.

Schoenbaum already knew Wian. "Bob, Dave, and I would talk a lot whenever we met in Chicago for the restaurant show," says Schoenbaum. "One day I finally figured it was time to get us all together to talk about this Big Boy thing. Bob knew darn well that other people were using his sandwich, but there was nothing he could do about it outside the state of California."

BIG BOY PACT

The three met in Cincinnati to work out an agreement. This meeting went smoothly, and an agreement was quickly reached that set the future course for Big Boy restaurants, transforming them from local operations into a powerful national force which one day would lead the coffee shop/family restaurant segment with some 1,200 units doing over $1 billion annual sales. But the agreement itself was rather different from what Schoenbaum had visualized. He had seen his role as director of merchandising, sales, and franchising for the entire chain. Instead, territorial divisions were charted. Wian would take responsibility for developing all territory west of the Mississippi. Frisch got the rights for Ohio, Kentucky, Indiana, and Florida while Schoenbaum had to be content with just West Virginia.

It wasn't long before people became aware of the great success Schoenbaum was carving out in West Virginia and began approaching him for franchised territories. Wian still held the rights to other states in the East, so Schoenbaum asked him for more territory. "You've got it," was Wian's prompt response. Schoenbaum was able to extend his Big Boy borders to Virginia, Tennessee, North and South Carolina, Maryland, and Washington, D.C. Eventually he traded off Maryland and Washington for a number of Southern states such as Georgia, Louisiana, Alabama, and Mississippi. Still later, Shoney's would acquire Big Boy rights for Arkansas and Missouri.

Now Schoenbaum had captured the merchandising tool to expand under the Big Boy emblem and just needed a name other than Parkette. He launched a much-ballyhooed contest to find a new name, offering the winner a new Lincoln. The audacity of such an offer took the city of Charleston by storm. Nobody had ever given such a prize for a local promotion, and the response was staggering. "I didn't know anybody who had ever given away a Lincoln," Schoenbaum says, "and apparently most other people didn't either. The idea of giving such a prize to a person who could conceive a name for a restaurant really caught the imagination of everyone in our area. What surprised me is that so few people came up with the name we finally selected. My dad's nickname always had been Shoney, and yet only five entrants came up with a name anywhere near that. All five of these spelled it a different way. We must have had tens of thousands of entries, and we had lots of prizes. Not only the Lincoln, but fifty other real good prizes."

Thus Shoney's was born on the basis of "Pop's" nickname and the contest. Schoenbaum was a master promoter and didn't just want to change the Parkette name to Shoney's Big Boy. Instead, he enticed customers with a teaser advertising campaign. The initial ads asked, "What is it? Where is it? When is it?" Shortly afterwards, he introduced the Big Boy name to his two Charleston area restaurants and then in 1951 expanded the name to Shoney's Big Boy.

ADVERTISING PUSH

Those early Shoney's days were memorable ones. Schoenbaum was one of the first restaurateurs to utilize the magic of television as a major portion of his advertising budget. His radio spots, developed by Bob Boser and Shirley Annand of a Charleston radio station, were forerunners of the comedy team spots which later became so successful. Some examples: "Shoney jumped in the Rappahannock and raided all the oyster beds" . . . "Shoney got caught stealing chickens so he could run special prices" . . . "Where's Shoney? He's out on those shrimp boats."

Schoenbaum had to be an innovator and an advertising leader in the early 1950s. West Virginia was in the throes of a serious recession. Automation had hit the coal mines, and 400,000 miners were out of work. Every other industry in the state was affected, and disposable income was at a low ebb. Price-off specials may be common today, but then they were original and exciting. He created new plates—shrimp dinners, oyster dinners, chicken dinners. He priced these dinners at 79¢, and traffic boomed in the midst of that recession.

He built a radio booth on the lot of his original location, and the place was jumping. When the United Nations began meeting in New York, he outfitted his carhops in different motifs representing all the United Nations countries. For thirty-one straight weeks he unveiled new costumes!

Advertising and promotion played a major role in the development of Shoney's but it was actually overshadowed by the attention to detail, product, and service quality. Jim Prentiss, later to become president of Shoney's South, joined Shoney's as an executive and stayed close to Schoenbaum and his philosophy. The two agreed on a credo, "Give the most of the best for the least amount of money. Whenever your food cost is too good, too low, we always add more to the plate. We always have tried to use the best quality food. We give our customers quantity, quality and price, and we give them modern buildings, clean surroundings, fast service."

When the Parkette first became Shoney's Big Boy, most Big Boy units around the country were drive-ins or carry-out places (although Wian did have some coffee shops on the West Coast). Schoenbaum was thinking along the same lines. "The drive-ins had been trashy," he said with a touch of affection. "We began to change the image. We built good buildings, pretty buildings, and made it a practice to remodel them before they became shabby. There have been times, and I don't like to remember them, when I didn't want to spend the money and I became ashamed of the building. When you don't spend to upgrade your building, it is a horrible mistake."

There just weren't any 9-to-5 days on Schoenbaum's schedule. He gave everything he had to do the job and expected those around him to do likewise. He started building an organization with those who had drive, ambition, curiosity, and foresight. Prentiss was in the forefront on these qualities. "To be at the top of the ladder," said Schoenbaum, "you must set goals that are beyond everyone else's imagination. Work harder and longer than anybody else." He did, and so did Prentiss.

FRANCHISEE QUESTIONS

Schoenbaum believed future expansion would have to be tied to franchisees who could handle their local markets, providing control and financing. But Prentiss questioned the idea of franchising and felt it might be better to keep the controls and money at home base during any expansion program. At first all of Shoney's Big Boys were company operated. Following the original three units in the Charleston area, Schoenbaum and Prentiss spread out to the Huntington, Parkersburg, and Ashland markets. But the operation thinned out too much and was no longer successful. "That's when I learned that getting away from your home base was a hell of a hassle," concedes Schoenbaum. "We just extended ourselves beyond our capacities. We didn't have the people to run those stores. When I couldn't see these stores every day in person, there would be constant problems."

He learned a valuable lesson from the initial setbacks. "Radial expansion (in a circle) is fine," he said, "but vertical or horizontal line expansion is extremely difficult." He compared his initial franchising ventures with a spider who builds a web to catch flies and insects. "That's their measure of success. We went out and made that web bigger. We just got more spiders to do the work. Each one of them lived right in the middle of his own web and stayed home to see that everything was going right. When your personal interests are at stake, you're going to take better care of the web."

Schoenbaum and Prentiss stressed a lot of color in those first buildings and were proponents of natural woods, stone, and lots of glass. Their kitchens were open ones so the customers could see and share the excitement of the food being prepared. It all seemed to be cost efficient and customer pleasing. But an opening in downtown Huntington wasn't so auspicious. Schoenbaum delegated it to others and wasn't there. Cars were lined up all around the building, out onto the street, and backed up for blocks. Employees ran out in the streets and tried to serve the customers. But it was a disaster. "We blew it," acknowledges Schoenbaum. "After that, I knew I had to be there in person to control a major event like this."

MANY ENTREPRENEURS

In any case Prentiss finally agreed that franchising was a necessity and that while company-owned units sounded great, there were limitations on how far they could extend themselves. Each organization franchised by Schoenbaum became almost a story in its own right as the Shoney's web started to spread. One of his two younger brothers, Leon, was the first franchisee and still operates eleven units in Virginia. The biggest franchisee is none other than Prentiss, president of

Shoney's South, which operates over 180 restaurants altogether. Another franchisee, Ray Danner, was looking only for a single Shoney's unit but ended up so successful that his franchise merged with parent Shoney's and he became chief executive officer of the entire company.

Others also learned the business directly from a working association with Schoenbaum: Chubby Young and Jim Pepper in eastern Tennessee; Ray Staab in Knoxville; Tommy Woodrum in South Carolina; Paul Young in North Carolina; Paul Holdren in Charlottesville; Chuck Sweeney in Richmond.

Marvin Kamisarow still remembers the day he drove to Charleston, West Virginia, and was awarded the Atlanta franchise by Schoenbaum. By 1981 he owned fourteen units with others on tap in what could become Shoney's biggest franchise expansion area. Bob Sinclair was a leading radio advertising executive but has become even more successful building his own restaurant chain in middle Georgia, with ten Shoney's becoming the capstone of his nineteen-unit system.

KIND HEART

Schoenbaum always had a big heart and would bend if he had intuitive faith in a person. He would go to Wheeling to collect money owed for back payments by franchisee George Boury and end up lending the Boury brothers additional money for their immediate needs. As of 1980 the Boury brothers were operating more than forty Big Boy restaurants in a wide geographic area, and were the very best of friends. When Schoenbaum celebrated his sixty-fifth birthday in Charleston, George Boury got out of a sick bed to attend the gala. "I don't know anyone else who could have gotten me out of that bed and into an airplane," George Boury says. "I couldn't have done that for anybody except Alex. Anytime I asked for help, he was always there. He never said no."

Perhaps Schoenbaum's kindness went too far in a business sense. Yet he had an intuitive knack for judging who could be trusted and who couldn't, and his batting average was high.

He helped many leading food service operators get their start. One of the most notable is Lou Fisher, a football player and Ohio State graduate who once worked for Schoenbaum. In the late 1950s Fisher started Ameche's coffee shops in the Washington-Baltimore area. Later he became chairman and president of Gino's (fast-food and Rustler budget steakhouses). Fisher relied on Schoenbaum for advice although he didn't always accept it. Schoenbaum helped many others too. When he talked about "my boys in the food service industry," he literally referred to a long list of people he had helped get their start and had continued to give advice. He simply loved the food service business and the people in it.

Shoney's gradually grew into a major company. In some ways Schoenbaum liked it more in the early days in the 1950s when his Charleston headquarters consisted of one large desk that he and Prentiss shared in the back of a converted garage. Two other tiny offices had space for a receptionist and waiting area and a bookkeeper and secretary. A small door opened into another part of the garage which became the commissary. He had his own bakery, made his own soups, stocked merchandise, ran a truck. He even had an office back there for his commissary manager.

Things were going well for Schoenbaum in the late 1950s and early 1960s. He wasn't in a hurry to build more company stores. "It really was like two separate companies," he notes. "I owned the stores in West Virginia, and the franchise company was simply exploding." He made sure that franchisee decisions were made by committee, with his own vote counting no more than any other single vote. But he supplied the direction, and one of the franchisees says that "when he wanted to be mean, nobody challenged him."

He was like a mother hen to the fledgling franchise company. He delighted in calling a franchise unit when least expected. If the franchisee was not in the restaurant, Schoenbaum would track him down somehow—at home, on the golf course, anywhere. "Who's minding your store?" he would ask.

No matter what situations he encountered, he never forgot his own humble origins. He was genuinely thankful for his own success, and because he remembered he found time for everyone—the store manager, the dishwasher, the waitress, the carhop, the short order personnel, the prep people. He would often drive some of his people home after a restaurant closed late at night; they had no other way to get home, and Schoenbaum wasn't going to let them walk five miles.

He remained a stickler for the details of food presentation. "If there was one thing that made Alex angry," says an associate, "it was if a franchisee cut back on food portions and didn't give customers a fair deal." Thus Shoney's always put pictures on the menu to show customers exactly what they were getting. Usually the restaurant delivered on what it portrayed in the picture although there were individual slipups just as there would be in any operation.

Drawing on his football background gave Schoenbaum a marvelous understanding of teamwork. He realized the importance of each individual and tried to involve every member of the restaurant personally in what was happening. He would often ask for his employees' opinions and suggestions for improving operations. Whenever Shoney's was ready to update its kitchen format, as happened every few years, he'd ask cooks and others for their ideas. He also sought improvements for the front of the house by asking employees on the floor what was really happening.

Schoenbaum was moving along at a steady pace in the mid-1960s and had the thought that perhaps he should or could acquire Kentucky Fried Chicken. He had some discussions with Colonel Harland Sanders, developer and owner of Kentucky Fried Chicken. There were a number of visits, but no deal ever emerged. Colonel Sanders finally sold Kentucky Fried Chicken to a group led by John Y. Brown (later to become Kentucky governor), and Schoenbaum was probably fortunate not to have become tied to such a large chain at that time.

MERGER DEAL

By the late 1960s Schoenbaum was fairly certain he wanted to concentrate on the Shoney's coffee shop side of the business rather than fast-food drive-ins. Despite continued success and growth, he found himself weary of the pace. He faced a difficult situation. Feeling that things just weren't jelling the way he wanted, he decided he couldn't keep carrying the burden alone. He opted to merge his Shoney's company of eight company-owned units and some fifty franchised stores with Ray Danner's Nashville-based Danner Foods.

Danner's career had paralleled Schoenbaum's in some ways. Danner had been successful in other businesses but never satisfied until he found his niche in the food service industry. He was a grocery store operator, bowling alley proprietor, drive-in movie operator, concessionaire, real estate salesman, and gasoline station operator. But once Schoenbaum had given him a franchise for a Shoney's operation in 1958, he was fiercely determined to surpass the rest.

Danner's units achieved higher sales and profits than those of any other area. He kept plowing back the profits into the continued growth of his company. He built a management staff and took the company public as Danner Foods. He was fully prepared for the 1970 merger with Schoenbaum, where he became Shoney's majority stockholder and chief executive officer while Schoenbaum was now board chairman. Schoenbaum urged Danner to look into food service concepts that could diversify the company—particularly fish and chips fast feeders which then seemed to have an excellent future. Danner eyed Kentucky Fried Chicken's H. Salt chain, one of the earliest entries in the fish and chips derby, as a possible acquisition but finally decided Shoney's could develop its own format. This was the start of what was to become the thriving Captain D's chain.

EGO ADJUSTMENT

Schoenbaum had to adjust his ego to accept the merger. "It actually made me do something that was a necessity—share the heroship and the burdens," he says. "Financially it was a terrific move, but it surely hurt my ego." And ego was a prime motivator for him just as it was for many other entrepreneurs. When he had opened his first restaurant, he assured a friend, "Some day I will have my restaurant advertised in the pages of the *Saturday Evening Post.*"

It didn't happen just that way only because the *Post* went out of business for a while. But by the mid-1960s Shoney's and Big Boy were prominently advertising in the pages of two leading weeklies, *Life* and *Look*. The fact that these two mass magazines went out of business temporarily too might have indicated that the prime middle market upon which Shoney's depended was eroding. But actually this market was now thriving with a new media hero called television. Schoenbaum long ago had anticipated the potential of TV.

FAST PACE

No longer president or chief executive, Schoenbaum was not ready to slow down. Up until he was sixty-five, he continued to maintain a pace that was the envy of executives thirty years younger. Most of all, he was continually aware of the pitfalls of success. "The danger point of potential failure is reached by executives who are acclaimed throughout the industry for the 'miracles' they have performed," he observed. "This is when complacency sets in and an operation can start going downhill fast in today's competitive environment."

To guard against complacency, he always felt it wise to turn over the executive reins to younger men with new ideas. "Other people should come in to run the show," he says. "You've got to make room for them. Once you've done it yourself, you must bring in others who are as hungry as you once were." Schoenbaum always followed through on this advice. In the 1950s he let the younger Jim Prentiss assume a good deal of the responsibility. In the 1970s Ray Danner as chairman and David Wachtel as president assumed increasing responsibility for the growth of Shoney's. Not wanting to interfere with the decisions of the younger executives at Nashville headquarters, Schoenbaum now spent much of his time looking after his Big Boy and other interests in Charleston. But if they felt they were getting off the main track, he would caution them loudly and clearly until hopefully they would listen to his sage advice. (Wachtel became chief executive in mid-1981.)

At no time did he become inactive. He kept visiting restaurants, talking to people and boosting the company's spirits as well as profits. In 1981 when he was Shoney's senior chairman, the company reported its eighty-eighth consecutive quarter of earnings growth. Shoney's was a Wall Street favorite and a powerful force with its Big Boy coffee shops and Captain D's fish and chips units. When Schoenbaum spotted complacency creeping into Captain D's in the late 1970s, he spoke his mind privately and publicly. "When unit sales stay the same for two years, even at a fairly high level, there's a definite problem," he warned. He suggested new approaches to get Captain D's back on top. While acknowledging that the downturn "perhaps is also part of the business cycle," he was delighted when Captain D's again began to raise its average per unit sales substantially.

"ONLY FIRST PLACE"

Much of Schoenbaum's philosophy was summed up through monthly columns that he has done for years in the company's house organ, *Shoney's Family News*. He started the column around 1960 before Vince Lombardi proclaimed "winning isn't everything, it's the only thing," and long before Shoney's selected as its theme for an operators' convention, "Good enough isn't good enough." One of Schoenbaum's early columns proclaimed: "How would you like to be second? I'll tell you how you can be. If you become complacent, satisfied with your operation as it exists; absent yourself from your business for long periods of time; deviate from preparation of food as it is pictured on the menu; allow carelessness to creep in, then I'll guarantee you, you'll be second! Second place is an attitude. To me it is an attitude of defeat, or of acceptance of the fact that you just aren't quite good enough to be first. There is one place we never want to be, and that is second. Never be second." And he wasn't—at least not very often.

As he approached his sixty-fifth birthday in 1980 he penned a column declaring: "We're not going to win this battle if we retreat and quit. It's not an original statement, but nothing is more true than 'when the going gets tough, that's when the tough get going.' I learned that early. It wasn't the easy football games that brought forth my best effort, but the tough games—the ones we knew could be lost if we didn't play our very best, get tougher with the enemy." Schoenbaum was tough when he had to be, but compassionate and charitable to others whenever he could be. That was the first principle he was brought up on, and he never forgot it. Behind his sometimes gruff exterior, there is a big heart.

When he became Shoney's senior chairman in the late 1970s, Schoenbaum supposedly "semi-retired" with his wife, Betty, to a splendid penthouse apartment overlooking the Gulf of Mexico in Sarasota, Florida. But he maintained an office in Sarasota and one in Charleston, West Virginia, to look after the family Big Boy and bowling interests, and one at Nashville corporate headquarters. He continued a rapid pace of racing around the country, visiting Shoney's and Captain D's restaurants, dinner houses, checking the competition throughout the country and talking over the state of the food service business in general with his friends and associates. He continually advises people in the industry on ways they can improve their position. On those occasions when he does choose to stay home in Sarasota, his phone rings constantly with personal and business friends calling from all around the country.

DEVOTED TO FAMILY

Betty and their fourteen-year-old daughter, Emily, share the story-book penthouse with Schoenbaum. One son, Jeff, thirty-five, lives nearby. After a stint as a Wendy's franchisee in Virginia he has his own real estate and brokerage business. The other son, Raymond, is a leading Wendy's franchisee in the Atlanta area and in other states. A daughter, Joanne, twenty-eight, is setting enviable sales records on the Coca-Cola field staff in California.

Schoenbaum certainly accepts the fact that his two sons didn't want to work at Shoney's. "A lot of young men don't like to follow in their father's footsteps," he said, "and I certainly can understand this. They wanted to make it on their own without my help. My boys chose to seek their own way of life. They didn't like the corporate way of life."

Even with all the honors, accolades, and accomplishments that have come his way, Schoenbaum was proudest of the moment when his young daughter, Emily, came running home from school all excited one day with a twinkle in her eye. She gave him a hug and kiss and said, "Guesss who's on page 141 of my new history book? You are. You're in my history book."

And he is. Eighth-grade students in West Virginia, reading of leading Americans and great West Virginians, learn about Alex Schoenbaum, his dreams, his ambitions, and the realization of those dreams.

Not bad for a former tough football lineman who started in food service with a tiny drive-in and through sheer grit, determination, and kindness became a living legend and an inspiration to others.

SECTION IV

The Irrepressible Independents

Any number of independent restaurateurs have added their individual touches to the industry and shown chains the meaning of creative quality. With their cost economies limited in contrast to chains, they've had to be more innovative. At the same time some of these independents have moved to expand into mini-empires of three restaurants and upwards. But they've resisted the temptation to be acquired by a larger company. They insist they can prosper on their own—and enjoy it more.

Two prime leaders among the independent entrepreneurs are New York's Warner LeRoy and Chicago's Arnie Morton. Some would argue that they are showmen or entertainers rather than restaurateurs. Actually they are both, and the combination is ideal. They have taken a large part of the old-time formality out of the restaurant business and replaced it with "casual fun" atmospheres in a whole new breed of restaurants.

LeRoy, brought up as the third generation of a prominent Hollywood movie producing family, was a theater and movie producer until deciding at age thirty-one that restaurants were a more satisfying form of show business. He launched a small Maxwell's Plum restaurant in the mid-1960s that revolutionized the industry with its cafe-style casualness and super-decor. A master craftsman himself, LeRoy left no stone unturned to fashion the most exciting decor even if it took millions of dollars. He later expanded Maxwell's Plum in New York, transformed Central Park's Tavern on the Green to his own image and opened a second Maxwell's Plum in San Francisco. Other Maxwell's-type restaurants were being formulated.

Wherever LeRoy went, he shot for big stakes—huge annual volumes of $10 million and higher. In the process he tried to maintain quality and appeal to a broad middle class and upper class market spectrum with great menu diversity. Customers always feel they are being entertained at his restaurants.

Morton, the Bill Veeck of food service, is a nonchain promoter and merchandiser if there ever was one. He has built his own restaurant empire adorned with some version of his name or his wife's: Arnie's, Arnie's North, Morton's, Zorine's Club La Mer. Each is adorned with his personality, too—flashy, exciting, holding back nothing.

Morton once was a guiding force in building up Hugh Hefner's empire of Playboy clubs and hotels during their peak in the 1960s. Some thought he belonged permanently at Playboy with his totally casual attitude. But after many years there, he started revolutionizing the Chicago restaurant scene in the mid-1970s. He has settled down and shown that beyond all the flamboyance is a fertile mind—one of the most imaginative and successful in the food service business.

9

Warner LeRoy

FANTASY CRAFTSMAN

When Warner LeRoy opened Maxwell's Plum one evening in April 1966, he had no idea what it could become. He had acquired the lease on a tiny 20-seat luncheonette next to his New York Cinema theater, known for showing some of the best foreign films. But a restaurant?

LeRoy, who was the son of a famous movie producer and had literally grown up on a Hollywood movie set, was a bit incredulous at his own nerve in ripping up the luncheonette and putting in his own restaurant format. He really knew nothing about restaurants but decided to give it a try. He managed to squeeze in eighty seats in an expanded 10-by-80-foot area, including an inadequate 7-by-12-foot kitchen.

The new place, designed by LeRoy as a personification of an ideal American cafe, resembled a junk food store more than a restaurant. He would have been thrilled just to fill half of the eighty seats that first evening. Instead, he was shocked to see a huge crowd stretching over a block waiting to get into the small place. He somehow managed to serve about three hundred meals that evening.

With calculation as well as a dose of luck, LeRoy had captured the essence of a new casual lifestyle at just the right time. His own exotic costumes meshed with a feeling that people "wanted to do their own thing," certainly not to have to dress up when going out for an evening's entertainment.

LeRoy, then thirty-one, viewed his restaurant as an exciting new phase of his show business career. It wasn't just the restaurant or the food, but a whole atmosphere package that pulled in the people. In his revolutionary thinking, he wanted all types of customers to have a choice of anything from a hamburger and coffee to a full dinner, within a $5 price. (This price ticket would more than triple in the next fifteen years.)

"JUNK STORE"

From this little "junk store," LeRoy gradually fashioned his own restaurant mini-empire. By 1981 an expanded Maxwell's Plum was grossing $6 million annually and yielding a spectacular $30,000 per seat annual sales; his Tavern on the Green restaurant, which he reopened at New York's Central Park in 1976, was doing $15 million annually; a new Maxwell's Plum in San Francisco was heading for at least $10 million; and he had a number of other versions of Maxwell's Plum on the drawing boards.

These types of volumes are astronomical for any restaurant. Yet in this context LeRoy—who finally had in fact learned the restaurant business so that he no longer had to operate just by instinct—was able to maintain a reasonable quality. He did concede that quality had slipped at Tavern on the Green in the face of massive crowds and an inadequate kitchen (a dilemma that seemed to plague him throughout his restaurant career), but he was determined to reverse this trend. He is indeed a showman and a mass merchandiser—with a sharp eye for and demand for quality and craftsmanship.

Maxwell's Plum was instrumental in transforming the entire restaurant scene. The idea of a casual cafe-restaurant was particularly appealing, and the outdoor cafe aspect along with the casual atmosphere took hold in many restaurants around the country. They catered to a diverse customer mix and were mainly successful in large cities.

LeRoy was interested from a young age in painting, sculpture, and crafts as well as the theater. Especially fascinated with stained glass and woodcarving, he saw the initial Maxwell's Plum more as a chance to display his craft work than as a business venture. "I simply wanted to have fun," he recalls. "I loved the cafes of Europe and wanted cafes to take hold here rather than the numerous saloons." Almost everything seemed to have been presented in the saloon format since Prohibition, but LeRoy quickly changed that. He fantasized a restaurant where customers could relax and have a cup of coffee or more if they wanted.

He was concerned about the stuffiness he found at many restaurants. He opted for casual dress and a comfortable, casual atmosphere. Betting on this theory against more conventional ideas of skeptics, he won.

Besides the unique atmosphere at Maxwell's, everything was handmade rather than being a collection of antiques. A craftsman at heart, LeRoy spent the better part of three years fashioning an entire ceiling in his own apartment for an expanded Maxwell's that opened in 1970. He also did much of the glasswork and woodcarving.

Although having to learn the operations and business aspects of restaurants, he has always had an uncanny intuition about what is right or wrong in a restaurant. One day he walked into Tavern on the Green and happened to notice something that didn't look just right about the chocolate cake. Sure enough, he discovered it was a synthetic chocolate—something that nobody else had spotted or else they simply had let pass. He wouldn't tolerate anything less than the real thing, and he immediately threw it out.

MOVIE STUDIO UPBRINGING

LeRoy was born in Los Angeles in 1935. He came from a family that lived and breathed theater. His great uncle was Jack Warner and his grandfather Harry Warner, founders of Warner Bros. His father, Mervyn LeRoy, produced some ninety movies—many of them on ranch stage settings outside the home where Warner grew up. Their house was on a 3,500-acre ranch which also happened to be the site of outdoor sets for Warner Bros. studios. Young Warner LeRoy was able to survey scenes from countries around the world and every type of movie setting. "It was a fantastic place to grow up," he recalls. It certainly gave an extra spur to his already active imagination.

When Warner was four years old, in 1939, his father produced *The Wizard of Oz* on another set away from the ranch. Warner spent much of his childhood surrounded by films, entertainment, and fantasy. He was precocious and became a Warner Bros. film editor at age eleven. He went to Universal Studios as an assistant director at age thirteen. As a teen-ager, he helped direct Abbott & Costello and other movies in an era when films were made in ten days. He quickly learned the intricacies of movie-making.

LeRoy had one younger sister, Linda. He felt secure in his childhood despite numerous moves and a succession of schools. When his parents, Mervyn LeRoy and Doris Warner, got divorced, he was sent to the Hotchkiss Prep School in Connecticut. He was familiar with the East since Warner Bros. headquarters actually were in New York. But he didn't savor the Hotchkiss way of doing things. "I'd been accustomed to a loose and free public school system in California," he says. "I just couldn't get adjusted to the tight discipline at Hotchkiss."

His mother married Charles Vidor, who was known for producing Rita Hayworth movies. LeRoy finally left formidable Hotchkiss for a fancy private school in Switzerland where his roommate was Ali Kahn, the future Aga Kahn and the son of Rita Hayworth. A friendship blossomed between the two families.

EUROPEAN INFLUENCE

From an early age LeRoy traveled extensively, especially to Europe and France. The first "great meal" he savored, at the age of twelve, made an indelible impression and was partially responsible for his later choosing the restaurant field to express his creativeness. He went to La Pyramide restaurant outside Lyon with his mother, Ali Kahn, and Rita Hayworth. "This is when I first realized food can be great," said LeRoy, who has always had a sensitive set of taste buds. "Once in a while you find something so incredible in a creative endeavor that you never forget it. This happens occasionally in the theater or in a restaurant, and it makes a lasting impression. Everything just falls together perfectly with a master chef like this and a few absolutely exquisite dishes." (Years later LeRoy's Maxwell's Plum would fall into this category in some ways.)

In any case La Pyramide and other European restaurants and cafes that LeRoy frequented from ages twelve to sixteen whetted his appetite for the food business. He didn't exactly have a tough time of it, gaining exposure to elegance and spending summers at the Riviera with his mother, Ali Kahn, and Rita Hayworth. They all ate and traveled together.

LeRoy returned to Los Angeles for his final year of high school and then went to Stanford College, Palo Alto, Calif. He majored in English and was active in the drama department at college and in the San Francisco area, producing fifteen plays. The enterprising young man, who adored show business, was also active with the local radio station.

Ahead of virtually everyone from an early age, he graduated from Stanford at age nineteen. He never saw any need for graduate school or further formal education after that.

Show business was in his blood, and he opted for it as a career—but not in movies at first. Actually he was disillusioned with the way children of Hollywood stars were handled. In contrast to the popular image of pampered stars' children, he found many of the children to be "mistreated." Although he was treated more than fairly, he didn't like what he saw happening to some of his peers. He never forgot an incident when a friend was thrown out of a Hollywood studio by the youth's own father and barred from ever returning. "I never knew the real reason," says LeRoy, "and I found this very cruel."

EARLY CAREER

After college graduation in 1954, he became a stage manager for Garson Kanin in New York City. He worked on a number of plays, including *The Diary of Anne Frank*. In 1959 he took over the old York Theater at First Avenue and 64th Street in New York. Obtaining investors, he produced and directed a number of plays over the next five years, including Tennessee Williams's *Garden District* and Maxwell Anderson's *The Golden Six*. Anderson was critically ill during production, and this was the last play he wrote. LeRoy felt the script needed rewriting, but nothing could be done because of Anderson's illness. Yet LeRoy was determined to make a box office success of this Roman spectacle. With his flair for the unusual, he put three stark naked slave girls on the stage—an exceptionally daring tactic for that era. Imagine his disappointment when theater critics insisted the whole thing was a posed gimmick and couldn't be real. Sadly, the three really naked young women were ignored rather than receiving the hoopla LeRoy had hoped they might cause.

One of his biggest box office successes was *Between Two Thieves*, which ran for one and one-half years. He also helped write the French play *Chin Chin* over a one-year period and produced it for Broadway. But primarily he was known as one of the first Off-Broadway producers. He proved this could be successful in its own way without the glittering lights of Broadway to help or distract.

In 1964 he converted the York Theater into the York Cinema, turning it back into a movie theater which it had been before he purchased it. He started showing Marx Bros. and Humphrey Bogart movies and experimented with foreign films. For the first time he began making a substantial living with his knack for innovation and grasp of what the public wanted at any given time in the fickle cycle.

His business prospered beyond his dreams. He paid a tiny amount for movie rights, and his packed theater grossed about $10,000 weekly with virtually no expenses. Yet he was to find later that the same space could gross and net ten times that much as a restaurant. More significantly for the man who always seemed able to make as much money as he wanted, he was to find the restaurant a more gratifying creative sphere for his talents.

NEW RESTAURATEUR

Perhaps it was fated that LeRoy would become a showman-restaurateur some day, but he got into the business almost by chance without having mapped any real plan. One day Huntington Hartford, editor of *Show* Magazine, approached him about the idea of doing something with the tiny luncheonette next to LeRoy's York Theater. Hartford thought of taking over the place in partnership with LeRoy and opening a "Show" restaurant. Hartford wanted 60 percent of the gross himself. LeRoy, always desiring control of what he touched, decided he could do it himself. Recalling his fabulous meals at La Pyramide and other great French restaurants and cafes, he now felt a sidewalk cafe next to his theater would be the ideal combination.

While the First Avenue Upper East Side area then was not considered a happy place for business, LeRoy saw plenty of taxis and people moving along the avenue daily and knew there must be a market for a cafe there. Most of all, he wanted to do a spectacular drama of some sort, and he had been frustrated in trying to implement this ambition in the theater. When he produced an artistically successful play about the Hungarian revolution called *Shadow of Heroes,* he nevertheless realized there was "no such thing as a feasible spectacular drama in the theater because it was all too expensive."

He had done quite a bit of painting, sculpting, and crafts and viewed a restaurant as an opportunity to display his craft work or simply to have fun. He also was addicted to the idea that open cafes would be far preferable to the enclosed saloons so prevalent on the New York scene.

As he planned his new-style cafe for the luncheonette where he had taken a long-term lease, he was concerned about the stuffiness he found at many restaurants. He doubted that most people really wanted to get all dressed up when they went out to dine. He also was concerned about the lackadaisical attitude of the help in these restaurants. "They weren't proud of their work as were the employees I had seen in Europe," LeRoy says. He opted to encourage casual dress among the customers and to hire employees who had a sense of pride in food service.

LeRoy really had no idea of any of the specifics of the restaurant business. He visited the famous P. J. Clarke's casual saloon-restaurant in New York a number of times and noticed that they somehow managed with their tiny kitchen and small operation. He also was influenced by ideas from cafes in France. Paradoxically, he adopted some of the physical touches he admired at the elegant more formal "21" Club. Noting toys hanging from the ceiling, LeRoy decided to hang stuffed animals from the Maxwell's Plum ceiling. He also used gaslights and stucco.

LeRoy did much of the work himself as he refashioned the entire luncheonette to his own aspirations. He made some of the crafts, etched the mirrors, and purchased the Tiffany glass. He emphasized Tiffany lamps. "I really was just trying to have some fun and exercise my creativity," he says.

Typically, he selected the cafe's name on a calculated hunch. He tossed around double-meaning names such as "The Silver Cherry" and "The Shanghai Hippopotamus" but finally thought of "Maxwell's Plum" when it flashed through his mind during a brainstorming session. He surmised it conveyed a certain feeling—perhaps of refined casualness. Luckily, he did not select a name such as "Warner's" or "LeRoy's" as he might have been tempted to do.

TRAFFIC-STOPPER

When Maxwell's opened in the spring of 1966, it stopped vehicular traffic in the area for weeks. Six policemen were needed outside to patrol the place. Waiting lines for dinner stretched all the way from First to Second Avenue. It was the "in" place, just as Studio 54 would be a decade later. But Maxwell's popularity was more sustained over a period of years though of course the novelty and excitement were never quite the same as in the first six months and when LeRoy opened his expanded version four years later.

LeRoy had positioned Maxwell's perfectly. Airline stewardesses, secretaries, and nurses flocked to the place, and it became a highly respected singles spot. It arrived just as the women's liberation movement and casual lifestyles were finding their niches. The openness, casualness, and uniqueness of this sidewalk cafe combined for maximum customer appeal.

With only eighty seats, LeRoy was suddenly serving some 500 meals daily. He featured a diversified "all-American" menu (later it would shift more to a Continental one) with a large hamburger not unlike Burger King's subsequent Whopper. A T-bone steak was selling phenomenally at $3.95, but LeRoy's manager warned him that each sale of a steak meant a $1 actual loss because the price was too low. "What did

I know about it?" says LeRoy. "I really had no idea about anything in such practical terms, but I just kept doing my thing." He did know that the restaurant and kitchen were severely overtaxed for the large amount of traffic passing through and that the place would have to be expanded.

With its open look, LeRoy's sidewalk cafe was the forerunner of some two hundred sidewalk cafes that would eventually dot the city. About the same time as Maxwell's opened its sidewalk cafe, so did TGI Friday's across the street and Mr. Laff's nearby. Political battles ensued for years as sidewalk cafes became a political football. Some felt they detracted from the esthetics of areas; others that they added greatly to the spirit of the city. No matter what, they changed the landscape of the city, and city officials launched a long series of discussions on what should be done about them. LeRoy has been a leading industry representative for cafes and continues as president of the informally organized City Sidewalk Cafe Association.

Interestingly, despite an elaborate glittering bar that he has always emphasized at Maxwell's Plum, LeRoy drinks no liquor. He has only an occasional glass of wine, perhaps once a month, at a wine tasting. "I simply don't like liquor," he says, "so why should I drink it?" He has never even sat at Maxwell's Plum's bar. "I put the bar in," he says, "because I felt an American cafe must have a bar." The bar has consistently helped pull in singles though Maxwell's evolved into a popular family place too. "After all, the singles scene *is* the cafe scene," notes LeRoy. "Young people were the first ones to come to Maxwell's Plum."

Almost from the first, he was bombarded with requests from people who wanted his help or wanted to do Maxwell's Plum types of places. He helped with the layout and planning for TGI Friday's restaurant in Dallas which became a standard for that chain. A number of concepts emerged bearing similarities to Maxwell's in decor, casual style, and appeal to singles. Houlihan's, Gilbert/Robinson's Kansas City-based chain, is one example. Clyde's in Washington is a close copy of Maxwell's Plum. LeRoy is delighted rather than miffed at the duplication. "I'll give other restaurants all the help I can," he says. "Anyone can try to do an exact copy, but it doesn't mean anything without the proper execution and implementation."

LeRoy loves to shock people, or at least draw their attention, with unusual costumes. From the beginning of Maxwell's, he dressed in any number of unique outfits. These ranged from a black velvet dinner jacket with large shining flowers of various colors to a Western outfit with lions' heads on the back or a Moroccan contraption with water cups, flashlights, and a huge hat adorned with silver bells. Whatever LeRoy did, he had fun doing it and so did his customers.

One of the major benefits of the original small Maxwell's was that it enabled him to meet his second wife, Kay. He met her one evening in 1968 when she walked into Maxwell's to have dinner. "I said to myself, 'There's a delicious woman,'" he recalls, "and went over and introduced myself." A whirlwind courtship and marriage ensued. LeRoy was perfectly capable of throwing himself just as enthusiastically into his personal life as his business. (When critics subsequently depicted Maxwell's as a "pickup joint," LeRoy's reaction was, "Fine, so what?")

A LARGER PLUM

In 1969, when he knew beyond doubt that Maxwell's would have to be enlarged, he met Charles Stein, chairman of the diversified Hardwicke Companies and an astute businessman and restaurant man. Hardwicke agreed to invest $500,000 in Maxwell's just when LeRoy was ready to spend a fortune redecorating the place. Some of the $500,000 actually was a loan, and Stein's company became an equal partner with LeRoy. But management of Maxwell's was still LeRoy's domain. "Try never to put up your own money," was the credo LeRoy had learned in Hollywood.

He was still showing movies at the York Cinema but was certain that restaurant space would be far more rewarding creatively and financially. He closed the theater and in 1970 opened an enlarged Maxwell's Plum with 240 seats (which still would eventually prove inadequate). The kitchen was much bigger, but not enough so to handle the entire volume. Yet there was enough space for LeRoy to concentrate on upgrading his food quality.

After its reopening in 1970 Maxwell's prospered even more. LeRoy never found it necessary to advertise. He let word-of-mouth and promotions carry the day. The new place offered a larger menu selection which later reached 180 items and was known for a variety of key dishes—not necessarily for one or two special signature items as are many restaurants. This variety personified his appeal to a broad market spectrum. Among the best-selling items for the next decade and beyond were black bean soup and onion soup; duckling, partridge, and pasta salads; seafoods; and desserts from Maxwell's own bakery.

If anything expresses LeRoy's outlook, it is the decor of his restaurant. A lighted Tiffany glass ceiling in Maxwell's 90-seat back room stands out as overwhelmingly spectacular. It was built from some 10,000 sheets of Tiffany glass which his wife had scouted from antique dealers throughout the country. LeRoy fashioned these into a ceiling and also designed and built antique mirrors, furniture, and a copper ceiling. He did much of the work himself, aided by a master craftsman. Ten lanterns and Tiffany lamps there were valued at as much as $30,000 each while three Tiffany windows were valued at over $50,000 each. One appraisal placed the entire value of Maxwell's interior adornments at over $1.5 million.

UNORTHODOX METHODS

LeRoy devised each detail of the restaurant to assure direct involvement of the customers, whom he sees as an audience at a theater. The women's room is situated in a spot where any woman has to pass through most of the restaurant to get there. This encourages maximum movement and involvement. He also created three separate levels, permitting a constant interplay at different levels with diners able to eye the singles at the bar in the center, the singles in turn looking at the people in the cafe, and the customers eating in the cafe looking at the passersby on the street. Of course, the people on the street are eagerly looking at the people eating in the cafe, establishing a rapport and a desire to at least try the restaurant if one hasn't already done so.

LeRoy uses unorthodox methods to achieve his goals. In the early days of Maxwell's Plum he placed an advertisement seeking "the best chef in New York for $50,000 a year." He held the box number replies for several months and then started calling some of the more promising candidates who had responded. He'd ask them if they'd be interested in being Maxwell's chef for $20,000 a year. Eventually he ended up paying almost $100,000. Frenchman Daniel Fuchs, once Charles de-Gaulle's chef, was his executive chef from 1973 to 1981 when Michel Bordeaux took the post.

LeRoy has persevered through a steady turnover of waiters since the beginning—a standard aspect of the restaurant business. He has kept the same general manager, Robert Willis, at the restaurant since 1971. Willis is particularly adept at the operations side.

LeRoy is a stickler for details and cleanliness. He has all the plants changed at least once every two weeks, and the cost of these plants runs to about $40,000 a year. But his absolute pride is the immaculate outside red awning. If it always seems unusually sparkling, that's because it is scrubbed daily and repainted six times a year at an annual $8,000 cost. Meanwhile, a garden of spices, herbs, and other experimental items always seems to adorn the manager's office.

LeRoy has a penchant for unique names and featured "deviled beef bones" as an item in the earlier days. When sales were going nowhere, he was smart enough to switch the name to "barbecued beef ribs." Sales on the same item quadrupled, confirming LeRoy's feeling that image is as important as the food itself. He once would allow only the food he liked on the menu. Thus broccoli, which he hated, was barred. Later he did add broccoli and other items he didn't personally like.

LeRoy firmly believes people should be entertained at their own budget level and not at the owner's. "A customer wants to go out and have a good time just the way he or she feels like it," he says. "Maxwell's Plum is for everyone," he emphasizes. The place's appeal cuts through a wide spectrum of the middle and upper classes.

Maxwell's also draws some people who can afford it just once a year. They save up their money for a special celebration, and they go. Birthdays, anniversaries, weddings and business achievements are celebrated there. "It pleases the senses, and it entertains," LeRoy says of his dramatic spectacle.

He does care what restaurant critics think since he has pride in his restaurant. Yet he is certain a place won't stand or fall on a critic's opinions. He accepts a reviewer's right to present a viewpoint about a restaurant but feels credibility suffers when reviewers discuss only the food. "A restaurant is a combination of food, decor, atmosphere, service, a lot of elements," he declares. "It's ludicrous to only talk about one aspect."

GREAT ADVENTURE

One project—great as it might be—simply wasn't enough for LeRoy's creative aspirations. As early as 1968 he was eyeing amusement theme parks as another form of the spectacular drama in which he gloried. LeRoy kept dreaming up ideas for such a park in the middle of New Jersey. When his new Great Adventure finally opened in 1974 at Jackson, N.J., it surpassed even his imagination. At a cost of $80 million he had built a 1,500-acre complex of a drive-through safari (his step-brother Brian Vidor purchased many of the animals in Africa) and an amusement park with a unique ferris wheel and unusual rides.

LeRoy's stamp was on the entire park and safari. He conceived and designed the varied rides. He also designed and built a wide range of restaurants and snack places which had an unusually high price ticket for an amusement park. But he felt quality would sell there, and the restaurants did reasonably well. Perhaps his most unique design achievement was the Best of the West restaurant, built like a log cabin with 100-foot-long trees and no nails.

He must have felt a special pride from the fact that the Great Adventure safari's main competition was Jungle Habitat some ninety miles north in New Jersey. Jungle Habitat, owned by Warner Communications, parent company of the family Warner Bros. studios, closed a few years later.

More the creator than the implementer, LeRoy sold his interest in Great Adventure in 1978 as other projects consumed his time. His imprint was clearly on the theme park, and by 1981 it was pulling in 4.5 million persons annually, a figure believed to be second only to Disneyland and Disney World.

TAVERN ON THE GREEN

Even before LeRoy dreamed about Great Adventure, he had visions and doodles about possibly taking over the prestigious Tavern on the Green restaurant in New York's Central Park and converting it into his latest version of fantasyland. He first dreamed about it in 1966, then started planning it in 1972. Finally, he got the approval from the City Fathers (actually a bevy of councils, commissions, and committees) and took over Tavern from Restaurant Associates. He wanted to transform the labyrinth of rooms and outdoor gardens into his own image. He also wanted to improve on the restaurant's $1 million annual volume at least tenfold. He was willing to spend $1.5 million on renovating it and actually has spent that sum annually in constant revamping ever since it opened.

When the Tavern reopened under LeRoy in the late summer of 1976, it bore his personal imprint. He took the craftsmen who had helped him with Maxwell's and put them to work on Tavern. His individual touches included a special brand of wormy chestnut for paneling; intricate sand-carved mirrors; four street lamps imported from Europe for the entrance; a banquet room chandelier adorned with hundreds of glass flowers made in Venice, and thirteen elegant chandeliers fashioned from foreign antiques.

LeRoy's attention to detail is legendary. He endlessly debated whether three-inch crystal balls would be the best and finally decided on four-inch ones as in the best taste to hang from a row of chandeliers. He had a total of nine linen companies apply for the contract before he found one that could do exactly what he wanted: produce floral designs with seven silk screens for the tablecloth.

If LeRoy's Tavern was an artistic and financial success with annual volume starting at $8 million and doubling by 1981, the 850-seat place was not necessarily a food hit. The food quality and service spread over a crowded complex of rooms posed severe difficulties. LeRoy concedes quality has been a problem. Trying to serve 2,000 meals daily from one kitchen was no easy task, he notes. He separated the facilities into one separate banquet kitchen and one dining kitchen to overcome the obstacles. Thus far he has established a pleasing environment but still fallen short on the food side.

ON TO SAN FRANCISCO

No matter how many restaurants he might do, LeRoy will always be known as the creator of Maxwell's Plum of New York. Still, he was determined to create something similar but bigger and better. In May 1981 at Ghiardelli Square overlooking San Francisco Bay, he opened another Maxwell's Plum. This one has 750 seats—not quite enough for his latest volume tastes but still far ahead of New York's 240-seater. This time he put in three kitchens, a bakery, and a butcher shop. These cost him over $1 million to build, and the remainder of the restaurant took over $6 million. To do it his way, he ripped out two previous restaurants at Ghiardelli Square and started all over again his way.

The restaurant is owned by Hardwicke, but it is run by LeRoy and almost entirely reflects his spirit and the ideas of Maxwell's Plum International president Charles Ramus, a twelfth generation French restaurateur. It is a combined product of the best of Maxwell's of New York, Tavern on the Green, and the thinking of LeRoy and Ramus. Here in LeRoy's "classic cafe," a customer can have a hamburger or a gourmet French dinner.

Again, he seemed more fascinated by his own craftsmanship in San Francisco than by anything else. He fashioned intricate displays of colors and textures, multicolored Tiffany glass ceilings, floral carpeting with matching tablecloths, overwhelming stained glass windows and antique chandeliers from nineteenth century India. His own company craftsmen carried out his ideas for these complex arrangements.

One major change that LeRoy made in San Francisco is in the bar's location. At Maxwell's in New York, it was in the center of everything— almost too intrusive. At Tavern it created a madhouse. In San Francisco the bar looks down on the restaurant rather than being in the center. This couldn't be bad since the San Francisco Maxwell's bar is doing double the volume of the New York Maxwell's one. Total volume for the San Francisco restaurant is hitting $10 million the first year—an astronomical figure for that city, generally known more for its food quality than massive volumes.

It falls considerably short of New York's Maxwell's on a sales per seat basis since the New York restaurant is doing $6 million on far fewer seats. Yet the San Francisco version appeared to be heading toward a financial success that would justify the heavy initial investment costs. A dance floor launched at the San Francisco Maxwell's could not be utilized the first few months as diners packed the place until 3 A.M. every night, despite predictions that LeRoy couldn't repeat his New York magic.

When LeRoy found he could not get top quality meat for the San Francisco Maxwell's, he immediately established a system of purchasing the meat in New York and shipping it to San Francisco. "I'm a nut for quality," he says in discussing purchasing procedures for his restaurants. He goes to extremes to implement this philosophy. Stringbeans are brought in from France. Butter is imported from Finland. Hearts of palms are grown by Indians for LeRoy on a Florida reservation.

LeRoy reduced the number of items somewhat in San Francisco as he felt quality could be enhanced this way. He is adopting a similar philosophy in New York where some items are being culled out of the mix of 180 each at Maxwell's and Tavern. But the balance will be the same with more daily specials added "so that the chef has time to produce quality dishes."

FAMILY LIFE

As hard-nosed as he is about business, LeRoy sets a priority to spend as much time as feasible with his family and to stay close to them. It is a tightly knit family consisting of his wife, Kay, and four children, Bridget, 17, from his previous marriage; Carolyn, 9; Max, 6, and Jennifer, 3. He tries to set aside some time for each of his children almost daily. The family travels together on LeRoy's business trips and dines in restaurants together. But LeRoy much prefers staying home for dinner at either his duplex apartment in New York's Dakota not far from his office or at his estate in Amagansett, Long Island, near East Hampton.

He is 5 feet 10 inches and often an amiable 250 pounds. Although his willpower is overwhelming in his business endeavors, it is less so in his eating habits. His weight fluctuates with solid reductions half the year and a ballooning the other half. He can't resist good food.

LeRoy has his own built-in alarm clock, rising automatically at a very early hour. Invariably no matter when he goes to sleep, he wakes up at 5:56 A.M. for no particular reason though he may be somehow programmed. When staying at his Amagansett estate where he feels he can concentrate more creatively, he works most of the morning, shuffling through papers, reading and checking financial figures. He takes time out for a leisurely breakfast with his family. Most of all, he finds time for "creative doodling" almost around the clock and comes up with some of his most brilliant futuristic ideas this way. Some of it may be just plain creative fun, but many of the ideas that he implements emerge from this process.

WORK HABITS

When LeRoy goes to his New York office, he spends much of the time working on new designs. He rarely ever takes time out for lunch. Perhaps once every two weeks he'll go to a restaurant—not necessarily Maxwell's Plum around the corner. He loves his restaurant, but he has learned to delegate responsibilities and he knows his very presence in the dining room can interfere with the normal flow of operation and inhibit the employees. In any case he prefers a light snack at his desk so that nothing interferes with his work.

He refuses to take any phone calls at the office except from his family. He simply wants to concentrate totally on whatever he is doing. On more than one occasion a famous celebrity or VIP has called, and LeRoy's secretary has urged him to take the call. Nevertheless, he sticks unswervingly to a policy of returning those calls he chooses to answer at his later convenience. "I have to be totally disciplined and consistent to accomplish my objectives," he observes.

LeRoy never dwells on the past. He doesn't keep clippings, reviews, articles, any momento of past accomplishments. There's simply no scrapbook for anyone to see. "I'm only interested in what I can achieve in the future," he explains, "and I'm sure the public is too. I don't want to be diverted by worrying about the past, pondering it or even thinking about it."

Work in effect is his hobby, but he does have other interests. He constantly reads about gardening, architecture, and other specialized subjects toward continued self-improvement. He particularly enjoys gardening and landscaping.

When he started as a restaurateur, LeRoy was admittedly an amateur. "I'm really still an amateur," he maintains, "but I think this is an advantage. I don't want to hear something can't be done because of technical reasons. I want it done, and I get it done."

NONSTOP CREATIVITY

His motivation is to always create more. He has more than enough money for total security with his extensive commodities trading business and other ventures. "My projects have to make money," he says, "but the creative challenge is the main thing for me." Food service is his art, his painting, his form of expression. He certainly doesn't mind acclaim, but his prime goals are the internal ones that he sets. "I have to think the food is good and that people who come to my restaurant have a good time," he says.

LeRoy has been offered fast-food companies, hotels, office buildings, numerous deals. He turns down most everything no matter how much financial gain might be involved. He only wants to tackle projects where his craftsmanship and skills are fully tested.

LeRoy's enterprises have grown to the point where he now has his own woodcarvers, foundries, independent craftsmen, and a factory that makes stained glass. "We make the only real color-crystal in the world," he says. These operations are so massive that LeRoy was partially responsible for the explosion in craftsmanship. "I couldn't find one person who worked on Tiffany glass when we first started," he notes, "but now there are hundreds."

With Maxwell's of New York still the basic model for future larger versions, LeRoy has chosen tentative sites for Maxwell's-type units (different names will be used to avoid any connotation of a chain) at Chicago's Lincoln Park; at the foot of the Potomac River in Georgetown, Washington; on Boylston Street in Boston; on the site of the old Schwab's drug store in Los Angeles, and on the Champs Elysées. He is depending on generating enough cash flow to do one of these each year at an initial average investment of $8 million. He envisions seating capacities in the 850 to 1,000 range and annual volumes over $10 million. If so, he would have an unmatched empire of spectacular volume places.

Only major cities with widely diverse customer mixes can accommodate massive restaurants like this. Such restaurants can help transform an entire city scene. At the same time LeRoy is confident he now can deliver maximum food quality along with these massive numbers. He is determined to keep building better-organized kitchens to support his artistic front-of-the-house flair.

LeRoy rarely stops and says anything is satisfactory. He is always trying to do something one better. He has an idea to tear down Maxwell's Plum in New York within the next few years, rebuild the kitchen and expand the seating. "The place is just too small," he concedes. "I want to make it more elaborate, more interesting and even more profitable by keeping more seats filled and adding private rooms."

He looks mainly at his cash flow when analyzing his restaurants' financial results. He figures that in 1981 Maxwell's Plum and the Tavern in New York made $3 million cash on a total of $21 million sales. This includes his having invested $1.7 million in renovations. Not bad at all for a "craftsman" and "amateur restaurateur."

He dreams of starting a new company to build "spectacular, dramatic" food service in national park settings. He envisions a park, entertainment and restaurant center which would overlook Niagara Falls. Space would be included for exhibits and dancing. Anyone who knows LeRoy realizes these dreams are not far-fetched.

A consultant for entertainment parks in Canada and Great Britain, another of his dreams is for a Tivoli Gardens type of place that would be bigger than the one in Copenhagen. In addition, he hopes to design a national park with restaurants, exhibits, and American history shows at Liberty Park in Jersey City, N.J. This would include Ellis Island and an immigration theme.

He likes to call his company LeRoy Adventures or Flash LeRoy. He handles all his operations from this base. The names are especially appropriate; for Warner LeRoy, everything is a flash adventure. Nobody—not even LeRoy—knows how each adventure will end. But each is guaranteed to be innovative, unique, "fun"—and almost certainly profitable.

10

Arnie Morton

MASTER ENTERTAINER

In his own grandiose but casual style, Arnie Morton has taken the Chicago restaurant scene to new heights, carving a permanent niche in the national restaurant industry as well. Once an executive vice president of Playboy Enterprises, he was involved in developing the concept for the Playboy Clubs around the world, combining Playboy Bunnies, food, and entertainment under one exciting roof. He has translated his expert knowledge of fine dining and entertainment into his own spectacular local food service empire. To dine at one of his restaurants is to experience high-quality cuisine in a totally entertaining environment.

Everything about Morton's restaurants spells quality. He knows quality food and how to produce a price-value package for his customers. In Newberry Plaza, a prestigious near North Side condominium building at 1030 North State Street, he has created four popular eateries: Arnie's, his first restaurant venture, an esteemed Chicago landmark and a popular attraction for out-of-towners; Zorine's Club La Mer, an elegant French seafood restaurant which Morton operates with renowned Chef Jean Banchet, owner of one of the crown jewels of

French restaurants, Le Français in Wheeling, Illinois (Zorine's Club La Mer was transformed in 1981 into a seafood restaurant from Zorine's, one of Chicago's first private discothèques, opened in January 1976); Morton's, a neighborhood saloon where the "who's who" of Chicago go for some of the finest steaks and fresh live lobster in town; and Arnie's Outdoor Cafe, a California-style sidewalk cafe serving Arnie's barbecued ribs, chicken, and burgers.

Morton also operates a sister establishment, Arnie's North in Highland Park, which recently added an upper-level deep-dish pizzeria to its Continental fare and lavish hot and cold buffet selection downstairs. In December 1980, he built, and now manages, the food and beverage operations for possibly the largest, all-inclusive indoor/outdoor recreational facility in the country, Chicago's East Bank Club. It includes The Restaurant, a clubby dining spot featuring a healthy nouvelle cuisine menu; The Grill; Riverfront Cafe, serving omelettes, sandwiches and salads; and full banquet catering facilities.

VEECK REINCARNATED

Arnie Morton is to the restaurant business what Bill Veeck was to the baseball business in Chicago—a master entertainer with a solid expertise in his profession. His flamboyant personality, coupled with his unique sense of flair, allows him to shape things differently and individually—always making a personal statement. The success of his main restaurant complex and his keen eye for promotional opportunities have played a major role in luring the highest caliber of customers to the Rush Street area. In fact, he can be viewed as a pioneer in the neighborhood. It was Arnie's that triggered a renaissance of trendy restaurants and saloons geared toward young professionals along Chicago's Rush Street. His uncanny knack for identifying a market and creating a restaurant concept to fill that need has catapulted him to the top. His goal is to be number one in each of his individual market segments—a target he generally achieves.

Morton's pride in his dining establishments can be experienced in just their names. He keeps the names in the family. Arnie's and Morton's were named after Arnie Morton and Zorine's after Zorine, his wife of twenty years and the mother of their five children.

The restaurateur lines in Morton's family run deep. His grandfather operated a saloon in Iron Mountain, Michigan, and his father, Morton C. Morton, ran one of the most successful restaurants and bars on Chicago's South Side. Born March 23, 1922, Morton began his restaurant career at a very early age in the company of two expert teachers, his grandfather and father. He began to "hang around" Morton's at the age of fifteen doing odd jobs, but left to attend the University of Alabama in 1941. He enlisted in the army infantry in 1943.

Returning home at the age of twenty-two, Morton began to examine expansion possibilities for his father's saloon. When an adjacent space became available, they cemented the deal and Morton's became both a restaurant and saloon.

In 1952, Morton's restaurant relocated to a larger space at the site of the Palm Grove Inn, an old-time Chicago landmark at 5600 South Lake Shore Drive. Later, Morton decided to set out on his own and in 1956 opened The Walton Walk on Ernst Court on Chicago's near North Side. Featuring top local piano entertainment, The Walton Walk became known as an intimate private bistro with a clientele of many of the city's leading socialites and celebrities. One of the regulars was Victor Lownes, then vice president of Playboy Magazine. A close friendship developed between Lownes and Morton, and subsequently between Morton and Hugh Hefner. In 1959 Morton joined the company as vice president to develop and operate the Playboy Clubs.

PLAYBOY ADVENTURES

Morton not only worked on keeping the Playboy Bunnies in the limelight but concentrated on keeping the dining facilities packed as well. Among his early promotions was to sell dinners for the price of a drink—which meant that anyone coming into the Playboy Club for a $1.50 cocktail could purchase the dinner buffet of ribs, chicken, and steak on a skewer for $1.50. With the added attraction of the internationally renowned Playboy Bunnies and Morton's in-depth knowledge of the food service industry, the Playboy Clubs rode an early crest of popularity.

While serving as ringmaster for the Playboy Clubs, Morton traveled the world over in an exciting whirlwind of chauffeured limousines and private jets. His hectic work schedule would take him to London one week, Manila the next, then Jamaica the week after to look after his hotels and clubs.

Although Lownes, Hefner, and Morton all shared a passion for power, wealth, and being surrounded by some of the world's most beautiful women, their individual styles differed. Morton, who traditionally rises at the crack of dawn, would arrive at work at 8:00 A.M.— just in time to see Hefner going home after conducting his work all night. Their schedules varied, yet they all worked together with astonishing success.

One of Hefner's parties at the Chicago Playboy Mansion proved fortuitous for Morton. It was there that he met a stunning twenty-year-old blonde theater student and Gaslight girl named Zorine Rejba. Morton, who had been married briefly and divorced years earlier, fell for Zorine and the two were married after a brief romance in 1961. He still endearingly refers to her as his "Polish Princess." He stayed with Playboy for fifteen more years while pondering the possibility of some day opening his own restaurant. Perhaps it was just as well that his thinking had not fully jelled to the point of action in the 1960s, for Chicago may not have been ready to accept his innovative concepts.

When Playboy went public in 1971, Morton's time to start on his own had arrived. Now the company was a large conglomerate and all decisions, large or small, had to be cleared through an intricate network of committees and directors. In 1973 he left Playboy and quickly threw himself into opening his own monument, Arnie's.

MORTON'S EMPIRE

As a contrast to Playboy's dark men's club style, Arnie's featured mirrors, plants, bright colors, and dazzling Art Deco and Art Nouveau artifacts. Instead of skimpily clad cocktail bunnies, Morton chose to dress his waiters and waitresses in Argyle sweaters, dark slacks, white shirts, and bow ties. In April 1974 the massive planning and construction was completed, and Arnie's restaurant made its Chicago debut.

The reaction of the public: an instantaneous success.

Soon Arnie's became known as "the place to see and be seen" as celebrities, politicians, and the city's leading business leaders began to frequent the near North's newest and most lavish restaurant. Hefner's reaction to Arnie's when it first opened was, "Morton, why didn't you do this for me?" Morton chided back, "I tried to but you wouldn't let me."

Although Arnie's was open to the public, it took on the aura of being a classy private club as many of Chicago's most prominent citizens became regulars. Morton reveled in it, spending every lunch and dinner hopping from table to table from one conversation to another, to meet and talk to all the customers.

In effect, Arnie's became a four-room meeting place for Chicago's "beautiful people," with each room reflecting a style all its own. The Bar, an Art Deco playground of nonstop action for Chicago's young professionals; The Wicker Room, an intimate neon private party room; the Garden Room with its lush greenery and plush banquettes; and the main dining room, an awesome paradise with a stained glass ceiling and mirrors overlooking a five-story atrium.

One startling creation was not enough of a challenge for the tireless Morton. Soon plans were underway to build Zorine's, one of Chicago's first restaurant/discos located in an adjacent space in the Newberry Plaza Building. Completed in January 1976, it became the hangout for Chicago's night-lifers with an elaborate cold and hot buffet table and the most contemporary of sound systems and dance floors. As a showcase for Chicago's glittery socialites and celebrities, Zorine's was a shrine that Morton dedicated to his wife.

With two flourishing restaurants under his belt, Morton went on to number three. In the summer of 1977 he transferred his unique dining and entertainment concepts to suburban Highland Park and built Arnie's North, taking an old grocery store and transforming it into still another spellbinding Art Deco/Art Nouveau palace. He surrounded the buffet table with six street lamps from early days on downtown State Street and twelve-foot gilded nude statues. This spectacular shrine turned out to be just what the North Shore was waiting for and Arnie's North, like its two Morton predecessors, became another local landmark.

With Arnie's North in its second year, Morton decided to go another route as a restaurateur. He opened his first steakhouse, Morton's, also in Newberry Plaza, in late 1978. Eyeing the market with close scrutiny, he determined that although there were many restaurants which featured good steaks, top quality steakhouses were few and far between in Chicago. He describes Morton's as a "comfortable saloon serving great steaks and fresh live lobsters." With a casually elegant decor flecked with photographs of local celebrities on its walls, Morton's is subdued in contrast to the flashiness of Arnie's and Arnie's North. Yet it shares one common trait with his other establishments; it too is a frequent meeting place for Chicago's elite.

Of course, there was still more to come. Morton opened three restaurants and rebuilt Zorine's in early 1981. The three dining spots were located at the East Bank Club, the centerpiece of which is The Restaurant, a 150-seat American-style dining room with a wine bar. His sixty-five-seat casual Grille serves fruits, salads, and hamburgers. And the Riverfront Cafe highlights a similar menu to the Grille but with outdoor charbroiling for steaks and burgers.

SIGNATURE PHILOSOPHY

In addition to his showmanship and wizardry, Morton also has an excellent grasp of the art of quality food preparation. He essentially revolves his restaurants around a handful of key items. "I take a few signature dishes and make them the core of my restaurants," he says. For example, in Arnie's the star menu attractions are pasta primavera, rack of lamb, and innovative chicken and veal house specialties. Some critics through the years have suggested that Morton focuses more on entertainment than food. However, he has proven himself to be masterful in both areas, continuing to provide Chicagoans with many of its most imaginative menus and visually arresting settings.

His goals are simple: he seeks to achieve the pinnacle within each market segment he enters. Despite the popularity of old-time Chicago steakhouses such as Gene & Georgetti's and Eli's Place for Steak, Morton's has already emerged as a frontrunner. Zorine's was the top discothèque in town until country-western and big band entertainment became a more trendy lure for night-lifers. Morton's solution was simply to transform the disco into a luxurious private French seafood restaurant utilizing the same membership roster.

"These things go in cycles," he explains. "After five years as a disco, Zorine's needed a new shot of life." Together with his partner, French chef extraordinaire Jean Banchet, Morton merchandised Zorine's Club La Mer into one of the city's most prominent seafood spots. As a Continental restaurant in Chicago, Arnie's continues to reign supreme. Whenever a local celebration takes place, Arnie's is more often than not the focal point.

Morton knows how to reverse his course in a marketing strategy if one of his original concepts doesn't seem to be succeeding. Arnie's North, with its elaborate decor and stringent dress code restrictions, was too flashy for most suburbanites. So he devised a method of turning the total space into individual specialty units. The bar area was transformed into Chicagoland's first Hamburger Bar, appealing particularly to families. The lavish buffet offers patrons a selection of forty hot and cold items for those desiring a more formal dining experience, and the Continental menu offers an elegant selection of beef, fowl, veal, and seafood entrees. In the spring of 1981 Morton opened a ninety-seat Pizzeria in Arnie's North's upper-level balcony.

By 1981 Morton's food service empire topped $8 million in sales with a diversity of formats and ticket averages. Arnie's alone climbed over the $3 million mark at an average $19 ticket per person. Arnie's North was hitting $1.5 million with an average ticket of $10.50 in the restaurant, $8.95 at the buffet, and $3.95 in the Hamburger Bar. Morton's was soaring with sales of $2 million at a $23 average ticket. Zorine's Club La Mer should top the $1 million mark its first year in business, with an average tab of $45 per person. But Morton had to shift strategies and open it to the public after it failed to attract a wide enough audience as a membership club.

MERCHANDISING SKILL

Morton's talents as a masterful merchandiser are evidenced strongly at Morton's. With his own unique approach, he set out to establish one of the country's leading steakhouses. He chose an English country theme with informal plastered walls and rough-beamed ceilings. The limited menu, which features 14-ounce double filet mignons, 20-ounce sirloins, 24-ounce porterhouses, and a daily fish selection, is only served for dinner. The freshest vegetables available and six dessert soufflés round out the menu.

Another marketing tool implemented by Morton is his spectacular use of buffets. The thirty-foot-long Grand Buffet at Arnie's North dazzles with over forty different dishes, leaving customers feeling like lost children in a candy store. A sumptuous array of fresh salads, sliced meats, an assortment of foreign and domestic cheeses, fresh cold poached fish, herring, stuffed tomatoes, steak tartare, chopped liver, and curried chicken with raisins are only a few of the featured items. This food presentation on a grand scale is part of Morton's trademark.

In addition to his culinary skills, his promotional savvy is outstanding. When Arnie's staged its seventh anniversary celebration in April 1981 for over five hundred of Chicago's most prominent citizens, Morton used the party as an opportunity to introduce many of his chef's new lighter specialties—boneless duck with wild rice and peaches, sea scallops printaniere, breast of chicken and veal citron. Subsequent business accelerated in the following months due to this spectacular introduction of the new Arnie's dishes.

This combination of quality food, expert merchandising, and promotional skills is Morton's flair. Always with an eye out for the unusual or the exotic, he goes to daring lengths for his restaurants, no matter what they cost. While dining in Paris in 1979, he experienced one of the best seafood dinners he had ever had at La Maree. He was so impressed by the food presentation that he invited La Maree's chef, Gerard Rouillard, to be his guest in America and cook for one week at Arnie's restaurant. Rouillard accepted, and throughout that week in August the French chef prepared a series of spellbinding five-course seafood suppers, at $20 per person. Estimates are that a similar dinner in Paris would have cost nearly $100. Morton went to great expense to accommodate the visiting chef, even constructing a special separate kitchen for his use. Long after Rouillard had returned to his native land, his La Maree house specialties were still being enjoyed at

Arnie's. His treasured secret recipes were shared with Arnie's own chef, Michel Teulet-Cote.

VARIED LIFESTYLE

Out of the dining room, Morton plays the role of corporate executive in an unpretentious crowded office, also located in the Newberry Plaza building. He prefers to have his office cluttered with restaurant memorabilia, old photographs, and magazines rather than be organized and tidy. Somehow order emerges from this chaos as is apparent in the efficient manner in which he runs his restaurants.

When he returns to his suburban Highland Park home, to his five children and Zorine, a different Morton emerges, more low-key and relaxed. Yet even when he's miles away from Arnie's, Morton still lives life at what to most people would seem like a frenetic pace. A solidly built six-footer, he seems to be in perpetual motion twenty-four hours a day. Ideas flow from his fertile mind constantly, and he is known never to be without a large yellow scribbling pad to jot down his flashes. One moment it's an idea for a new restaurant, the next minute he's jotting off a letter to Mayor Jane Byrne suggesting a dining complex at the Navy Pier. But unlike some grand-scale thinkers, Morton's ideas are not all pie-in-the-sky—most of the massive plans he sets out to accomplish he plots out carefully and sees through.

One of his closest friends calls him "creative, flamboyant, and stimulating." He adds: "Morton sometimes jumps off the deep end. I have to remind him that he's not playing with Playboy money anymore. He's now using his own."

Along with his creative outbursts, Morton also has an uncanny knack for getting along with people. Much of his clientele became regulars at his restaurants because Morton made them feel like they are in a warm family setting. He asks them how their children are—he always remembers each child's name—and just generally "kibbitzes" with each table. More than anything else, this is the reason why so many Chicagoans keep coming back for more.

He tends to be a perfectionist in his business dealings and doesn't always project this "nice guy" image in transactions. "Arnie Morton really expects a lot for his money," says James Miller, who has been the interior designer of some of his restaurants. "You have to be on call twenty-four hours a day," Miller attests, recalling that during the one and one-half years he worked on Arnie's restaurant, he was on the job seven days a week.

Margie Korshak, who has handled public relations for the Morton empire since its inception, says that at first she felt Morton was nearly impossible to work for. "He would upset me terribly, screaming about a publicity item that didn't get into the newspaper society columns and slamming the phone down," she recalls. But gradually Korshak became accustomed to Morton's high-powered ways and grew to respect his creativity and openness.

Says Morton of his firecracker style: "I know I'm not a pussycat. I don't want to be one. If I get upset, I let it out right away and then it's over."

As his restaurants expanded in the late 1970s, Morton had to become more of an administrator and less of a "saloonkeeper," a transition he resists. He hates offices and much prefers to be out on the floor mingling with his staff and the customers. Yet by comparison to some of his earlier and wilder days, his life is extremely stable.

TIME FOR FAMILY

His first marriage took place at a fling on a weekend house party just before he entered the army. When the thirty-eight-year-old Morton married Zorine, his life took a more traditional turn. He adored her and listened to her business and personal advice, which helped to establish him as a pillar of both the Highland Park community and the city of Chicago.

Despite his nonstop business pace, Morton always manages to spend time with the kids, who in 1981 ranged from ages eight to eighteen. They frequently ride bikes together as a family on Sundays and have taken several fascinating vacations as a group around the country. He considers himself to be both a father and grandfather to the children, calling them "the best thing I've ever done."

He had twins by his first marriage, Pam and Peter, now aged thirty-three. Pam works for a movie production company, and Peter is a successful fourth generation restaurateur. "If you want to talk about somebody really innovative in this business," Morton beams, "talk about my son Peter. He's a chip off the old block."

Peter opened a restaurant in London at age twenty-two and called it the Great American Disaster, a high-class hamburger emporium which was sold in 1972 to a group which franchised it. The Morton drive deeply engrained in his blood, Peter's next venture was London's Hard Rock Cafe, a restaurant that catered strictly to a youthful audience who queued for hours to sample a casual menu of steaks, hamburgers, salads, and milk shakes. In 1980 Peter returned to the United States and opened Morton's Steakhouse in Beverly Hills, regarded as one of the most star-studded hangouts in the Los Angeles area.

NEW VISIONS

Arnie Morton will never be content with the status quo. He always aspires to try something new, something better. His happiness comes both from running great restaurants and dreaming up new ones. His next ambition? Perhaps a Lido Parisien Revue in Chicago, complete with waterfalls and circus performers. An extravaganza to top all extravaganzas for Morton, but if you look at his past track record, you'll know that this too can be done. He already has a site selected for the 500-seat club within a block of his complex of restaurants, but negotiations are indefinite.

Or, he may sell all his restaurants and concentrate on creating a dining and entertainment spectacle on the Navy Pier. He has already mapped out his game plan: a monorail for transportation to the tip of the pier; fifteen white tablecloth restaurants; twenty fast-food vendors; a 600-room hotel; a marina; a half-acre flower garden; and exclusive retail shops—all enclosed by a glass roof. Just another day and idea in the life of Arnie Morton.

Sounds like a dream? For someone who has made most of his dreams come true—running the top attraction of Rush Street, the best steakhouse, the finest French seafood house, conceiving of Chicago's annual "Taste of Chicago" food festival (a weekend food fair featuring eighty of Chicago's fine restaurants coming together in Grant Park, which draws nearly a million "tasters")—nothing is impossible.

With Arnie Morton, even the most illogical brainstorms become realities because he carries them through with the foresight and courage to stick to his convictions.

Some of his ideas may make Zorine turn prematurely gray, but after all these years she knows that Morton can make the most wildly impractical idea into a profit-making venture. One thing is sure: don't bet against Arnie Morton encountering success in any direction he turns.

SECTION V

The Creative Consultants

For more years than anyone cares to remember, restaurants and evolving chains made their way laboriously on their own. They either failed, succeeded, or finished somewhere in between, based on their individual efforts. But in the 1970s a new breed called "restaurant consultants" sprang up, capitalizing on a need. The restaurant industry had grown so complex that expertise was required in many areas within and outside an operation. This ran the gamut from just plain advice to interior, exterior and kitchen design, menu planning, and devising entire restaurant concepts.

Some felt the idea of an outside consultant was an unnecessary expenditure of time and money. Nevertheless, they were here in force for the maturing restaurant industry and now an entire new industry of restaurant consultants has sprouted around it!

Two of the giants in this consulting field are Joe Baum and George Lang. Each once was an executive with Restaurant Associates. Each operated his own restaurants. Each is based in New York and ranges around the world. Each is obviously expensive. But each has his own distinguishing characteristics and is fiercely competitive.

Baum, with an early upbringing in the Catskills and in hotels, led Restaurant Associates in its peak years of the 1960s with such innovative restaurants as the Newarker, La Fonda del Sol, and the Forum of the Twelve Caesars. His ideas reflected brilliance, but he was often ahead of his times and not all the restaurants were so profitable. His crowning achievement was the intricate web of diversified food service and retail facilities at New York's World Trade Center, topped by the famous Windows on the World restaurant. Now Baum is busy inventing new directions such as "healthy" fast food. He is visualizing the future and realizing his creative dreams through his food service achievements.

Hungarian-born Lang, an expert violinist and skilled in numerous other endeavors, has also brought the focal point of his creativity to restaurants. He has created and designed restaurants throughout the world, to the point where some think he has spread himself too thin. Yet he remains convinced that he can handle the myriad projects. His crowning achievement probably is his own restaurant a few doors from his New York office, Cafe des Artistes. This attracts celebrities from far and wide and offers an appealing value package. He is busy designing combination food service and retail space for a number of shopping centers, fashioning a Middle Eastern fast food chain called Shehi based in Saudi Arabia, and creating a bevy of other projects. One thing is sure: nobody has more projects going at once than Lang, and nobody's mind can focus on ten different points at once as his does.

11

Joe Baum

RESTAURANT MAGICIAN

One day in the early 1960s Joseph H. Baum walked into his Forum of the Twelve Caesars restaurant for lunch and asked the maitre d'hotel, "Did you solve your problem with the consomme yet today?" The stunned maitre d' asked Baum how he could possibly have known there was anything wrong with the consomme, and said it was all right now. "That's fine. I'm glad to hear it," replied Baum.

"How did I know there was anything wrong with the consomme?" Baum asked rhetorically years later. "It's easy. There's always something wrong with the consomme." He could take the obvious like nobody else could and convert it into a masterful way of raising the alertness and quality of his operations.

Joe Baum pays careful attention to every conceivable detail of a restaurant operation, from matchbook covers to wine quality to menu graphics. He calls it plain old common sense, but it's really a special knack of intuition. Using his unorthodox methods, he likes to find out what's wrong with a place, not necessarily just what's right. If a customer nods or shrugs his shoulders in the dining room, Baum knows exactly what the gesture means and takes appropriate action. He also knows from memory what items are on every shelf of the kitchen and senses when things aren't as they should be.

He is a stickler for important details like getting exactly the right table heights and the correct level of lighting. But he also keeps his eye on the broad picture to make sure a restaurant is doing what it's supposed to be doing in terms of carrying through a specific theme with the consumer. He almost always seems to be able to recall applicable information relating to any problem at hand. He has the instincts of a gambler, but never seems to lose. He has a knack for making the right moves in conceiving a restaurant, in the kitchen, and in the front of the house.

CREATIVE MIRACLES

At 5 feet 7 inches, Joe Baum nonetheless towers over everyone. He has an insatiable appetite to excel and inexhaustible enthusiasm to propel him forward on almost any project or series of projects. Rarely does he seem to realize the true food service miracles he has achieved; he is always busy planning for the next one. He reaches for the world of tomorrow before his contemporaries do. He is never content with what is but rather reaches for what can or will be.

Give Joe Baum just one idea for anything, and he'll come up with a hundred ideas to top it. His imaginative mind ranges all over, and he is constantly pondering new concepts for the future. "You've got to stay ahead of the consumer," he says. "Our job is not to react to changes after they happen but rather to initiate changes and new concepts in advance. We've got to be right on target for the future."

This is a man whose creativeness and boldness have revolutionized the food service industry and, to an extent, the American way of life. In the 1950s Joe Baum dared to imagine that an airport restaurant could indeed become a prime attraction for fifty miles around. The Newarker restaurant—which had been deemed by some of the foremost restaurant experts as utter madness—grew and prospered for more years than could be expected at, of all places, New Jersey's Newark Airport.

In the 1960s he dared to imagine that there could be a twenty-four-hour restaurant that wasn't a coffee shop. The result was the Brasserie, a forerunner of similar concepts around the country. He also created, under the banner of Restaurant Associates, the spectacular Four Seasons restaurant with its rotating decor for each season, the Latin American La Fonda del Sol and the Roman Forum of the Twelve Caesars. The latter two did not survive through the 1970s, but they are still regarded as among the great restaurants of the era. Baum's experiments ushered in a Golden Age of restaurants and proved a restaurant didn't have to be French to be great. Nor did it need red plush banquettes and crystal chandeliers.

In the 1970s Joe Baum created an astounding interlocking of multiple diverse food service operations at New York's World Trade Center. They range from the elegant 107th floor Windows on the World to a bevy of informal places, health food places, convertible facilities for retail food, and dining rooms on the main level.

In the 1980s he launched what some felt was an impossible paradox—a nutrition-minded healthy foods chain that was also fast food. And he is intensifying his efforts to find the most potent combination of food service, retail, and merchandising facilities in buildings.

While many of his most notable achievements were accomplished under the corporate umbrella of Restaurant Associates, Joe Baum really is the opposite of a corporate type (which may explain why he and RA came to a parting of the ways in 1970). He is dedicated to individual excellence, but is not unmindful of the practical need for profit. It's just that he wants to attain these goals along his own lines. In essence, he is an entrepreneur—but with a wider vision than just one restaurant. He seeks to influence consumers and their habits and is never content to merely open a place and then stand on his laurels.

It's quite natural that Joe Baum's highest achievements have been in and around New York City. He has had a love affair with the city all his life. He feels much of the grandeur of the city stems from its restaurants—and not vice versa. One of his great personal thrills is the awe-inspiring view of the entire New York area from the Windows on the World restaurant.

FAMILY BACKGROUND

Baum was born August 17, 1920, son of Louis and Anna Baum, owners of the 165-room Gross and Baum Family Hotel in Saratoga Springs, New York, and of a winter resort hotel in Lakewood, New Jersey. Baum took an interest in cooking and food service from the time he was five years old. At the family dining room his mother ran the back of the house, his father the front, and he worked in the pantry. The family had a close identification with Saratoga where Louis and Anna had met when Louis was driving a bakery truck.

Baum was heavily influenced by his parents' tender concern for the customer. "Everything they cooked was done with love," he recalls. His parents would travel to many markets to locate the freshest fruit and vegetables, and they followed with close care every item that was served at meals. This tender, loving care was an attribute that Baum carried over to his restaurants.

Among his courses at Lakewood High School in New Jersey was home economics. After graduation in 1937, he took on an assortment of odd jobs at various hotels, washing dishes and waiting on tables. Then came the Cornell School of Hotel Administration, as Baum sought to combine his love of cooking with formal training in hotel and food servi ɔe administration. To help pay his way through college, he worked as a busboy, waiter, and cook at hotels in New Jersey and Florida. It was on one such job as a desk clerk in Miami that he met a pretty young blonde named Ruth Courtman on the beach. She later became his wife, and they have three children, Hillary, Charles, and Edward.

Baum received a B.S. degree in 1943 from the Cornell Hotel School. But he also made sure he obtained a diversified education, studying Russian and other general subjects as well as the specific hotel administration courses.

After graduation Baum underwent nine months of training in the navy. He became a navy supply corps ensign on a destroyer-minelayer in the Pacific. On the fateful day of April 12, 1945—the day President Franklin Roosevelt died—Baum's ship was cruising off Okinawa when it was attacked by two Kamikaze planes. Baum and the entire crew had to abandon ship. But before going overboard he managed to open the safe, destroy the code and save $70,000 in small bills which he carried off the ship. He and two-thirds of the crew were plucked from the water by another ship hours later. The rest perished. While on the new ship, Baum discovered he had lost some of the small bills in the confusion. To avoid what would have been horrendous red tape when the ship landed, he simply replaced the missing bills with his own money.

He apparently learned more about persistence and detail from his wartime experience, than about food service per se.

CAREER APPRENTICESHIP

Baum's first full-time job after the war was as a management services consultant with Harris Kerr Forster, a consulting and accounting firm. Baum, who had specialized in accounting at the Cornell Hotel School, earned fifty dollars a week, a respectable starting salary in those days. He did extensive reports on food and beverage controls at the Lexington Hotel in Manhattan and at the Hotel St. George in Brooklyn. He would look into how many martinis were sold in any given week or month compared with the same period the previous year. He would often stay up half the night with his wife working on these reports which may have seemed of questionable value. But young Baum was learning discipline as well as statistics.

Visiting a number of Harris Kerr's restaurant clients, Baum found that while creativeness and innovation were highly commendable, the bottom line and investment return on the client's dollar always had to be respected. "You must make good things pay," is the way Baum has always put it. He launched a new beverage accounting system at Harris Kerr.

By 1947 he had risen to supervisor in charge of food and beverage controls for the firm's hotel and restaurant clients. He then became manager of one of the clients, the Monte Carlo restaurant and night club. It just happened that William Zeckendorf, Sr., was owner of the Monte Carlo—and a demanding one at that. Baum marveled at the way Zeckendorf could focus on ten different things, jumping from one to the other with intense concentration on each. Baum himself soon was able to work with chefs, service staffs, customers, and others without missing a beat.

He learned from Zeckendorf how to juggle a variety of responsibilities and to keep track of exactly how many customers were being drawn every night so that adjustments could be made if the counts didn't keep climbing. Zeckendorf once called Baum at 4 A.M. from Mexico to inquire how many covers there had been at dinner that night.

By this time the twenty-nine-year-old Baum knew the basics of food, wine, and management, but he wanted to learn more about styling. He always had a feeling that restaurants were really another form of theater, so he signed on with Norman Bel Geddes for two years as a director. Bel Geddes, known for his lavish designs of Broadway productions, also was a hotel and restaurant designer. He wasn't afraid to take risks and try new things, and he constantly encouraged Baum to do something different in design at each hotel or restaurant.

It wasn't long before Baum was ready for the next challenge, and he joined the Schine Hotels group in Florida as restaurant operations director. His father, who had moved to Miami Beach in the 1930s, had told him during the Depression that Miami was overbuilt and a good place to stay away from. "I really didn't believe him then," Baum recalls, "but by 1979 it finally was overbuilt for the business that was available. It took a long time, but my father was proven right."

The Schine chain included the Roney Plaza in Miami Beach, the Boca Raton Hotel and Club, the Ambassador in Los Angeles and fifteen other properties. Baum proceeded to launch all types of innovative concepts for the hotel chain's restaurants. He couldn't do otherwise, for he was never content with continuing the same formula. His new styles of service and table settings attracted attention from New York executives visiting Florida.

NEWARKER SURPRISE

An interesting development was taking place in New York at the time. Abe Wechsler, a coffee supplier, had turned over the presidency of his Riker's chain of twenty-four-hour counter restaurants to his young son-in-law, Jerry Brody. Total annual sales for the twenty-four lunch counters and two cafeterias were only $4.5 million. Brody knew something would have to be done to spur the fledgling company's growth and decided to take a chance. He signed a lease to open a restaurant at Newark Airport under the banner of his newly formed company, Restaurant Associates. But now he had to find someone to launch and operate the restaurant, someone with a creative flair who could persuade customers that they should go to the airport to eat rather than to fly.

Brody heard about Baum's innovations in Florida. He set up an appointment to meet Baum one day in 1953 and was so impressed that he hired him on the spot. Brody was then thirty and Baum thirty-two, and they were to prove a potent team.

They agreed a superb chef was needed to make the team complete. Baum recalled that a few years earlier he had met Albert Stockli, a Swiss who wove his own magic in small Atlantic City hotel kitchens. Baum never forgot a lunch he had with Stockli in a basement kitchen. Anyone who could make Swiss barley soup and other superb dishes as did Stockli could be invaluable in developing a quality airport restaurant. He was hired as the Newarker chef and was delighted to move northward along the New Jersey Shore. His creativeness would help spark the food at a number of Restaurant Associates restaurants over the years.

When Baum and Stockli got the Newarker open in late 1953, everyone in the industry was predicting disaster. Even Restaurant Associates itself wasn't sure. After all, the restaurant was two flights up and had no escalator. Since there was little air travel at Newark Airport then because of a series of plane crashes in nearby Elizabeth, most of the business would have to come from residents within twenty-five or even fifty miles who would make a special trip to the airport to dine. It hardly seemed plausible, but Baum made it so.

He poured in time, money, and effort to fashion a restaurant better than he had envisioned. He insisted on quality china. He thrived on unique merchandising touches that would lure the customers from miles away and on projecting a price-value image. He served seven oysters instead of the usual six and dramatized it by placing the extra oyster on a small plate next to the main plate. He also served huge Absecon oysters which customers had to cut with a knife.

Other Baum touches, implemented by Stockli, were flambéed

shashlik, shrimp in fruited mustard sauce and flaming desserts. The initial investment in the Newarker was so large that it lost money as expected for two years. But by 1955 word had gotten around New Jersey and New York about the sensational airport restaurant, and it began to prosper. It is said that more people went to Newark Airport for the restaurant than to fly. Children would plead with their parents to take them to the new airport restaurant so they could partake of desserts topped with fiery sparklers. Annual volume reached $3 million at its peak.

The way Baum sees it, "We created at the Newarker a truly hospitable aura, with warmth and personal service, in food service, appointments, and control." More than that, the successful experiment indicated to Brody and Baum and Restaurant Associates that this same magic need not be isolated to airport locations, that it could be repeated in new types of New York City restaurants.

RESTAURANT EMPIRE

Over the next decade, Baum fashioned an empire of restaurants that sparkled with his resourcefulness and were the envy of the industry—at least artistically. They were highly profitable too for a while until soaring rental, food, and labor costs started outpacing the volume growth. Baum was aided considerably in these innovations by a wide range of top creative talents brought into Restaurant Associates. They included George Lang, Stuart Levin, Tom Margittai, Paul Kovi, Allen Lewis, Jim Armstrong, Pat Terrail, and others who today read like an all-star cast through much of the industry. It was the greatest assemblage of restaurant talent ever in one place, and so perhaps it was inevitable that the most creative concepts would emerge under Baum's leadership.

Baum's array of leading restaurants under the Restaurant Associates banner included La Fonda del Sol, Forum of the Twelve Caesars, the Four Seasons, the Tower Suite in the Time-Life building, Mamma Leone's, Trattoria, Charley O's, and Charlie Brown's. There also were more popularly priced places such as Zum Zum, Hungry Charley's on college campuses, the International House of Pancakes (a franchise), and Brasserie, one of the first of a new generation of "coffee shops" that were not really coffee shops.

Baum thrived on individual challenges. When he was given the task of building a restaurant on the ground floor of the Time-Life building, he immediately thought of his long-term interest in Latin America. This was the origination of La Fonda del Sol, which he liked to call "a fantasy fairyland." To implement his theme, he traveled all over Latin America collecting puppets, dolls, and toys to decorate the restaurant. He and a crew of decorators and chefs obtained colorful artifacts from Peru, Guatemala, and Mexico to adorn the walls.

The $3 million investment in this restaurant was immense, and in those days even New Yorkers did not expect to pay such high prices for Latin American food. Peak volume barely topped $3 million, and Restaurant Associates' management finally felt it had to cut back on the scope of the operation and on the fancy decorations. After fifteen years La Fonda closed, a wrenching personal blow to Baum. He maintained it could have succeeded had it stuck with its original objectives, lavish as they were. He later was at least partially vindicated in the sense that if Restaurant Associates could have held on for another few years until New Yorkers understood and craved for Latin American cuisine as they did in the 1970s, La Fonda could have been a financial success. It might be doing $12 million annual sales today.

Although not everyone agreed with Baum on his ambitious projects, he was respected for remaining true to the original objectives. When he launched the Forum of the Twelve Caesars at Rockefeller Center, he insisted on calling it a Roman rather than Italian restaurant. Everything had to be truly representative of the Roman empire. When spigots representing busts of Roman emperors were screwed on, they were stolen. Baum promptly ordered replacements from Italy and this time had them welded on. He researched the Roman theme completely in museums and libraries throughout Italy. Wine glasses, silverware, and service plates in the Forum authentically reflected the Roman era. The Forum prospered as a complete theme restaurant for over a decade, but the neighborhood and finances changed. After twenty years the Forum finally closed.

THE FOUR SEASONS

The Four Seasons was another Baum special, in the Seagram Building on New York's fashionable upper East Side. Revisions in the menu and decor were implemented quarterly, and New Yorkers loved the change of pace, the elegance, and the nouvelle cuisine that was being launched. Baum's designs for the glassware became part of a permanent collection at the Museum of Modern Art. Volume soared to a $4 million annual peak, and then started dropping.

An elemental lesson emerged that might apply to some of the other great restaurants. While Restaurant Associates as a corporation was running the Four Seasons, the restaurant didn't receive the sustained commitment that it did in the late 1970s when Paul Kovi and Tom Margittai took it over as entrepreneurs. Just the idea of their being on the scene constantly and having full ownership worked wonders as the volume—which had plummeted to $1.5 million—again climbed to the $4 million mark and beyond. Joe Baum's magic could not continue indefinitely on any restaurant in a corporate environment. Or perhaps the Restaurant Associates empire had grown to a point where it was exceedingly difficult to control.

Baum conceived the Four Seasons as an American classic restaurant. He launched wine merchandising on a grand scale there and created a sensitivity to wine as part of the meal. He also was one of the first to emphasize California wines in an elegant setting. He offered the incredible bargain of two bottles of wine for $8. When Kovi and Margittai ran the Four Seasons under Restaurant Associates, objectives were different. A corporation could not take risks and devote total concentration to the restaurant as Kovi and Margittai could once they personally owned it. This was their baby, and they made the most of it.

VARIED THEMES

With La Fonda del Sol, the Forum, and the Four Seasons, Baum introduced the idea of serious theme restaurants as opposed to the "offbeat" types of themes prevalent in so many places. Baum would go to any extreme to carry through his theme of changing foods for each season at the Four Seasons. He did not hesitate to fly in items from countries throughout the world to represent each season: wild mushrooms, grouse, cheeses, oysters. He also insisted on making wine available to the public at reasonable prices.

Each of his restaurants was designed to capture a different segment of the market. For example, Trattoria was a lighter-type Italian restaurant while Zum Zum catered to a different type of customer with German counter girls and Bavarian-type fast service. Charlie Brown's, near Grand Central Station, was geared to the commuter market.

Baum moved up to Restaurant Associates president in 1963, and by 1965 Restaurant Associates had diversified under his leadership to a wide-ranging 130 restaurants and food service operations. These included food service facilities at Bear Mountain State Park, Central Park, the World's Fair, and the Orange Bowl stadium in Miami. In addition, there were now Restaurant Associates food service operations at airports, schools, and various stadiums.

Baum loved it best when he was creating a new concept, when a restaurant was in its formative stages and new ideas were being born. He loved to see the mix of customers at his varied places. But by the late 1960s some of the glitter was gone from his efforts. Although Restaurant Associates sales had jumped to over $100 million, bottom line pressures were building. The order went out from the boardroom to curb many of the creative efforts and stick with basics. Restaurant Associates wanted to diversify outside of New York City. It didn't have the same tender feelings for the city as did Baum. He understood the reasoning but was severely disappointed at the board's action.

Baum's ability to immerse himself totally in the food service challenges at hand was dramatically demonstrated when he kept feeling severe stomach pains during Restaurant Associates board of directors meetings in the last several months he was there. He assumed the severe pains were caused by pressures during the meetings, and he kept to a business-as-usual attitude throughout. He finally discovered, however, that the pain had a definite physical cause when his appendix burst and he was seriously ill with peritonitis. But he managed to recover from the illness and build a whole new team somewhere else.

NEW ENTERPRISE

Discouraged but not defeated, Baum left Restaurant Associates to form his own Joseph H. Baum Co. This move was almost inevitable from the first as Joe Baum was always an entrepreneur in spirit. Most of all, he sought control of situations—something not entirely feasible in a corporate environment with multiple authorities. So it was altogether natural that he would take his energies and creative talents to his own company and set out on what was to become the key challenge of his career—developing food service at the huge World Trade Center.

His first task as a consultant was to devise a master plan for food service in the World Trade Center. He didn't do things on a small scale, so the plans he drafted were monumental. In fact, only one person was probably capable of implementing such plans: Joseph H. Baum himself. By 1974 the Port Authority of New York and New Jersey, which owned the World Trade Center, awarded the food service contract to Hilton International. Hilton International in turn formed a special subsidiary called Inhilco and named Baum president. It seemed inevitable that Hilton International would be chosen as an international company for the new center that had an international flavor. It was equally inevitable that Joe Baum would be chosen to run it. He had the creative flair to accomplish anything, and given the wide-ranging spaces of the 107-floor World Trade Center he now had the latitude to put all his creative instincts to maximum use.

WORLD TRADE CENTER

Counting the time he first signed a contract in late 1970 to design the whole feeding system at the World Trade Center, Baum spent six years developing the thinking and actuality for the vast spectrum of twenty-two diverse food service places in one building, ranging from fast-food units to full-service restaurants with a variety of food service and retail shops in between. He wanted to have everything available in the World Trade Center to serve all types of palates and pocketbooks. He also had a commitment to serve everything as fresh and natural as possible on the premises.

Just as experts had confidently predicted people would not go to an airport for dinner during an earlier phase of Baum's career, they now said nobody would go all the way downtown to the World Trade Center for dinner or drinks, or both, at night. They were just as wrong then as they had been earlier.

The intricate web of food service operations at the World Trade Center turned on one large central kitchen. This was the center of Baum's new glittering galaxy and it made everything economical and feasible. He built in central system efficiencies and bulk purchasing which enabled him to save a critical 2 percent on food and beverage costs, compared with what the costs would be if each place were operated as a separate restaurant.

While weaving all the food service operations together into a delicate blend, Baum also tried to treat each as his own individual restaurant. He constantly refined and refigured the tones of each one. He was never satisfied that things couldn't be further improved.

A stickler for maximum quality control, Baum tried to prove that one could feed huge numbers of people without sacrificing quality and variety. His concept at the World Trade Center was to reduce massive spaces into personalized smaller operations that would sport diversity and quality. These smaller, personalized units—in preference perhaps to huge cafeterias—had a feeling of freshness. In the midst of this individuality, cost savings were realized with a central kitchen and central services for baking rolls, dishwashing, garbage disposal, and other functions.

WINDOWS ON THE WORLD

The crown jewel of Baum's new empire was the 107th floor Windows on the World complex with its spectacular fifty-mile views and food that was of remarkable quality for what in some ways was a mass feeding complex. On a clear day one could almost see forever from these windows. Baum overcame the age-old problem of customers vying for the best view seats by somehow creating them equal. All the tables had equally perfect views. They were designed methodically so that each one appeared to be on a special high level. In the circular format each table was easily accessible from the kitchen. (No detail is left untouched by Baum.)

Windows on the World actually consists of a main dining room called The Restaurant, an Hors d'Oeuverie with wide assortments, a Cellar in the Sky where five special wines are served with dinner for thirty persons each evening, numerous banquet rooms and banquet facilities on the 106th floor, and meeting rooms. Total volume by 1981 was pushing toward $20 million. Even with some 2,500 persons eating there daily, Baum managed to maintain quality and a price-value which offered full price-fixed dinners in the $20 range. He emphasized a cold buffet table with appetizers from around the world, selections of varied entrees and outstanding desserts. The legendary main bar was called the Great Bar or City Lights bar. It carried some thousand different labels, and a mirrored ceiling enabled customers to see drinks being poured. Windows on the World converted into a private club for lunch and was taking in $1 million annual dues for 4,000 members.

A full 107 floors below, on the Concourse level where thousands emerge and converge daily from the subways and PATH trains, is Baum's Market Square of food service operations. These are strategically placed to grab the commuters going both ways and for the 50,000 occupants of the building (some of whom are numbered among the 80,000 daily business visitors there).

One section is a Coffee Exchange, a small kiosk which manages to serve some 1,000 breakfasts, then gears up for lunch, and still later becomes a coffee and tea retailing place. There there's the Market Bar and Dining Rooms which at a luncheon price of perhaps $10 per person some consider preferable to Windows on the World. Desserts and a number of the other items are the same as at Windows on the World and come from the same central services.

INTRICATE SYSTEM

Within the Market Square, a Big Kitchen complex consists of the Coffee Exchange, a Raw Bar, Nature's Pantry healthy foods restaurant with a retail annex, a delicatessen, bakery, rotisserie, grill, and soda fountain. All cooking areas and grills are in the open for the customer to see. In this intricate web each server at each counter takes care of the food preparation and the money. This speeds service and makes the individual server responsible for food quality. Then all the places convert to retail space for commuters who want to buy food on the way home. Baum has left no stone untouched in this ingenious complex.

But how does food in daily abundance travel from the central services basement to the 107th floor? This has always been a challenge for top-of-skyscraper restaurants, but particularly so in this much higher case. What happens is that a specially padded elevator transports the food. There is a complete system for controlled distribution and purchasing projections.

Oh yes. Perhaps as an afterthought but still very much in the picture, Baum launched a 44th-floor Sky Dive snack shop to lure customers for breakfast and lunch from surrounding floors within the building. This one proved a disappointment for years as Baum and others struggled to find the right combination which in effect could successfully compete with some of the Concourse level places—particularly Eat and Drink and the Corner, both of which served breakfast and lunch.

By 1981 the World Trade Center food service that Baum created was grossing over $32 million in annual sales, including over $20 million from the Windows on the World complex and extensive banquet facilities. Baum's multi-use of each food service operation for different meal periods and for retailing made this an exceptionally productive use of large amounts of space. Other buildings such as New York's Citicorp Center would try to blend in a number of restaurants and fail; any such combination needed the fine tuning that a master such as Baum could provide.

DIVERSE PROJECTS

Meanwhile, he had retained his own consulting company and by 1978 had designed Anderson's Food Center in Hiroshima, an eight-floor retail and restaurant complex in a landmark building. He also created and opened food services at the National Gallery in Washington, D.C., and a lunchtime community for the Lutheran Aid

Association in Appleton, Wisconsin. Nobody could say that Baum wasn't diverse in his projects. But whatever he did, he saw a unique vision that nobody else did.

In late 1978, while remaining a food service consultant to the World Trade Center, he resumed the presidency of the Joseph H. Baum Co. He liked to create and innovate and not necessarily to merely implement once his creative systems were in place. Thus he was ready to move on to new challenges. Over the next few years he redeveloped the food service and food retailing space in the Crown Center, Kansas City; translated Sesame Street into a learning center for food and nutrition with a fast-food operation called the Sesame Food Factory; set up the themes and merchandising for consumer amenities at Fisher Brothers' Park Avenue Plaza; was an adviser on a new master plan for consumer services and amenities in Central Park, and was a restaurant consultant for W. R. Grace.

"HEALTHY" FAST FOOD

The Sesame Food Factory, opened in eastern Pennsylvania in late 1980, was one of his most intriguing concepts. It introduced a new market segment called nutritional fast food. Whole grain and natural fresh ingredients predominate in the menu, which still offers fast-food prices of under $2.50 per person and fast service. It remains to be seen whether other such places will spring up, but Baum's idea was a revolution in itself. It personified his conviction that the consumer would seek natural wholesome foods in any form whether it was fast food or gourmet dining. The 1980s would be the true nutritional decade, Baum felt, as he continued to size up future trends before they became obvious to other people. He also knew how to implement specific concepts for these trends once he had thought about it long enough.

"Why can't we change the form of fast food?" Baum asked when people questioned his nutritional approach, which actually was a cornerstone of his World Trade Center operations too. "After all, fast food is well-known to the public. When you combine this with consumer drives for nutritional food, you have a winning combination." If it had been done before, Baum didn't want to do it again. He wanted to completely change the form and direction of what others had done. Not that he wasn't closely aware of almost everything that was happening in the industry. It was just that he wanted to change it.

Baum focused on retailing ideas just as readily as food service. He saw both as a form of theater or entertainment and wanted to make them enjoyable experiences. He radiated happiness whenever his cash registers indicated by consistent strong sales that his intuition about what the consumer wanted had been proved right again. His uncanny instinct, based on solid research and "hunches," was correct on so many occasions that one would have thought he had a foolproof crystal ball, although he modestly would claim it was simply trial and error.

QUALITY DRIVE

Quality and flavor are the two prime ingredients that customers will demand for the 1980s, Baum insists. Price, value, decor, and other factors may enter into it, but as he aptly puts it, "The customer today wants to sense and taste certain textures and flavors." This was the theme of his Market Square complex at the World Trade Center, a monument to his personal aspirations. It also was the theme of Sesame Place and of Baum's entire future thinking. He always looked for self-satisfaction by trying to top yesterday's project with a better one tomorrow.

He declares that customers are "hungry for real foods, the smell of cooking, strong tastes, care and human contact." He warns that as a noted psychologist said, "If you eat enough precooked, frozen, reheated foil-and-plastic lunches out of machines, part of you will starve to death."

Baum deplores an industry philosophy which, as he terms it, says "automate, eradicate jobs and entire job categories. Keep employees away from customers as much as possible. Let customers do the work themselves . . . at salad bars or cook-your-own-dessert cop-outs." He points out that one of the reasons franchise units have encountered difficulties is "because their cold, hard impersonal efficiencies weren't what the customers really wanted." In short, Baum says, customers don't want to be fed by machines or robots. "They want to be served, not fed . . . and by people, not contraptions."

Some of Baum's thinking which he puts into practice: "Improve the workplace. Intensify levels of service. Become more expressive in your products and less stereotyped. Increase the opportunity for customer contact with employees. Build in more human contact."

He feels that every type of food service must be kept individualized and humanized. "If we persist in the mindless elimination of service from a service industry," he warns, "if we let machines dehumanize the restaurant workers and the restaurant patrons, we're deceiving ourselves. We must not confuse efficiency with excellence."

TASTE AND TEXTURE

It's not enough to produce textured brick walls and rough-sawn wood counters, Baum emphasizes. "But we must begin putting taste and texture on the plate . . . People must be able to feel what they're eating." Convinced that as an industry "we have to produce the kind of food that people will trust us for," he warns that "if a big chunk of America lies awake at night listening to its arteries slamming shut after eating in our restaurants, we are all in trouble. If that means no more frying, if that means we must develop new methods of cooking, that is a proper application of technology." At the present pace, he speculates there simply won't be enough "fresh, pure unadulterated food to go around."

In Baum's view a restaurant reflects the fashion and temper of its times and doesn't create anything per se. He saw the 1960s as "roaring, soaring, glittering times" and noted that "the good restaurants expressed that exuberance. They brought drama and excitement to eating out. They were great fun. My mistress (restaurants such as La Fonda del Sol, Forum of the Twelve Caesars, and the Four Seasons) was everybody's darling."

Describing "the greening of the restaurant industry," Baum says that by the early 1970s this mistress was "losing some of her charms, sagging a bit. Her basic sincerity, the honest value of her hospitality, was too often cheapened by operators who misjudged her crowd of admirers. In place of my lady's true virtues, the crowd began to find overpriced imitation, dressed-up pretension, second-rate quality. Instead of considerate, personal attention, they found standardized, prepackaged formulas. And those admirers, the best market the food service industry ever had seen, stopped coming around. They felt my mistress had done them wrong. She had lost the essence of what they'd found so attractive."

A recession was only one factor in a slump which hit the restaurant industry in the early 1970s. "What really destroyed the faith of the faithful," Baum says, "was the business itself. It became its own worst enemy." But the slump was followed by an upturn from 1976 to 1978, then a downturn again. This was part of the business cycle. Baum felt that to gain extra momentum during an upturn and to resist downward tendencies during a minus cycle, one has to be prepared with dramatic innovations that will give consumers the texture and feel they are seeking in an entertaining atmosphere.

DOWNTOWN REVITALIZATION

Baum's molding of the World Trade Center into a vibrant food service complex was probably his outstanding achievement. It must be remembered that when the idea was first germinating in the early 1970s, the downtown area around the site was a depressed zone. Few people would venture there at night. Basically there were no restaurants of note in the area. But the World Trade Center and Baum's food service facilities became highly desirable to the public. They created a viable seven-day retailing and restaurant business with underground parking in the building, complete security, and easy access. This was the catalyst that transformed the entire area and caused other first-class restaurants and hotels to sprout in places that previously were regarded as unpopular.

Windows on the World is literally the foyer of New York City. It lifted the spirits of the area and the entire city when it opened in 1976 in time for the bicentennial celebrations. People always told Baum throughout his career that each project he tackled was admirable but wouldn't jell. "Never say never," was Baum's advice after each success.

He fell in love with each project he approached. His enthusiasm and confidence generated one unique restaurant after another. He consistently carried through on his idea that a restaurant's function was to give pleasure to customers. He fashioned each restaurant into a practical fulfillment of his fantasies.

Joe Baum was born to make a difference, to make an impact on humanity. He has done it through food service in the most positive sense.

12

George Lang

MAN FOR ALL SEASONS

When George Lang was born at his parents' home in Hungary in 1924, the midwife kept dipping him back and forth between ice water and hot water as was her habit. It was her way of confirming that everything was fine with the baby. From then on, Lang lived by the credo, "pleasure in variety." Literally almost from birth people have been asking the question: What makes George run?

By the time he was a teen-ager in Hungary, he was able to write a special Latin inscription in one of his most treasured school books to project his philosophy. To nobody's surprise it read *varietas delectat,* "pleasure in variety." George Lang is a personification of the adage that variety is the spice of life. He has never wanted to be confined to one field or one interest although he concentrates much of his limitless energy on the area where he has built his reputation in the United States—restaurants and restaurant consulting.

Lang at various times has been a master violinist, tailor, waiter, chef, busboy, maitre d'hotel, caterer, manager of leading restaurants, food and travel writer and columnist for *Travel & Leisure* ("Table for One"), television food commentator for CBS's "Sunday Morning" program, photographer, author, calligrapher, designer of tableware, collector of antique watches, and master cook for legendary events and parties in his own kitchen-dining room.

Although he had accomplished a great deal by 1981, when he was in his mid-fifties, he had hardly scratched the surface of his multi-faceted talents. But it's not from lack of trying. In one typical week he would speed from New York to Phoenix, to Beverly Hills, to Dallas, and perhaps end up in Europe for a day. He thrives on his racehorse pace and is probably unhappy only when he has a chance to completely relax and "do nothing," which just doesn't happen. There are too many thoughts filtering through his mind for him ever to be without a creative idea or a multiplicity of such ideas.

Sometimes his ideas are not related to design, accouterments, food beverages, interiors or any other connected subject. Rather they are mental doodles as a form of relaxation. Examples of some of Lang's creative future plan "fun" doodles which he never really intended to implement—most of them are clearly spoofs—are lobster-flavored soda, a soup plate with a built-in blower, a typewriter with each key a full sentence of cliches, a world map with movable borders, a see-through apron for bottomless dancers who want to cook, and a bathtub made of soap. His recent *Lang's Compendium of Culinary Nonsense and Trivia*, showing another facet of his talents, is a notable success.

Lang is usually on the go from 6 A.M. to midnight, moving in every direction. He knows the virtues and ingredients of virtually every gourmet dish, but as a practical matter often prefers a salad and cottage cheese to save time. He enjoys whatever he is doing at the moment although he always has a specific short-term and long-term plan for his crowded schedule and for every project. He thrives on five hours' sleep and has an alarm clock implanted in his mind. When an idea penetrates his subconscious while he is sleeping, he leaps up and jots it down on a note pad next to his bed. This can happen any number of times a night, and many of his most creative ideas originate just this way.

Lang's appearance can be deceptive. Balding and rather short, he fixes his blue-eyed gaze with absolute concentration on the person he is talking to. This can overwhelm some people. He has a unique physical and mental energy—either a born talent, developed, or a combination of both—that carries him through sleepless days and nights, endless meetings, wine tastings, and food tastings. It's no wonder he has earned a reputation for possessing a "stainless steel stomach."

WIDE-RANGING ACTIVITIES

He has bottled burgundy under his own label; arranged parties for Queen Elizabeth II, Premier Khrushchev, and dozens of heads of state in various hotels and restaurants; designed restaurants and nightclubs for luxury cruise ships; was probably the first American restaurateur to visit China in 1977; operates his own restaurant, Cafe des Artistes; wrote the restaurant and gastronomy entries for the Encyclopedia Britannica; designed a kitchen, called one of the finest, in his own home; serves on the board of Carnegie Hall, and has written articles for a number of major magazines.

Among other things he has been called "the Herman Kahn of food and drink"; "the renaissance man of the restaurant industry"; "the maestro of restaurants"; a person "whose purpose in this world is to think about restaurants"; and "certainly someone who the planet will know was here." *The New Yorker* seemed to sum it up best, saying that Lang combines "the head of a scientist with the heart of an artist, and the ingenuity of a used-car salesman with the energy of a marathon runner."

CREATIVE INNOVATION

When it comes to innovation, Lang is at his best. In the late 1970s he designed the food service facilities at Loews Monte Carlo Hotel and emphasized certain individual touches to capture the prevailing mood. Thus it was that for the hotel's poolside menu, he had a portrayal of a pretty woman lying on a beach with real straps that the customer must open to see the menu. For whatever reason, business thrived at this particular location.

In New York's new luxury Palace Hotel he designed a dessert wagon which holds ice cream for the meal period. And in Los Angeles he is

designing a club where each booth will be an information center and
club members can obtain information about the weather, flight schedules, and stock market quotations as well as communicate with office
or home.

Lang even managed to transform the former space that housed the
Democratic National Headquarters to productive restaurant use. With
three years of effort in the late 1970s, he designed the plush forty-two-
seat Jean Louis restaurant on the site of the renovated Watergate Hotel.

Darting about in every direction and to every corner of the globe as
president of the George Lang Corporation, he numbers among his
recently completed and present projects a new Middle East fast-food
prototype called Shehi; merchandising the Beverly Center, a 100,000
square foot rooftop complex of thirty-five restaurants and food shops at
a new shopping center being spawned in Beverly Hills; a multi-
purpose restaurant and "music room" at the Doubletree Inn, Kansas
City; a new casual self-service dining concept called Jennie's Cookery
for W. R. Grace in Southern California; the food and beverage facilities
for a new addition to New York's Museum of Modern Art; restaurants at
New York's Palace Hotel; the Soho Charcuterie at the Ann Taylor
specialty store off Fifth Avenue in New York; with the personal
involvement of President Marcos, the restaurants at the luxurious
Manila Hotel in the Philippines; and the King Cole restaurant at New
York's St. Regis Hotel.

This list is just a sample of the scope of his many projects. Lang
indeed oversees an empire of diversified projects around the world as a
restaurant "consultant." Some view a consultant's role as "the last stop"
or "the end of the trail." But for Lang, it's really just the beginning as he
tries to put together all the ingredients to achieve his dreams. He is a
realist but a perfectionist and is seldom fully satisfied with the results
of his latest project.

He views his business as primarily pleasure, not work. But there are
times when he has to drive himself and exercise intense discipline to
accomplish an objective. He knows how to jump from one thing to
another and concentrate each time on the task at hand. By conservative
estimates he travels 250,000 miles a year and eats in as many as fifty
restaurants a week during special research trips.

STEADY CLIMB

Lang is strictly a product of on-the-job training. He learned many different disciplines over the years but had to coordinate his skills to be successful at whatever he tried. He never had a natural progression from one thing to another and thus was constantly in the position he relished—of learning by doing. He actually had the advantage of dealing with most problems from scratch and being able to devise original solutions, whereas most people rely on knowledge previously gathered. "Others use their minds as computers and reach solutions based on past experience," Lang says. "I opt for the innovative solution to problems rather than being dragged down by what's gone before. I am aware of the background, but I'm not consumed by it." (This is what's behind his drive always to find fresh angles in a situation.)

Lang was brought up in Hungary in the 1930s when the upward mobile middle class was striving to achieve more status. He recalls his own parents trying to emulate certain elements of the manners of the upper classes even though the middle classes were the educated ones. In the process, however, he received a "proper" upbringing—with all the elements of good manners—which he feels everyone should have.

Seeking a broad background in liberal arts, Lang studied Latin, Hungarian literature, and philosophy at the University of Szeged in southern Hungary. Interestingly, years later he would urge his son, Brian Simpson Lang, to strive for a specific education geared to a definite vocation. Yet Lang would continue to cling to his insistence that the best training and discipline were unstructured ones where an individual could obtain a broad educational background and then progress in a series of challenging jobs.

VIOLIN MAESTRO

Lang fell in love with the violin at an early age and also tried his hand with moderate success at poetry and short story writing. He studied the violin avidly and although he wouldn't have become a Heifetz, with his native talent and dedication he might have come close. In his early twenties he decided against it as a career because he wanted a field and a lifestyle that would allow far more individual freedom. "Being a violinist was a very limited life," he notes, "and I never wanted to be tied down to any constant 9-to-5 routine, or any routine at all." Certainly 6 A.M. to midnight would be more Lang's speed. Decades later, Harold Schonberg, senior music reviewer of *The New York Times*, wrote that "George Lang invented food and probably music too in one afternoon."

With an instinctive knack for improvising, Lang put on his most virtuoso violin performance as a twenty-year-old youth in Hungary at the end of World War II. One day he found himself facing a number of Russian soldiers who invaded the basement of the apartment house where the tenants had taken refuge. When they spotted the violin case, they insisted he play the violin for them, and play he did throughout the night for almost eight straight hours at gunpoint. Whatever selections he may have chosen, they apparently kept the Russian soldiers happy enough so they finally left without doing any further harm.

If Lang wasn't totally disillusioned with postwar Europe then, he certainly was within another year. "It represented everything I didn't want," he says. "The new world in the United States seemed much closer to my spirit and my way of life." This was true; yet Hungary and Central Europe always remained very much in his blood. Years later, when he was well-established as director of the Four Seasons restaurant in New York, he was delighted that his staff fashioned him a birthday cake shaped like a globe. Only one country—Hungary—covered the entire globe. He also wrote *The Cuisine of Hungary* in 1973 and launched his own Hungaria restaurant in New York in the late 1970s.

In any case Lang managed to escape in 1946 from Stalinist Hungary to Austria where he won a scholarship to the Mozart Academy of Salzburg. Eventually he found his way to a U.S. Army troop movement ship and—packed in like a sardine—made his way to the promised land. He was amazed at the variety of foods offered on the ship. It was his first exposure to any real diversity of food, and he was impressed and overwhelmed. He had been accustomed to no choices in food, but rather only specific courses for each meal. He had an arduous time trying to decide which type of soup or which dessert he wanted in the ship's cafeteria. He would finally make his decision when sailors advised him not to dawdle on the line.

LIFE IN THE UNITED STATES

When Lang finally arrived in New York, he was fascinated by the Horn & Hardart automats (leading attractions for years until they were converted to more profitable Burger Kings in the late 1970s). He also discovered a favorite store at Forty-first Street and Ninth Avenue off Times Square, where he could buy a loaf of old bread for a penny.

One of his earliest jobs in the United States was as a violinist with the Dallas Symphony Orchestra. Here he did well but was not the star. He wanted to establish his own uniqueness in a creative field and decided to try something else. He recalls going to bed one night as a musician and waking up as a cook. He was a $46-a-week cook (a standard wage in those days) and earned his citizenship in 1949. How Lang managed to cut in half the usual five-year wait to become a citizen was never explained. But it was typical of the way he always carved a path around red tape to accomplish his objective.

Within a four-year period, he worked in a couple of dozen restaurants and nightclubs in every position from potager to chef in the United States, Italy, and Austria. When he felt he had learned what one place could offer, he moved on to the next one.

At one point Lang wanted to gain experience with a "name" restaurant and took a job as a busboy with the old Reuben's restaurant in New York. He then rose through a series of restaurant jobs. He was successively a waiter, captain, headwaiter, and manager. Then he found himself operating a wedding catering firm near the Bowery. One of the customers liked what Lang was doing so much that he recommended him to the famous Claudius Charles Philippe of the Waldorf Astoria. Philippe, a taskmaster, was impressed with Lang and hired him. He proceeded to teach Lang showmanship as well as food merchandising. Lang recalls learning "how to sell what were blintzes on Wednesday morning as crepes Suzette on Saturday night."

Lang learned from Philippe how to juggle numerous tasks simultaneously and do them well. He would watch Philippe concentrate intently on three different things at the same time. "If he could do it, so could I," Lang figured.

Utilizing the diversified talents he had learned and acquired, he next became a vice president with Brass Rail restaurants, known for family dining and—of all things—cheesecake. During his two years there he opened several restaurants at Kennedy Airport and in other cities. Soon he made the jump to Restaurant Associates, diversified operator of a multitude of restaurants in the New York area and the home in the 1960s of the most creative talent in the industry. Lang began as a project director for the Tower Suite restaurant and Hemisphere Club.

He headed Restaurant Associate's World's Fair Restaurants in 1964-65, which included private clubs, dining rooms, an employee cafeteria and perhaps the first luxury restaurant based on American regional cuisine (Festival 64/65). He set aside one private dining room especially for Henry Ford, should he drop by, which he did only rarely. But it never hurt to be prepared.

For a while he operated the Four Seasons restaurant, following the World's Fair period, during which time he produced the first Four Seasons cookbook.

NEW CONSULTANT

Inevitably, after 10 years with Restaurant Associates, he grew restless in a corporate environment despite the latitude he was given on many projects. He started thinking seriously in 1970 about going into his own consulting business where he could exercise his creative talents to the maximum. Fate and contacts moved him quickly along his path. No sooner had he started thinking than the phone rang. It was Marriott Corp. president Willard Marriott, Jr., asking if he could help develop specialty restaurants for the food service and hotel chain. Just a few hours later, Loews Hotels chairman Robert Tisch called to see if he might be interested in helping with European expansion plans.

Lang was in business as a consultant within a week, based on these two initial major accounts. His staff consisted of one secretary, but he already was a pioneer with his bunched-asparagus logo for the George

Lang Corporation. Today food service consultants are so plentiful that—like some segments of food service operations themselves—the field may face its own saturation dilemma. But in 1970 Lang was the first to offer creative help to operators on a wide range of services. As the food service business grew astronomically in the 1970s, more and more consultants joined the fray.

Throughout the 1970s Lang gradually built up his client list and his reputation for innovation. "You may not always love what George does," was the word in the trade, "but at least you're going to see something different." George himself was never totally satisfied with what he was accomplishing. He always looked to the next project as a possible fulfillment of his dreams. By the late 1970s there was no one specific project but rather a myriad of challenges and a full staff to carry them out.

HOTEL DINING UPGRADED

Some of Lang's biggest successes were in the hotel food service field—an area where restaurants often had been relegated to a mere supporting role. But Lang made sure the restaurants were the stars of the hotel and sparkled with their own individuality. When he designed the food service facilities at Loews Monte Carlo Hotel, the local people assumed he would try to outdo the fine French restaurants all around the area. Instead, he created a special niche with an Argentine steak restaurant along with a series of quasi American-style dining areas. One sported quality hamburgers and ice cream sodas, another a mixed grill and sangria, and a third chili dogs, barbecued ribs, tacos, and pita. Who would expect to find good old-fashioned American restaurants in the middle of Monte Carlo? George Lang gloried in doing the unexpected. A 1920s Russian-style night club, Folie Russe, completed the hotel's features.

At Loews Anatole in Dallas, he decided on a series of finely tuned ethnic restaurants. After all if he could build American restaurants in Monte Carlo, he could build a Chinese restaurant in Texas. He designed a French restaurant and a Mexican restaurant for the hotel. But the unique one in the mix was Chinese. He visualized a banquet for the customer who wanted to go to a Chinese wedding or feast but couldn't. He commissioned scrolls and a bronze Buddha from owner Tremmel Crow's collection to give character to the place and made the rest of it comfortable and contemporary. He named it the Plum Blossom, emphasizing that "you have to think of positive names with positive connotations for the customer, yet keep it within the mesh of the place."

Lang also created for the Loews Anatole a Crocodile disco, Danish-style coffee shop, a twenty-four-hour food kiosk for casual offerings, and two lobby bars. A person could hardly walk anywhere in the hotel without bumping into some sort of food service. It's no wonder that in its second year of operation—1980—Loews Anatole achieved $24 million food and beverage sales, higher than the revenues it obtained from rooms. This was unusual for the hotel industry, where rooms normally outperform food service by a wide margin.

Tackling two Sheraton Hotels in New York, Lang put his own streamlined touches on them. He helped on a $20 million project to enhance the Sheraton Centre Hotel. He has always despised wasted unproductive space, and agreed with Sheraton's Klaus Ottman to do away with half the massive lobby and produce a European-style cafe. A tightly packaged kitchen and an invitingly designed bar made the cafe extra profitable. After that Lang added a Northern Italian restaurant, Ranier's, which competed with nonhotel restaurants when it opened in late 1980.

He helped refashion a 1904 structure at the St. Regis Sheraton on New York's Fifth Avenue. Since he realized any alterations in the historic seventy-five-year-old hotel would be akin to sacking the temple, he had a photographer take numerous pictures of the existing space at the King Cole Room restaurant. He and his associates then redesigned the entire place down to each detail of the chandeliers. When some critics recoiled at the total transformation of the "exquisite" old dowager, Lang simply sent them the 8 by 10 glossies of the old King Cole Room with its formica tables, pseudo-medieval plaques, and plastic seats.

He also designed restaurants at hotels in Washington, Montreal, Quebec City, Budapest, Hamburg, and other cities. But his biggest achievement under difficult circumstances was at the Manila Hotel in the Philippines. There he worked with designer Dale Keller to find the right combination, at the personal request of President Marcos. "We wanted to emphasize pride-boosting for the people," Lang says, "because that's what they needed then (in the late 1970s)." He decided that each of the five restaurants should be based on Philippine art, history, and design. He proceeded to study each of five separate regions of the Philippines carefully for months before settling on each design. For example, he had recipes tested and retested for such items as a dessert soufflé related to Philippine rituals.

While testing Lang's recipes in Manila, Paula Wolfert was so dedicated that when flood waters rose to peak heights, she persisted in testing the food even though the water almost reached her knees at times. (If the food could survive that test, it could survive anything.) This was the type of intense dedication Lang expected and received from people. He set the example by going the last extra mile on each project.

PIZZAZ IN DEPARTMENT STORES

A field where restaurants had been treated even more as stepchildren was in department stores. They tolerated restaurants only for their traffic-building potential and to keep customers shopping in the store after they would eat there. Lang tackled a tough situation at Alexander's department store on New York's upper East Side in 1977. He was given a poor fifth-floor location with no real exposure. He devised a mix of wine, beer, espresso, and light snacks with a casual atmosphere and called it Cafe A'Lex (off Lexington Avenue). It prospered with a per person check average under $2, yielding annual volumes upward of $1.5 million. Out of what essentially had been a break-even restaurant at best, he created one of the most profitable areas per square foot in Alexander's entire department store.

Another store that benefited from Lang's touch was Ann Taylor's specialty store off Fifth Avenue. He and an architect created a sixty-seat charcuterie restaurant with retail-food sales in a wide street window exposure in a relatively small space.

PROJECTS GALORE

His projects in the past few years have offered a highly diverse mix. These include consulting for the Hotel Roosevelt and Crawdaddy restaurant in New York; designing restaurants in Germany for Miami-based Hardwicke; working with Cunard Line to improve the cuisine on the *Queen Elizabeth II*'s 100-day around-the-world cruises; Resorts International in Atlantic City; the Royal Orleans Hotel in New Orleans; Saga Corporation, Menlo Park, California; designing a new restaurant at the Sheraton-Carlton in Washington, D.C.; the Statue of Liberty's new food facilities, and the recently opened food kiosks at the Park Avenue Plaza building in New York.

Among projects he was undertaking in 1981 were a new prototype for General Foods's Maxwell House division, a project Lang considers unique in nature and scope; a restaurant in New York for the Swiss-based Movenpick firm; an entire floor of restaurants for the huge Stamford, Connecticut, Town Center shopping center; and a tie-in to develop a new hotel and restaurant china and crystal line for Villeroy and Boch, a highly prestigious European manufacturer, and the first of a new Lang design line.

It all prompted some observers to wonder whether Lang was overextending himself. "How much can any one person and his staff accomplish in quality if he is spread out over the world?" was a prime question. Lang acknowledges that like anyone else, he has had his share of failures "for various reasons, some related to my own concepts and some to extraneous factors." But he points to his large number of successes and emphasizes he is still dedicated to quality, not just quantity. The mix may be achievable for Lang, who runs five times as fast as almost anyone else.

The project that seemed to intrigue him the most in the early 1980s was a highly improbable one—a plan for an Arabian Middle Eastern fast-food chain. Lang first dug in and read everything he could find about that part of the world—even the Koran—to obtain the feel of the society and what would be required in food to reflect customs and traditions. "You have to know what the customers will really want and will accept . . . particularly in this case," he noted. "We have to readjust our whole design vocabulary and our tastes to meet the situation." He decided to reflect outdoor Arabic life with a casual place that would in effect be entertainment for the people as so little of that exists there. He settled on a concept that would combine some Arabic foods with foods from India, Mexico, and California.

Sponsored by the Arab Food Services Company of Kuwait, which is owned by the well-known Alghanim family, the chain was to be called Shehi. An initial unit is to open early in 1982 in Kuwait, with other pilot units envisioned for Jedda in Saudi Arabia, Dusseldorf, London, and selected locations in the United States. It is planned as an eventual wide-ranging franchise operation.

Shehi was aimed at an untapped Middle Eastern market whose food service had been dominated by either local mom and pop operations or by major United States chains such as McDonald's and Kentucky Fried Chicken. These chains tried to add doses of local items to their usual fast-food repertoires. But Lang and his group showed more flair for local merchandising with the first "true" Middle East fast-food chain. Yet crucial decisions remained, such as whether to operate an initial commissary in the Middle East or else produce the food in the United States, freeze it, and ship it over.

Another major challenge facing Lang in 1980 and 1981 was in planning a huge complex of thirty-five potential restaurants on the 100-acre eighth (top) floor of the contemplated Beverly Center shopping building in Beverly Hills. Each restaurant will be operated separately in the super-modern building. Many of the restaurants would serve a triple purpose of retail, takeout, and eat-in food. Lang also planned to include a large farmers' market and fifteen small movie theaters (eighty seats each) on this floor, with each movie starting five minutes apart. (Would this make it possible for a shopper or restaurant goer to see fifteen movies in one full day and night?) Outside glass-enclosed escalators would lead to Lang's top floor in the spectacular complex.

But he faced a severe problem since the traditional sales mix of a shopping center was 7 percent in food service. The Beverly Center developers gave him the task of at least doubling this percentage. They obviously realized food service could be every bit as profitable—if not more so—than retail space. Lang found this challenge to be inspiring rather than threatening.

He also was turning some of his attention to the Town Center in Stamford, Connecticut, where a fourth-floor complex of fourteen restaurants by Detroit-based tycoon Alfred Taubman (who is also a partner in the Beverly Center complex) was being planned. Lang envisioned European-style cafes, four diverse anchor restaurants, and an ethnic-type casual dining section as the hub of this project. Both Beverly Center and Stamford Town Center were to open at the end of 1981.

One of his most interesting projects was in response to the challenge of developing a new restaurant concept for W. R. Grace. By 1979 Grace had purchased a multiplicity of food service chains: Far West Services (dinner houses and Coco's coffee shops), Del Taco Mexican fast-food units, El Torito Mexican dinner houses, and Gilbert/Robinson (Houlihan's). Grace also was hoping to develop something on its own that would be particularly suitable for high traffic shopping centers. Lang and his associate, Alan Reyburn (now head of Bloomingdale's food service), developed the idea of Jennie's Cookery, which would use convenience foods but also would cook items fresh daily on the premises and would offer a serve-yourself pasta bar. An initial Jennie's opened in 1980 at Mission Viejo, California, with salads and fruits featured. Lang describes it as a "soft-edged healthy food place serving people from twelve to ninety-two." He sees it as "less fancification and less dazzle," as a reaction to high costs. Yet the interior is elegant.

Lang doesn't confine his creativity to restaurants though they play the dominant role. He worked on a new food package for ITT Continental Baking, a flexible retort pouch that places completely cooked foods in soft packages that can be kept for a year without refrigeration. This refined a concept originally developed by the army.

FAILURES EXPLAINED

He has always maintained his own dreams of excellence and doesn't feel he has come anywhere close to achieving all his objectives. Yet out of perhaps a hundred projects, only a handful can be said clearly not to have succeeded. One of his most notable "failures" was with La Folie restaurant in New York. He did manage to design one of the most spectacular men's rooms ever created, but his best efforts in other parts of the restaurant went for naught.

"The road to intention is paved with hell," Lang says of his La Folie experience. "If a restaurateur knows the limits of his dreams, he'll stimulate the consultant and get the best combination. But if he is in another business, taking the non-stop ego trip, and wants to jump from step one to step four and hurry through the whole process, it can be a disaster." The way Lang sizes it up, the project bogged down in a hodgepodge of too many outside experts. "One person did the logo, another did part of the interior, two or three others did parts of the interior, and so on. It just didn't jell."

Yet, when he was able to switch ownership and former manager and member of his team, Romeo Mattiussi, together with Chef Bernard Norget, took over La Folie, they made a success out of it. So Lang feels a good restaurateur will conquer in the end.

A second "hodgepodge" was The Ports restaurant complex in Toronto. This much-heralded project involved five restaurants, a disco, and bars. It was part of an effort by a number of owners, but it never lived up to its potential. "There was nothing wrong with the design or the merchandising," says Lang. "It was like a well-designed auto that the driver can't drive." The owner apparently was stronger on the liquor side of the business than in food.

Perhaps the biggest disappointment in Lang's career was the gigantic Porto Carras project in Thessalonika, Greece. Ambitious plans were set by a Greek corporation to create a huge resort village rimming the bay, with several hotels, night clubs, nurseries, stables, vineyards, olive oil and other food manufacturing plants, and just about anything else needed for a totally self-sustaining village. Also included were extensive dining facilities for large cruise ships there. Top experts from all over the world were assembled but after all the efforts of the most talented groups had implemented many of the plans, it became commercially untenable in its original form. Parts of it are presently operated by a British hotel group.

A basic error had been made in strategic planning. Lang had asked the owners whether it would make more sense to build a seasonal complex that could prosper half the year and have an underground convention center for the other half. But the owners showed him elaborate charts indicating the complex could prosper all year. No underground convention center was built, and the complex faltered in the cold weather. All of which illustrated once again either that too many experts can ruin a project or that strategic planning must take into account every conceivable weather eventuality, or both.

Lang enjoyed some of his greatest successes with hotels, but one of the hotel deals didn't bear fruit. Holiday Inn was trying to overcome its image as a staid place for dining and hit upon the idea of a Pipers theme restaurant to liven up things. Lang was selected to implement the idea. But it never really took hold as a series of management changes at Holiday Inn resulted in signals for the Pipers project constantly to be changed. Even Lang was hard-pressed to figure out what management really wanted. (Later Holiday Inn was able to get more on the track with relative management stability, the acquisition of Perkins Pancake Houses, and some other in-house food service projects that helped take away some of the staid image.)

OWN IMPRINT

While Lang's main career is as a consultant to others, he has put his own imprint on a restaurant he operates in New York—Cafe des Artistes. This is unique and a powerful expression of his personality and philosophy.

For Cafe des Artistes, just a few doors from his headquarters, Lang tried to create a 1917 world in 1976. The way he sees it, food service merchandising can be successful by creating an ambience with which a customer is unfamiliar or by creating a fantasy which will be only slightly familiar. When he redesigned Cafe des Artistes and took it over himself, he shot for the second category. "Some customers will say it's like Europe, but others will think it's turn-of-the-century New York," he said. Lang retained a collection of nude paintings on the walls that are conservatively valued at $1 million. He put into action his philosophy that a restaurant "must be a blend of harmonious elements . . . food service, accouterments, atmosphere, innovation. None of the elements should overpower another."

In keeping with his desire for relative simplicity—or at least to reach a diverse market—Lang's average per person dinner ticket at Cafe des Artistes was under $16 even in 1981. This did not include wines, which added a few dollars to each check. The whole restaurant radiated value amidst Howard Chandler Christy's ephemeral floating nudes—an image of luxurious surroundings with food at lower prices than most of the better New York restaurants. Proof of Lang's success here may be that where Valentino ate there in the 1920s, Mayor LaGuardia and other celebrities in the 1930s, and Fanny Hurst and Noel Coward in the 1940s, in the early 1980s Mayor Koch, Governor Carey, Diane Keaton, and Warren Beatty are among the many regulars who dine there. Celebrities and knowledgeable diners from far and wide seem to feel comfortable and to know their privacy won't be invaded.

HUNGARY OVERDONE

Yet Lang's other restaurant, one so close to his homeland and his heart, didn't make it. In a sense he overshot his market with this one. Called Hungaria, it opened in 1977 in the new Citicorp building on New York's upper East Side. It closed in late 1980 around the time that a number of other adjacent restaurants in the building closed. They were victims of a general failure by the building's management to promote the area for nighttime business. While sales were brisk at Hungaria and the others at lunchtime, they faded to a trickle for dinner.

Beyond the difficulties in the building, Lang concedes he made a strategic error in launching a truly authentic Hungarian restaurant with decor that was different than "the typical cutesy cliché design that non-Hungarians expect in a place like this." The restaurant had to depend on non-Hungarians to succeed; but 80 percent of the dishes were unfamiliar to them. Moreover, the location for this type of business was poor. In an ethnic neighborhood or an area like Lincoln Center, it could have fared much better.

Lang worked out a deal with Hungarian government officials and imported three of their top chefs and two pastry chefs who had won almost every culinary prize in Europe for the last two decades. A gypsy orchestra was brought out of Hungary, and its staff actually occupied half a floor of a New York hotel. None of these flourishes mattered. Hungarians alone couldn't support the moderately expensive place, and it was ahead of its time for the rest of the market. Although it broke even, Lang closed it lest it drain his energies from other projects.

He has clear likes and dislikes in his personal and business dealings. He is unequivocally opposed to the idea of trying to gain the absolute last square inch of space in a restaurant by crowding together all the customers. He prefers a reasonable space allotment of ten to fifteen square feet per person and as much as twenty-two square feet in luxury-type restaurants. He also thinks along-the-wall banquettes—increasingly popular in many restaurants—are often a mistake and not conducive to the eye-to-eye contact necessary in business dealings. He abhors recessed or high-hat ceiling lights—just to mention a few of his tenets.

Lang deplores "unfair penalties" which hit restaurants that try to innovate. "If anyone innovates in our business," he says, "the effects will be marginal. Instead, the restaurant with the same old safe concept is rewarded." Specifically, he refers to reviewers not understanding the historical process or the necessity of being courageous in design and merchandising. "Why shouldn't a restaurant also be judged on what new contributions it has made and what new ideas it has presented?" asks Lang, who has received his share of excellent and mediocre reviews. "A 'laundry list' of dishes in lieu of an overall review picture reminds me of the book which was published in Germany in the nineteenth century about the Taj Mahal. It gave painstaking details about every angle, arch, and texture, but since it did not discuss the whole structure and published no picture of the building, the reader had no idea what the Taj Mahal looked like."

Lang isn't sure why he does things the way he does. He doesn't like to spend much time analyzing himself. "I'll leave that to the pundits," he says. But he feels he has utilized only a small portion of his total ability. "I haven't done yet what I am capable of doing," he says with a wink, "but I will." His own philosophy is that the sign of an effective person is one who has enough energy, knows his limitations, and has unceasing curiosity.

Some consider Lang difficult to work for since he is demanding of himself and of others. But he tries to consider the needs of his subordinates and brings an infectious excitement and self-propulsion to his people. He has lost some of the best to bigger jobs elsewhere and is convinced that "when they're ready to go off on their own, they just will and should. In fact, sometimes you do better by bringing in fresh thinking before the patterns are too established."

THE HUMAN SIDE

There's a human and sensitive side to Lang amid all his business mechanizations. He prides himself on having a "soft" office that is more library, greenhouse, and museum than anything else. He shares the office with business visitors and two cats, Truffles and Escoffier. They too taste foods as the chef or outsiders bring in morsels for them.

Lang often begins his workday before sunrise by practicing on his 1709 Stradivarius. When not setting a frantic work pace later, he can be found in his own kitchen whipping up a new recipe or designing a new china pattern, or a nonexistent accouterment.

To food connoisseur James Beard, Lang in human terms simply is a man who is "devoted to fine music and loves cooking a great chili or a super Gulyas for his friends, but most of all turns out a neat loaf of bread." People tend to put Lang on a pedestal because of his creative talents. But with all his diverse interests and abilities, the one thing that keeps driving him is a willingness to dream and to actually achieve some of these dreams.

When Lang arrived in the United States as a refugee in 1946, he applied to Cornell University and was rejected. To augment his earnings as a cook, he sold the Encyclopedia Britannica and turned pages for Carnegie Hall artists.

Years later he addressed a Cornell Hotel School graduating class as a preeminent food service leader who wrote the latest Britannica restaurant entries and was a Carnegie Hall trustee. George Lang is indeed the poet of the possible.